RESEARCH METHODOLOGY

Ratan Khasnabis
Retired Professor and Honorary Director,
Department of Business Management,
Calcutta University

and

Suvasis Saha
Professor,
Department of Business Management,
Calcutta University

UNIVERSITIES PRESS (INDIA) PRIVATE LIMITED

Registered Office
3-6-747/1/A & 3-6-754/1, Himayatnagar,
Hyderabad 500 029, Telengana, India
e-mail: info@universitiespress.com; www.universitiespress.com

Distributed by
Orient Blackswan Private Limited

Registered Office
3-6-752 Himayatnagar, Hyderabad 500 029 (T.S), India

Other Offices
Bangalore / Bhopal / Bhubaneshwar / Chandigarh / Chennai
Ernakulam / Guwahati / Hyderabad / Jaipur / Kolkata
Lucknow / Mumbai / New Delhi / Noida / Patna

ISBN 978-81-7371-952-3

First published in India by
Universities Press (India) Private Limited 2015

Cover and book design

Typeset in Minion Pro *by*
MacroTex Solutions, Chennai 600 091

Printed at B B Press, Noida

Published by
Universities Press (India) Private Limited
3-6-747/1/A & 3-6-754/1, Himayatnagar,
Hyderabad 500 029 (T.S), India.

Preface

The aim of the book is to introduce 'Research Methodology' to students at the graduate and postgraduate levels. The book has evolved out of more than two decades of experience in teaching courses on Research Methodology in the Department of Business Management at Calcutta University. The methodologies considered in this book are related primarily to social and empirical research. Natural science and theoretical research have not been dealt with in this book. Students of any branch of social science can use the book to learn the techniques and tools of empirical research. However, the primary target is students of Business Management whose special needs are taken care of without undermining the needs of students of other branches of social sciences.

A book on Research Methodology is usually designed with the tools of descriptive and inferential statistics with some chapters on descriptive accounts of 'methodology' of utilising these tools. However, we felt that it should emphasise 'methodology'. Statistical tools are introduced (at the elementary level) only to meet the need to explain the methodology of research. The issues related to methodology of empirical research have been discussed at length to equip the readers with domain knowledge and enable them to use the tools of research efficiently. A researcher who is thus equipped is expected to contextualise statistical tools more efficiently to his/her specific research issue(s). Any book on statistics will provide information on utilising the required statistical tools.

The textbook contains fourteen chapters and a select bibliography. Chapter 1 is an introductory chapter in which the subject is contextualised. Chapter 2 discusses the concept of research design and the problems of constructing an appropriate research design. The major element of empirical research is 'data' whose worth is often not realised. Thus, in Chapter 3, the genesis of data and the nature of the data source are discussed. The discussion is extended further in Chapter 4, with a detailed discussion on preserving the quality of data under various settings of data collection. The chapter ends with an appendix that lists specific organisational or institutional sources of secondary data and the dimension of the data collected by such agencies.

In sociological studies, economics (experimental economics) and business management, data are often generated by 'experimental technique'. Chapter 5 discusses various types of experiments, the settings for such experiments and the possible types of errors that might occur while the researcher conducts such experiments. In Chapter 6, the issues related to the tools for collecting data through questionnaire method (primary data) are discussed. Classification of questionnaires, steps involved in designing a questionnaire, merits and demerits of open-ended and closed questions along with the techniques of minimising ambiguity while collecting the data through the questionnaire method are detailed.

Chapter 7 deals with the challenging issue of error-control. The types of errors, methods of minimising such errors, editing the data set by detecting the outliers are discussed. The features of four different scales used for measuring data are discussed in Chapter 8. Appropriate scaling techniques for various types of data with special emphasis on the techniques of analysing qualitative data, specialised scales and their functions and limitations are discussed.

Chapter 9 deals with methodological issues related to sample surveys. The difference between sample and census study, technical issues related to sample design and methods of sampling as well as practical problems that the researcher faces while conducting the field survey have been discussed.

Chapter 10 provides an overview of the basic statistical tools of data analysis along the lines of a ready reckoner for the tools that are widely used in social research. The chapter also introduces the concept of econometric modelling which is widely used in causal research. Chapter 11 deals with sampling theory, sampling error and testing of statistical hypotheses at an elementary level.

Chapters 12 and 13 concentrate on report writing and research administration. This discusses preparation of tables, formats for reports, problems associated with research administration and suggests methods for bridging the gaps between the company and an external agency. In Chapter14, the researcher is taken through a 'walk-the talk' exercise using a live situation—how a problem is first defined in terms of a research design and then analysed on the basis of research output.

Most of the chapters are provided with student-focussed assignments. The successful handling of each assignment will help the student in understanding the basic issues of social research. Each chapter also has a set of multiple choice questions for the reader to test his/her knowledge.

We are thankful to our family members for providing relentless support when we needed seclusion to put down our thoughts in the form of a textbook. All the batches of students in the Department of Business Management, Calcutta University, whom we interacted with require a special mention. Much of what is in the book has grown out of teaching the subject in the class room. As we look back, we understand that class room teaching is possibly the most effective way of learning; the inquisitiveness of the budding minds has helped us learn while teaching. Our heartfelt thanks to our students.

We are obliged to our colleagues of the academic fraternity, particularly to Dr J B Bhattacharya, Former Professor, Burdwan University, for his advice, from time to time, regarding the content and concepts. We also thank Dr Gita S Dattatri and Ms Dharani Kothandapani, Universities Press, for editing and polishing our manuscript and taking it to publication. Thanks are due to the reviewer of the initial manuscript for comments and suggestions which were extremely helpful in shaping the final manuscript. Needless to say, only the authors are responsible for the errors and omissions in this book. We will consider our efforts rewarded if students/readers find this book helpful in their study on social research. Feedback is invited to rkhasnabisl@ gmail.com or dr.suvasis123@ rediffmail.com.

Ratan Khasnabis, Professor (Retd)
Suvasis Saha, Professor
Department of Business Management
University of Calcutta

Contents

Preface iii

1. Introduction **1**
- 1.1 Introduction 1
- 1.2 Issues in Social Research 2
- 1.3 Theoretical and Empirical Research 3
- 1.4 Methodological Issues 4
- 1.5 Management Uses of Market Research 5

2. Research Design **10**
- 2.1 Introduction 10
- 2.2 Steps in Research Design 11
- 2.3 Types of Research Design 11
- 2.4 Exploratory Studies 12
- 2.5 Descriptive Studies 16
- 2.6 Causal Studies 18
- 2.7 Concluding Observations 23
- *Assignments* 24

3. Sources of Data **27**
- 3.1 Introduction 27
- 3.2 Stimulus–Response Relationship 28
- 3.3 Alternative Formats of Data Collection 30
- 3.4 Forms of Communication and Modes of Data Collection 31
- 3.5 Nature of Data under Various Settings 32
- 3.6 Concluding Observations 34
- *Assignments* 35

4. Maintaining Data Quality Under Various Settings **38**
- 4.1 Introduction 39
- 4.2 Data Quality Under Verbal Mode of Communication 39
- 4.3 The Advantages and Disadvantages of the Oral–verbal Method of Communications 43
- 4.4 Observation 44

4.5 Content Analysis 45
4.6 Secondary Data 46
Assignments 49
Appendix 4.1 51

5. Experimental Techniques **53**
5.1 Introduction 54
5.2 Types of Experiments 54
5.3 Settings for Experiments 55
5.4 Errors in Experimentation 58
5.5 Experimental Design Notation 59
5.6 Designs of Experiment 60
5.7 Application of Experimental Design 65
Assignments 70

6. The Questionnaire Method **73**
6.1 Introduction 74
6.2 Questionnaire 74
6.3 Types of Questionnaires 78
6.4 Designing a Questionnaire 85
6.5 The Methods for Communication 89
6.6 Projective Techniques 90
Assignments 96
Appendix 6.1 98

7. Errors in Data: Measurement Error **100**
7.1 Introduction 100
7.2 Response and Non-response Error 101
7.3 Other Sources of Measurement Error 107
7.4 Other Checks on Data 112
Assignments 114

8. Measurement and Scaling Techniques **117**
8.1 Measurement 118
8.2 Measurement Scales 119
8.3 Scaling Techniques for Measurement of Attitude 129
Assignments 150

9. Methods of Data Collection **153**
- 9.1 Introduction 154
- 9.2 Sample Versus Census 154
- 9.3 Cost Effectiveness and Optimum Sample Size 156
- 9.4 Sampling: The Basic Framework 158
- 9.5 Methods of Sampling 158
- *Assignments* 170

10. Tools of Processing and Analysis of Data **173**
- 10.1 Introduction 174
- 10.2 Quantitative and Qualitative Data 174
- 10.3 Interpolation of Data 175
- 10.4 Tools of Data Analysis 181
- 10.5 Regression Analysis 193
- 10.6 Use of the Tools of Regression in Time Series Analysis 198
- 10.7 An Outline of Econometric Modelling 204
- 10.8 Use of Analysis of Variance (ANOVA) in Quantitative Research 207
- *Assignments* 223

11. Sampling, Sampling Errors and Testing of Hypotheses **228**
- 11.1 Introduction 229
- 11.2 Population and Sample 230
- 11.3 Population Distribution and Sampling Distribution 230
- 11.4 Confidence Limits of Estimates 233
- 11.5 Reliability of an Estimated Mean 235
- 11.6 Reliability of Estimated Standard Deviation 236
- 11.7 The Significance of Difference Between Two Means 236
- 11.8 Testing of Hypotheses 238
- 11.9 Chi-square as a Non-parametric Test 242
- *Assignments* 248
- *Appendix 11.1* 252

12. Data, Analysis and Report Writing **254**
- 12.1 Introduction 254
- 12.2 Interim Report and the Final Report 255
- 12.3 Preparing the Final Tables 256
- 12.4 Analysing the Data 258

12.5 Some Common Mistakes 259
12.6 Outline of a Final Report 262
12.7 The Research and its Limitations 264
Assignments 266

13. Research Administration **268**
13.1 Introduction 268
13.2 In-house Agency 270
13.3 External Agency 271
Assignments 276

14. An Illustration of Research Methodology **279**
14.1 Introduction 280
14.2 Identifying the Research Issue 280
14.3 Type of Research 281
14.4 Generation of Data 281
14.5 Methodology Used 281
14.6 Coverage Area 282
14.7 The Questionnaire 283
14.8 Tabulation and Compilation 288
14.9 Report Writing 290
Appendix 14.1 291

Appendix 1 294
Appendix 2 295
Appendix 3 296
Appendix 4 297
Appendix 5 298
Appendix 6 299
Appendix 7 300
Appendix 8 301
Appendix 9 302
Appendix 10 303
Appendix 11 304

Bibliography 305
Index 309

INTRODUCTION

LEARNING OBJECTIVES

After going through this chapter you will understand

- What research is
- Types of research
- The genesis of good research and issues involved with reference to research
- The essence of theoretical research and empirical research
- Social research envelopes the areas of research in business management and its functional areas and these need to be explored and understood

1.1 INTRODUCTION

Good research stems from a good research idea. Where do we get a good research idea from? 'All essential ideas in science were born in dramatic conflict between reality and our attempt at understanding the same', said Albert Einstein and Leopold Infeld on this issue in their book, *The Evolution of Physics.* Our attempts at understanding scientific reality result in ideas, which when translated into research work, contribute to increasing our knowledge of the subject. The quality of the idea determines the quality of research.

Primarily, one needs an idea to pursue a research project and the idea originates from one's own grasp of the subject. A proper grasp of the subject results from the assimilation of the available knowledge that has been accumulated through the endeavours of other researchers. The genesis of good research lies in the wisdom of the researcher. The researcher must be wise enough to know what the available knowledge is and where the research gap lies.

If knowledge of the subject and the researcher's wisdom is the *raison-de-tout* of good research, why should one undergo training in the methodology of research? Einstein did not take a course in research methodology at a university. Even researchers of less repute do not take up courses on methodological issues in most cases. In fact, research methodology is a subject of recent origin. With the passage of time, academicians understood that a new entrant in the field of research will benefit from a well designed course on research methodology. When a research programme is envisaged, it therefore includes a coursework that a researcher is supposed to undergo before working on his own area of research. The expected benefit is that the research will be more methodical and scientific and the researcher would gain in terms of efficiency if he is exposed to a course on research methodology.

In the social sciences, with the development of university-level courses in sociology, applied economics and management science, a course on the issues in research methodology has also been developed. Coursework on the subject has become necessary in order to equip the student better in his endeavour to translate his ideas into research output. This is mainly because, thanks to research on methodological issues, a vast amount of literature has developed that may contribute to the researcher's effort to enhance his efficiency in handling research issues. Without undermining the importance of a course on research methodology, we would add that the contribution of research methodology to the quality of research is of secondary importance; the quality of research is basically determined by the quality of the research issue which, *inter-alia*, is the product of the researcher's understanding of the subject.

1.2 ISSUES IN SOCIAL RESEARCH

Research in the academic area of the social sciences is often described as 'social research'. This nomenclature is introduced in order to distinguish it from issues in the natural sciences. Social research entails research in any area of social science, including Economics, Sociology, Psychology and Management. The issues in social research that we will discuss here involve the methods that help in the study of human behaviour—behaviour in the context of human relations vis-à-vis society. Human relations are designed with reference to the economic, political or sociological parameters of society. Often, the issues involve the behaviour of the individual in an organisation. The behaviour of the individual in various areas of society can be brought into sharper focus. Thus, the behaviour of an individual as a consumer or a member of the workforce in a factory or the behaviour of an individual as a member of a sales organisation—all these could be discussed as separate areas of study. Human psychology in the behavioural world of the individual or a group can also be considered as an area of study in social research. Research in the area of social anthropology is also a very important area of social research. An interface between anthropology and sociology is often identified; the interrelationships among various socio-economic forces are also highlighted as an area of social research. In fact, a multi-disciplinary approach within the general ambit of the social sciences is often advocated. There is growing literature in the area of social research which takes up a multi-disciplinary approach.

One example of such a multi-disciplinary approach is what has developed in recent years as *The Science of Management*. This is a branch of social science which discusses various issues of business management. Most of the issues are economic in nature. However, it is not a part of economics. It includes several issues of organisational behaviour, which draw heavily from the field of pure and applied psychology. Again, this science discusses the issues of jurisprudence that involves business decisions. In discussing the business climate, it draws heavily from sociology and political science. In the applied area, the subject discusses the tools and techniques and equips the practitioner in arriving at better business decisions. In a nutshell, the subject is a hybrid developed out of various branches of the social sciences. However, the hybrid is developed in order to help one reach a better business decision.

Although social research would include a research issue in any area of social science, in the present volume, the issues that we take up are broadly confined to the science of management. The tools and techniques of social research that we discuss here can be used for research in other areas of social science as well. However, the emphasis here is on those topics of social research which are mostly used in a particular branch of social science, namely, the science of business management.

1.3 THEORETICAL AND EMPIRICAL RESEARCH

A theory is basically a generalisation based on some observed features of a phenomenon. But theory, being an abstraction, may not correspond directly to the observed phenomenon. Often, the theoretical conclusion may not be observable. When a textbook on micro-economics describes the behaviour of a firm with the help of a U-shaped cost curve, it is the creation of a theory which banks heavily on the assumption of certain laws of production (the law of variable proportion in this case). Empirically, such a firm that moves along the U-shaped cost curve may not be visible. Again, a perfectly competitive market which is discussed in textbooks of economics is also not observable in reality. The theory is not weakened due to this problem. There is a realm of theory in which the robustness of the theory is tested with the help of the tools of pure logic. The validity or otherwise of a theory is tested in terms of its logical consideration. There exist certain axioms that initiate the theory. The axioms may or may not correspond to the reality as it is observed in the world of phenomena. The robustness of the theory is not disturbed due to the absence of a correspondence between the theory based on abstraction and the observed reality. Axiom-based theory provides a model that may not directly correspond to the reality. By relaxing the axioms or resetting them, one is expected to obtain results which would correspond to the observed reality to a great extent.

Such an interrelation between the theory and reality is derived from a particular theory of knowledge—the *Theory of the Positivist School* of 19th century Europe. August Comte (1798–1857) is generally recognised as the founder of positivism. According to positivism, the unobservable causes of phenomena are abandoned in favour of a search of law-like regularities among observable phenomena. Following Comte, there developed a school of thought, which worked out the epistemological rules for research in both the natural and the social sciences. This is known as *logical positivism* or *logical empiricism of the Vienna Circle*. This is the most influential school of thought in the philosophy of the science. According to logical positivitism, an axiom-based theory is to be developed in terms of the causal factors explaining a phenomenon. The validity or otherwise of a theory should be tested in terms of empirical research to the extent that such testing is possible. One thus gets a rationale for empirical research in the theory of knowledge. A theory should be empirically tested for justifying its validity to the extent such an experiment is possible. Empirical research by itself cannot constitute a theory. It needs the help of the logic of induction to derive a theory out of empirical research.

In social research, we usually follow these philosophical guidelines of the theory of knowledge. Briefly speaking, research in the social sciences contains elements of both theoretical research and empirical research. Empirical research is taken up to test or validate a theory based on empirical observations on the causal factors of a phenomenon. Theorisation is also possible, but this would require a sufficiently large number of observations to strengthen its power of induction. A logically consistent structure is, of course, the basic requirement of a robust theory.

1.4 METHODOLOGICAL ISSUES

The interrelationship between theoretical and empirical research as defined in logical positivism is the basis for the methodological orientation for every book in social research. A book on social research never addresses the theoretical issues contained in a particular branch of the subject. Such issues are adequately dealt with in books on the theoretical part of the subject. For example, organisational behaviour as studied under management studies, considers the theory of motivation as a part of the text that develops its logical structure. The empirical validation of a theory on motivation is not usually taken up in the text. Some case studies are cited, but the student is not expected to test the theory by taking up a field survey, that is, by considering the empirical part of the phenomena. However, according to logical positivism, a theory should be tested and a practitioner of the subject must know how to test it. This is particularly true with respect to branches of the social sciences which have an immediate use as they are used by professionals who are expected to intervene in the process and reap the best of the outcome with respect to the issue under consideration. In the literature on methodology, this is known as the process of social engineering. In those branches of social science in which social engineering is of immediate use, a trainee in the subject must know how to apply the theory in the empirical world; in other words, he must be equipped with the tools and techniques to take up empirical exercises arising out of the theories he learns and the phenomenon that he observes.

Training in social research would therefore effectively mean training in theory and training in empirical research as well. A textbook in social research is expected to cover such areas of knowledge that help the reader understand how best to utilise empirical facts to test a theory. The products of research are very important, particularly with regard to management-related issues, because they may be used to derive an effective strategy for management, so that the business goals of the organisation are achieved in an efficient way. We shall discuss how such an idea works in the world of marketing research.

1.5 MANAGEMENT USES OF MARKET RESEARCH

A look into the different kinds of market research conducted by various firms will reveal the kind of usage and benefits that the corporate entity is expected to derive from such research.

A few major areas are highlighted below. Broadly speaking, there are five main areas into which market research may be categorised. These are:

(a) Corporate responsibility,
(b) Business and corporate economics,
(c) Product research,
(d) Sales and market research, including market forecasting, and
(e) Advertising.

The most common phenomenon in the management profession is the setting of goals, establishing strategies, developing plans, putting plans into actions and devising the necessary control and appraisal processes.

Viewing management in the light of this administrative process, it is necessary to visualise forthcoming events; this is very important for management. The management sets goals according to its perception about the future. Goal setting has to be precise. Research in marketing, if utilised by the management, brings precision to the goals and that helps in planning the course of action to be followed.

One may therefore suggest that *market research fulfils the management's information needs.*

Some information needs may be identified in advance; some may not be. Management information needs are to be met through an administrative process. The administrative process can be divided into four stages:

(a) Goal setting and establishing strategies,
(b) Developing a plan,
(b) Putting the plan into action, and
(d) Designing control and appraisal procedure.

We now elaborate in the context of management's information needs with reference to the various stages of the administrative process.

(a) **Research during goal setting**

Suppose a new television brand is to be launched, the company would like to arrive at a strategy for the introduction of the product. *The nature of information that market research should provide at this stage are:*

(i) Dissatisfaction and needs in the relevant target segments (market gap),
(ii) Demand size and trends,
(iii) Market structure and nature of competition,
(iv) Projected market share, return on investment and profitability,
(v) Technological and material innovation needed,
(vi) Supply conditions and prices,
(vii) Environmental hazards (pollution or factors reflecting environmental degradation),
(vii) Legal requirements, if any, with reference to the introduction of such a product,
(ix) Distribution and pricing that is likely to be acceptable to the consumer, and
(x) Promotional effort that would be required.

A successful and precise collection of data through empirical research will help us in addressing these issues.

(b) **Research during the planning phase**

While one is planning a product, advertising or promotion, the nature of information that marketing research is expected to provide is quite different from those enumerated above. Suppose we consider the previous example of launching a new brand of television, the information that will be needed are related to:

(i) Identifying the key market segment(s),
(ii) Identifying the attitude of the specific market segment towards existing products, prices, promotions and advertising,
(iii) Testing the appeal of the potential product attributes, and
(iv) Understanding the needs and attitudes of channel members.

Having the information in the proper form will help the organisation to look forward to putting the plan into action.

(c) **Research during the time the plan is being put into action**

When a plan is being put into action, the prime function of market research is to *monitor* the action. This is quite different from the planning phase, when the role of market research was restricted to the identification of the key target segments. Thus, the nature of management information that market research will provide here is quite different. Let us continue with the example of the new TV brand. Now that the television manufacturing firm has specific information with reference to a specific target segment, the product having been introduced, *the nature of information to be collected is as follows*:

(i) Total industry and product class sales,
(ii) Firm's sales, by product and market share,
(iii) Product availability and end user patterns,
(iv) Cost and effectiveness of the firm's marketing effort with reference to product and market,
(v) Cost and effectiveness of the promotion drive and/or advertising,
(vi) Awareness of the new product and the enhanced value it offers,
(vii) Trial rate and purchases, and
(viii) Changes in competitive spending levels and strategies with relevance to price, package, promotions and others.

Such information is most important in the after-launch situation. But what should be understood is how to tie up the loose ends for the product in question, and also, to gauge the standing of the product vis-à-vis competition. It is also important to discover how to overcome the gap between the actual and the projected, expected or intended information. This would call for research in devising control and appraisal.

(d) **Research for devising control and appraisal of the plan's effectiveness**

The firm producing the new brand of television would now like market research to address the following problems:

(i) Understanding the value compatibility of its offerings to that of the customer's value orientation,
(ii) Aggregation of the operating data and the trends and available navigable gaps through which the expected or projected target could be achieved, and
(iii) Attitudes towards repurchase prices and perceived price preferences, promotional gaps that could be blocked.

As pointed out earlier, the management sets goals according to its perception about the future. The issues for market research are set accordingly. There are, however, information needs that cannot be identified in advance. Macro-economic factors, which are less deterministic and less controllable for the firm in question, largely account for the information that cannot be identified in advance.

For example, if the publisher of a newspaper suddenly finds that the regulation curbing the import of newsprint has been withdrawn, he/she will opt immediately for strategy-oriented market research to identify how to derive the maximum monetary benefit from this opportunity.

Once this newspaper company is able to identify a few key opportunities, it would like the market research team at the planning stage to address the problem of developing alternative plans for each alternative key opportunity. Once the market research team is found to handle the issue successfully at the planning stage and the management, armed with the new research output is able to identify the key plan to be followed, the next step in research is to determine how to put the plan into action.

The research in the next two stages is more or less the same as in the case of management—information needs being identified in advance, discussed earlier.

Finally, it should be pointed out that much of the market research, in cases where the management's information needs have been identified, is quite routine and regular. In cases where the management's information needs have not been identified, the market research is ad hoc. However, appropriate research design is a crucial factor for the success in each type of research.

This information provided by market research for the use of management, can be categorised on the basis of marketing functions as enumerated below:

(a) Advertising research:
   (i) Studies of advertising effectiveness,
   (ii) Media research, and
   (iii) Motivation research.

(b) Corporate responsibility research:
   (i) Ecological impact and assessment study,
   (ii) Legal regulations affecting launch and promotion, and
   (iii) Consumer's right to know.

(c) Business economics and corporate research:
   (i) Short-range forecasting,
   (ii) Long-range forecasting and trend analysis,

   (iii) Pricing strategy, and
   (iv) Plant and warehouse location sites.

(d) Sales and market research:
   (i) Measurement of market share,
   (ii) Determination of market characteristics,
   (iii) Market audit,
   (iv) Sales analysis,
   (v) Sales force management research,
   (vi) Store audit,
   (vii) Consumer panel studies, and
   (viii) Promotional research.

(e) Product research:
   (i) New product concept,
   (ii) Competitive product studies,
   (iii) Simulated market research, and
   (iv) Research on launch of the product.

These are some of the main areas of information made available to corporate management as a result of research. Of course, this list is not exhaustive. In all such areas, a researcher needs training in research methodology to impart efficiency in handling these issues.

CHAPTER 2

RESEARCH DESIGN

LEARNING OBJECTIVES

After going through this chapter you will understand

- The steps that a researcher should follow in empirical research
- The alternative ways of planning a research or concept of research design
- A specific research design has a specific in-built system by which the steps in the problem are approached
- There are three broad types of research designs—exploratory design, descriptive design and causal design
- There are specific features for each of these designs
- The researcher has to apply his own judgement regarding the suitability of a particular design in the context of a given research problem
- Flexibility in research design is the key to good research

Key words: Research design, research hypothesis, exploratory studies, descriptive studies, causal studies, types of causal studies

2.1 INTRODUCTION

Research begins with identifying a research issue. As the researcher identifies an issue, he also identifies his research objective. The researcher then has to finetune the research objective to bring precision to the research issue. To achieve this precision, specific research questions have to be formulated. The researcher may also have a research hypothesis (a tentative proposition which has to be tested), that he wants to verify or test in the course of his research work. However, every research need not necessarily start with a research hypothesis.

After identifying the specific research question, the researcher should work out a plan of action for addressing them. This involves methodological issues that the researcher has to address, usually without having received training in research methodology. While there is nothing wrong in solving problems through an educated guess or by the 'learning by doing method', *a priori* knowledge of how to handle the methodological issues is still advocated because such knowledge provides a more efficient way of solving the problem.

Discussion on research methodology starts with research design which is the plan of action of a research project. There are several ways of planning a research; however, each plan of action follows certain broad steps will be described first.

2.2 STEPS IN RESEARCH DESIGN

Research design acts like a navigator for the researcher and guides the research through the following steps:

- identifying the research questions,
- survey of literature and documentation to identify research gaps,
- the formulation of the research hypothesis, if any,
- identifying the empirical part of research,
- identifying data requirement,
- sample design and data collection,
- data analysis,
- testing the research hypothesis, if any,
- interpreting the tested results,
- or, interpreting the findings to suggest a hypothesis,
- identifying limitations of the study,
- identifying the areas of further research,
- arranging the bibliography, and
- writing the final report.

These are the steps that every empirical research follows. However, *a specific research design has a specific in-built system by which these steps are approached.* Before following these steps, a researcher should therefore identify the research design that is best suited to his research issue.

2.3 TYPES OF RESEARCH DESIGN

Research design can be classified into three broad categories—exploratory, descriptive and causal. Each category has an in-built design described in terms of steps through which the research question is addressed. Depending on the type of research that the researcher is going to undertake, he should first identify the type of research design that he would follow. This makes research less time consuming and therefore more efficient.

We shall discuss the steps involved in each of the research designs that follow. However, before we elaborate on the steps, it should be pointed out that a researcher should opt for a specific research design after taking certain factors into consideration. These factors are enumerated below.

(a) Research goals in terms of the utility and applicability of the result in decision making and/or in policy making,
(b) Availability of data,
(c) Availability of time, money and manpower,
(d) The limitations of the researcher (for example, his level of skills and knowledge), and
(e) The magnitude of the problem dealt with by the researcher.

Studies that follow explorative design are known as *explorative studies*, those that follow descriptive design are known as *descriptive studies* and those that follow causal design are known as *causal studies*. We shall discuss the features of each of these designs of research subsequently.

2.4 EXPLORATORY STUDIES

Exploratory studies are conducted for the following purposes:

(a) Formulation of problems, and/or
(b) Formulation of alternative courses of action.

In an exploratory study, the researcher has a research issue and therefore a research objective. At this stage, the researcher has still to finetune the research objective. He has research questions derived from the research issue but he is not in a position to formulate a research hypothesis yet. In an exploratory study, the researcher takes up the research issue without any *a priori* research hypothesis. Further, the findings of the research may or may not provide the basis of a hypothesis or a set of hypotheses for further research. Basically, an exploratory study is exploratory in the sense that the research issue is new; there has not been any previous work in this area of the study. The purpose of the research could be *to formulate the research problems on the basis of the exploratory work*. In the areas of market research, the purpose of an exploratory study could even be the formulation of a new/alternative course of action.

Let us suppose there is a sudden fall in demand for an established brand of washing powder. The reasons could be many, ranging from internal reasons to external ones, such as market-driven forces. The researcher cannot have an *a priori* hypothesis to explain the phenomenon. He may list all the possible reasons based on an educated guess. But testing all of them may not be cost effective. Therefore, some preliminary studies can be carried out at major department stores and it may be necessary to interview some knowledgeable persons regarding this. The required study has to be exploratory in design.

The research design in an exploratory study must have flexibility for the obvious reason that the researcher does not have a hypothesis that he is going to test. However, it should be noted that despite the necessity for flexibility in exploratory study design, there are certain stages that are usually included in such studies:

(a) Search for secondary information sources,
(b) Interviews of knowledgeable persons in the subject area, and
(c) The examination of an analogous situation.

2.4.1 Search for Secondary Sources

Secondary sources of information are the rough equivalents of 'literature' on the subject. In an exploratory study, there is no literature that matches the research issue exactly; however, the researcher could try to get an exposure to the area of research by consulting the literature related to an analogous situation. Reports, case studies, classified information and the data collected by various agencies on analogous cases may provide the necessary information that the researcher may need for exploring research problems on which there is no previous work.

There are two basic sources of secondary data. These are:

(a) *Publications by the government or by government-affiliated institutions*: Various international bodies such as the United Nations, the World Bank and the WTO are also good sources of official data. State and Central Government offices maintain websites from which the relevant data can be downloaded. The Central Statistical Organisation (CSO) and one of its wings, the National Sample Survey Organisation (NSSO) are very reliable sources of macro-level data.
(b) *Non-government publications*: In the annexure to chapter 4, a list of the major sources of secondary data which are available in India has been included. The *Centre for Monitoring Indian Economy (CMIE)*, Mumbai, is a major non-government organisation that compiles available secondary information in its regular publications. Along with hard copies, the researcher may also get these publications on compact disks or even online. It is also possible to update the data. However, CMIE data presents a problem in that the original sources are not mentioned in the data that the CMIE publishes.

There are advantages and disadvantages to using secondary data.

Advantages

(a) Access is often easy and the cost is usually low, particularly when the data set is collected from government organisations.
(b) Secondary data, particularly the data generated by the Central Statistical Organisation (CSO), Government of India, is very reliable. The non-sampling error is low, particularly

with respect to the data provided by the National Sample Survey Organisation (NSSO) because the data collection machinery of the NSSO is robust. The decennial census on population and other related issues is particularly useful, because it is based on complete enumeration involving every household in India.

(c) Often, it provides good leads in gap analysis when the researcher fails to get the desired information from the primary data that he has collected from the field.

Disadvantages

(a) Though the data come faster, it may not meet the specific requirement of the researcher; often, it needs modification and updating.

(b) The accuracy of the data and its reliability is not always good; much depends on the quality of the source (that is, research design of the source, quality of its survey personnel). While the government and the research institutes usually meet this requirement to a large extent, private agencies often fail to meet the standards when they try to compromise on quality to economise on the cost. In many cases, the data are not revalidated. As a result, it often loses reliability. A researcher must check the authenticity of the data collected from secondary sources, before utilising such data for his own research.

2.4.2 Obtaining Information from Knowledgeable Persons

Information from knowledgeable persons can be obtained by using the following methods:

(a) Pilot survey,

(b) Referral survey.

The method used to collect information from knowledgeable sources is usually the interview method. In other words, the setting for data collection is informal. The questionnaire method or the structured interview method often elicits a poor response.

(a) *Pilot survey*: The pilot survey is done using a group of competent (knowledgeable) respondents, not usually chosen through a random sample. After a search of secondary sources or a review of literature is over, the researcher locates the area of the problem in which primary information is necessary. This is done as a part of the preparatory work. The researcher takes it up as a pilot survey as the results will help him understand the problems in the field area. The researcher will utilise this information to finalise the framework of the field survey and to prepare the list of questions for which responses have to be elicited. The interview in the pilot survey is usually informal and non-structured. Often, this is utilised for a further study of secondary sources.

(b) *Referral survey*: Competent groups of people who are knowledgeable about the issue often refer others to the researcher and informal interviews are arranged with members of such groups to ascertain their views. It is not a randomly chosen sample and the issues of discussion are usually presented in an unstructured form.

2.4.3 Study of an Analogous Situation

An analogous situation consists of a phenomenon which is similar to the phenomenon that the researcher would like to take up for study. Study on an analogous situation is done so that the researcher gets an idea of the nature of the variables that might be involved in his study and would also see how such variables behave, with respect to the phenomenon from which the analogy pertaining to the issue under study can be drawn.

The approach is based on studying case histories. Examination of case studies in an analogous area may help the researcher understand the nature of his problem. It may also suggest which variables are important and the nature of the relationship that may exist among the variables in the analogous study. It may also suggest the variables with respect to which an exploratory study has to be performed. The result of the study is expected to be suggestive. The idea is to get as much information as possible so that exploration in the area is facilitated. We may discuss one such situation where studying an analogous case could be rewarding for the researcher.

Let us suppose a market research organisation in India is entrusted with a study of the problems of marketing a cell phone service; let us also suppose that the product is a new one, and so no previous study in this particular area is available with respect to the Indian market. The researcher understands that the study is going to be exploratory in nature, the study will not have a set of *a priori* hypotheses and a great deal of flexibility will exist in the survey design.

The researcher may feel that along with meeting knowledgeable persons and collecting information from various sources (such as the turnover in the cell phone industry in other countries), it would be prudent on his part to study an analogous case from the services industry. The researcher may, after a series of discussions with competent persons, identify the specific market that can be taken as an analogous market, such as the market for pager services (which were there in the 1990s). Case histories, published reports and even research output in that area may be collected for building up the analogous case. The researcher may even go in for simulation (see Assignments).

The target of an exploratory study is not to formulate a research hypothesis which may or may not be a result of the study. One point, however, must not be missed—an exploratory study provides the researcher with a research question based on which further studies can be taken up.

After conducting exploratory research, the investigator is expected to have derived substantial knowledge about the research problem. It would therefore be easier for the researcher to formulate a research hypothesis. Exploratory research thus serves as the foundation for further research, which might consist of either descriptive or causal studies.

2.5 DESCRIPTIVE STUDIES

A descriptive study, as the name suggests, is basically the description of a phenomenon. The description in this context, implies that the rigour which is necessary to describe the phenomenon is not missing. Most research, particularly, those in the area of market research, belong to this group. For example, a study on the users of particular consumer goods may basically be the outcome of descriptive research that constructs a profile of the clients with the necessary information on income, age, sex and other characteristics of the group. The researcher is not particularly interested in studying the cause and effect relation that may exist among the variables. The research is different from exploratory studies in the sense that *it has a formal design*. Since the purpose of a descriptive study is to portray the characteristics of a particular phenomenon, it may or may not have a set of initial hypothesis about the nature of these characteristics.

While a descriptive study may not have a set of hypothesis to start with, it would end up with a rigorous description of the phenomenon under study, so much so that the descriptive study would usually end up with a set of hypotheses. The researcher may take up a follow up study that would test the hypothesis in the framework of a causal study (see below).

The descriptive study, as pointed out, has a formal design. A formal design ensures that the research covers all the phases that the researcher may envisage, with respect to that particular research problem. It entails a precise statement of the problem and from this precise statement, specified methods of selecting the source of information should be stated; if it involves a field survey, the survey design will have to be drawn up. The idea is to eliminate inaccurate or inappropriate information, as far as is practicable. For a market survey, a careful design of the descriptive study is particularly necessary in order to ensure cost efficiency to which the professional market research organisations assign much importance.

In order to ensure cost efficiency, it is advisable that the researcher, after formulating the research problem with necessary precision, constructs a set of dummy tables to describe the nature of information that the researcher would need to address the problem that he has formulated. This would reduce the cost to the researcher, because a researcher usually collects more information than is necessary, in order to eliminate the necessity of a repeat field visit. If the researcher has precise understanding regarding the information that he would utilise in his report, the necessity of a repeat survey is automatically eliminated; it will not be necessary to prempt a repeat survey by incurring the cost of collecting unnecessary information at the very first stage.

The drawback of 'descriptive research' is that it has the limitation of formality. In the case of exploratory work, flexibility is the main advantage, as it results in the proper identification of the problem. In a situation where the problem is not properly identified, a descriptive study should be preceded by an exploratory study.

2.5.1 Steps in a Descriptive Study

As we have pointed out, a descriptive study may or may not have a set of hypotheses to start with. Thus, as a first step, a researcher identifies the research issue, specifies the research question and analyses whether or not the issue involves a set of hypotheses that can be specified as *a-priori*.

Theoretical knowledge of the subject and exposure to secondary information is necessary for the researcher to build his own judgement about the need to introduce a set of hypotheses on the research question. This, however, is the necessary first step in descriptive research.

Descriptive research is aimed at describing the phenomenon under study with quantitative and qualitative information. Such research does not aim at controlling the variables and simulating the results. The information that is necessary in the context of the given research issue will have to be identified. The second step involves identifying this information.

The researcher then compiles and analyses the information. The analysis is not expected to involve a rigorous study in terms of cause and effect relations among the variables. Statistical tools are utilised; however, sophisticated econometric tools are usually not used in such studies. This is so because a descriptive study does not insist on having a set of research hypotheses that are to be tested *precisely* with the tools of quantitative analysis. The researcher is expected to furnish his research findings in terms of simple statistical tables, without the rigour of analysis, to lay bare the precise relation of causality among the variables captured in terms of econometric models. This is done in a separate research design which is known as the design of causal studies. However, pre-planning is needed for carrying out statistical analysis, regardless of the level of sophistication of such studies.

2.5.2 Main Characteristics of Descriptive Research

The main characteristics of descriptive research are the following:

(a) The researcher does not exercise control on the variables—he can only report what has already happened and what is happening at present.

(b) The research work is pre-planned and has a structured design. It has a research question – with or without research hypothesis(es) – and it ends up with some conclusions which could be tentative, forming the basis of further research.

(c) Since the purpose of the study is to provide information to specific issues which constitute the research question, the issues must be selected carefully. The findings of a descriptive research might suffer from systematic (non-random) error culminating in a wrong description of the phenomenon under study unless the researcher remains vigilant about this problem. Since the purpose of an exploratory study is to provide the researcher with a research question based on which further studies can be taken up, the risk that the research would end up with a wrong description of the phenomenon is minimum. The causal structure which is contained in the research hypothesis(es) of a causal study provides an in-built check against this problem (see below). But no such check is available in descriptive study. One would therefore conclude that more precautions need to be taken against the possibility of systematic (non-random) errors in descriptive study than in an exploratory or causal study.

2.6 CAUSAL STUDIES

Although descriptive studies are predictive, they do not aim at attaining precision in prediction. Usually, the researcher tries to attain precision in prediction by identifying the cause and effect relations among the factors that describe a phenomenon. Precision can be achieved by describing the factors as variables and then identifying the underlying relations among the variables. Usually, this is done by understanding the relation of causation in the phenomenon under study. The study is therefore called a causal study.

The basis of a causal study is the understanding that there exists a cause and effect relation that explains the features and the behaviour of the object under study. The philosophical root of causality as a method of study is positivism, which is usually applied in the study of natural phenomena. Ordinarily, the causation is studied in terms of variables, which are usually taken to be quantifiable. However, the logic of causation is also applied in cases where the variables are qualitative in nature.

In empirical research, usually, the causality is first conceived in a theory that describes a phenomenon in terms of the cause and effect relationship. The relationship is then tested empirically for which the researcher shall have to collect information in the form of data with respect to the variables under study. Sometimes, the theory is found to be inadequate for developing a working hypothesis for empirical research. In such a situation, the researcher takes recourse to an experimental study for unfolding the causality that might be hidden in the phenomena. In market research, an experimental study is of wider use (see Chapter 5 for a detailed discussion on experimental study).

In causal studies, the variables and explanatory set of variables are first understood as explained. Casual variables are known as *explanatory variables* and the outcomes or the effects of the causal variables are noted as *explained variables*. For example, the quantity demanded with respect to a particular product (assumed to be captured in sales figures) might be taken as an explained variable. From theory, one understands that the sales values of the product is explained by several factors such as the price of the product (P_x), the price of the related products (P_y, P_z), the purchasing power of the customers [captured through the disposable income (Y) of the target group of customers] and also the residual factors, that is, the factors that have not been taken care of in the theoretical construction. If the sales data describes the amount of the product sold and we note it as quantity demanded (X_d), then X_d is the explained variable and according to the theory, X_d is explained by a set of explanatory variables such as P_x, P_y, P_z, Y and R which is the symbol for the residual term. In simple mathematics, this is a description which is written as $X_d = f(P_x, P_y, P_z, Y, R)$; Here, f indicates that X_d is related to the variables indicated within the bracket. The exact nature of the relation is not specified in this description. However, in empirical research, the researcher will have to specify the exact form of the function and tests the validity of the relation by taking recourse to statistical analysis.

Given this broad outline, we shall now discuss the types of causation that we may conceptualise, while taking up empirical research.

2.6.1 Deterministic Causation

Causation is considered to be deterministic, if the identified explanatory variable can explain the behaviour of the explained variable completely. Consider the previous example regarding the behaviour of the sales data that is supposed to describe the demand behaviour of the product. If it is assumed that the demand of the product described through the quantitative information of the sales data and the quantity sold is explained by four explanatory variables, namely, price of the product (P_x), price of related products (P_y and P_z) and the level of income of the consumer (Y), then in effect, it is being suggested that the volume of sales is completely determined by these four factors. The implication is to be noted carefully. If we know the exact relation by which these four explanatory variables are related to the explained variable, then for various given values of P_x, P_y, P_z and Y, we can determine the quantity demanded of the product (X_d) with precision. A causal study which is performed under this framework is known as a study under deterministic causation. For example, when we run a regression with X_d as the explained variable and P_x, P_y, P_z and Y as explanatory variables, it may so happen that the regression cannot explain X_d completely in terms of the four explanatory variables. Still, the model will be considered a deterministic model because the model states with certainty, which part remains unexplained by the selected explanatory variables.

2.6.2 Probabilistic Causation

Let us try to look deeper into the problem. How does one know that X_1, X_2 and X_3 are three variables, which are necessary as well as sufficient to capture the movement of the variable Y? The answer could be that we get it from the theory—in this case, from the theory of demand for the product under consideration. How the theory is developed is a different issue and is not in the purview of the present discussion. The researcher accepts the theory as a robust one, so much so that he or she believes the theory has the power to explain fully the behaviour of X_d from the given information on P_x, P_y, P_z and Y.

However, no theory is so robust from the empirical point of view. If we test the theory for empirical verification, it will be observed that even with an exhaustive set of explanatory variables, one cannot explain the behaviour of the explained variable in totality. A gap will still exist—the gap between what the theory explains and what occurs in reality. The gap will be low, given that the theory is sufficiently robust. A robust theory will minimise the gap, but the gap is still expected to exist. *The reason is that there is basic randomness in the behaviour of the variables under the study.* The root of this randomness is, of course, the incompleteness in knowledge. How and when this problem will be resolved is a different issue. The researcher in the empirical area of the subject needs a tool to tackle such a situation. A probabilistic model that contains/captures the chances of occurrence of the explained variable, given the occurrence of one or more explanatory variables, can be suggested as an effective way of handling such a situation. Instead of taking a deterministic model, one may gain by replacing this with a probabilistic model where the researcher enters a disturbance term in the proposed regression. The disturbance term is taken as a random variable, with a given probability distribution and the whole exercise now becomes a *stochastic* one.

2.6.3 Causal Relation: Framework for Quantitative Analysis

For quantitative analysis, a researcher may start by studying the extent of association among the variables under discussion, *without specifying the possible exact relation among the variables.* In statistical theory, this part of the analysis is done by measuring the correlation coefficient between or among the variables. In case the correlation is found to be low, the researcher understands that a further study to explore the exact form of the cause–effect relation is not necessary. The correlation coefficient also indicates the direction of the relation between two variables (if the correlation coefficient is negative, the relation is that one variable moves in the opposite direction to the other variable).

The other method for studying the extent of association among the variables is to apply a statistical tool for the analysis of variance. A non-parametric test, known as the *Chi-Square Test,* is often used to study whether the hypothesis of having any relation among the variables can be accepted with reasonable probability. These tools of analysis will be discussed later. The point that we want to highlight at this stage is that the pursuit of quantification of the relation in terms of cause and effect should be preceded by an exercise that checks whether the variables under discussion are at all related or not.

At the second stage, we study the extent of the exact relation among the variables within the framework of a cause and effect relationship. Needless to say, this part of the exercise is taken up only after the researcher is convinced that the variables are indeed correlated or that the possibility of association among the variables is not ruled out. The issue at this stage is to study the exact nature of relation in a function form in which the independent variables are the explanatory variables and the dependent variable is the explained variable. Usually, such relations are explored in terms of regression analysis.

Suppose it is observed that there is a positive correlation between the level of family income and the percentage of expenditure on the consumption of fruits, this indicates that there is a relation between two variables—the family income and the percentage of expenditure on the consumption of fruits. The possible direction of the relationship or association is described by the sign of the correlation coeﬃcient. The correlation coefficient also describes the strength of association among the variables, the family income and the percentage expenditure, on fruits in this case.

Now, the subsequent step is to study the direction of relation, namely, the relation in terms of the cause and the effect and the precise amount by which the quantitive change in the causal variable affects the effect variable. Technically speaking, this issue can be addressed by regression analysis. A detailed discussion of regression analysis will be taken up in Chapter 10. At this stage, it should be pointed out that regression analysis presupposes a functional relation in an exact form. In this particular example, the relationship is developed with one variable as the dependent and the other as the independent variable (demand for fruit is reflected in the expenditure on fruits as the function of family income, that is, $Y = f(X)$ in the context of the present example). Once this is specified in the form of an exact function, we can find out the regression coefficients. From the estimated coefficient, one can find out the effect of change in income on the consumption of fruits.

For non-probalistic regression analysis, the researcher starts with the hypothesis that there exists an exact relation between or among the set of explained and explanatory variables. The form of such a relation could be linear or non-linear. Thus, in the case of a two variable model, the exact form of relation with $Y = f(X)$, could be captured in terms of the following exact relations, $y = a + bx$ which suggests a linear relation, the estimated parameters in this case would be $\hat{a}$ for a and $\hat{b}$ for b.

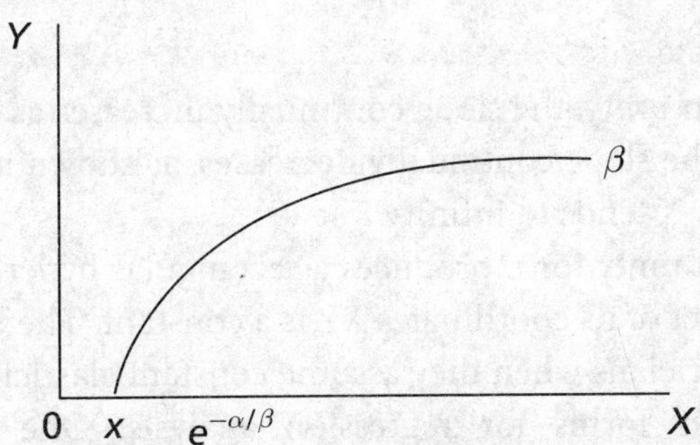

Fig. 2.1 Semi-log transformation

It is not always expected that the relation between X and Y would be linear. It may be non-linear as well. A widely used form of the non-linear relation is $X = AB^y$. The econometric model that attempts to describe such a relation is often developed with a semi-log or a double-log transformation.

$$Y = \alpha + \beta \log X; X = AB^y$$

$$\frac{dy}{dx} = \frac{\beta}{x}$$

so that the slope decreases steadily as X increases. When $Y = 0$, $\log X = -\alpha/\beta$, so that the point of intersection on the X axis is at $-e^{-\alpha/\beta}$.
The exponential form of this function is $X = e^{-\alpha/\beta} e^{y/\beta}$, which may be written as $X = AB^y$, where

$$A = e^{-\alpha/\beta}$$
$$B = e^{1/\beta}$$

This is the steady growth function employed.

Double-log transformation

(1) $\log Y = \alpha + \beta \log X$
(2) $\log Y = \alpha - \beta \log X$

These functions may also be written as

(1) $Y = AX^{\beta}$
(2) $Y = AX^{-\beta}$

where $\log A = \alpha$
For case (1),

$$\frac{dY}{dX} = A\beta X^{\beta-1}$$

so that, if β is greater than unity, the slope continually increases as X increases, while if β lies between zero and unity, the slope continually decreases, as shown in Fig. 2.2. For either value of β, Y tends to infinity as X tends to infinity.

For case (2), a value of unity for β produces a rectangular hyperbola, that is, the locus of a point such that the product of its coordinates XY is a constant. The double-log transformation is employed by econometricians when they assume constant elasticity between Y and X.

There could be other forms for regression analysis. One such form is reciprocal transformation and logarithmic reciprocal transformation. Readers will get more exposure to these mathematical forms in a book on econometric analysis.

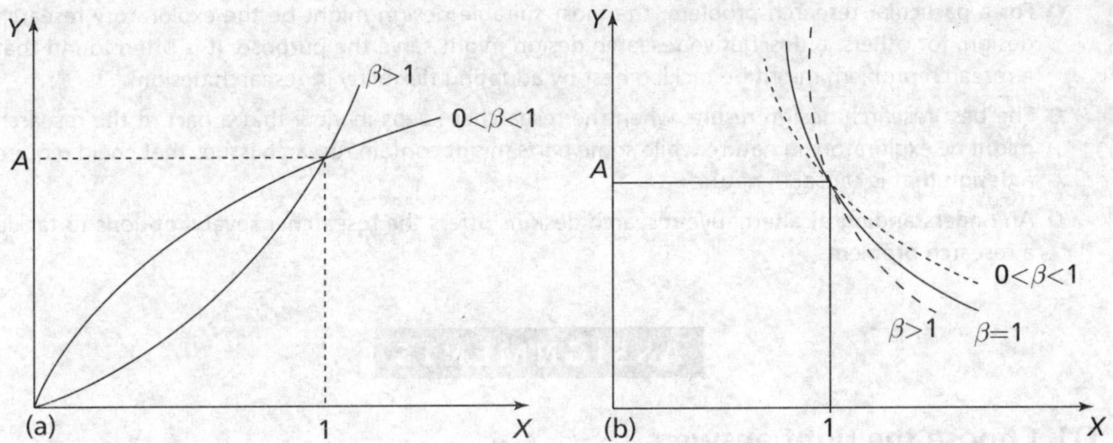

Fig. 2.2 Double-log transformation: Case 1

Fig. 2.3 Double-log transformation: Case 2

2.7 CONCLUDING OBSERVATIONS

While planning the research design, a practitioner should note that a research design should be drawn up on the basis of the suitability of the proposed design in the context of the research problem. The researcher has to apply his own judgement regarding the suitability of a particular design in the context of a given research problem. It is not necessarily true that the causal research design would be the first choice for a researcher because it contains more mathematical rigour. For some research problems, the most suitable design might be the exploratory research design. In some cases, a descriptive research design might best serve the purpose. *It is often found that a research problem can be best tackled by drawing up a research design which contains the elements of the various designs that have been outlined above.* In other words, *flexibility in research design is the key to good research.* The researcher will be rewarded if he draws up the research design according to his perception of the research problem, keeping in view that a part of the research may be exploratory in nature; but at the same time, there might exist some other parts which contain research issues that may be better addressed if the design is set as causal. A knowledge of alternative research designs helps the researcher understand the nature of options that he may apply while pursuing a research problem.

SUMMARY

- While finalising the research design, the researcher has to apply his own judgement regarding the suitability of a particular design for a given research problem. The causal research design need not be the first choice for a researcher just because it contains more mathematical rigour.

- For a particular research problem, the most suitable design might be the exploratory research design, for others, a descriptive research design might serve the purpose. It is often found that a research problem might be tackled best by adopting flexibility in research design.
- The best research design results when the researcher keeps in view that a part of the research might be exploratory in nature while some parts might contain research issues that could require a design that is causal in nature.
- An understanding of alternative research designs offers the researcher several options to tackle a research problem.

ASSIGNMENTS

Q1 Choose the right answers

1. Research designs are of the following types:
   (a) Exploratory, decisive and causal
   (b) Opportunity oriented, decisive and causal
   (c) Exploratory, descriptive and causal
   (d) Opportunity oriented, decision oriented and causal
2. Analogous situational studies are normally:
   (a) Part of causal design
   (b) Part of descriptive design
   (c) Part of exploratory design
   (d) None of the above
3. To find a meaningful conclusion, the research design sequence should be:
   (a) Exploratory, causal and then descriptive
   (b) Exploratory, descriptive and then causal
   (c) Causal, descriptive and then exploratory
   (d) None of the above
4. Deterministic causation is said to occur when:
   (a) The causal variable is controllable
   (b) The causal variable is the only necessary and essential condition for the effect
   (c) The causal variable is uncontrollable
   (d) None of the above
5. Probabilistic causation is said to occur when:
   (a) The effect has a probability of occurring
   (b) The causal variable is partially responsible for the effect
   (c) The causal variable is both necessary and sufficient condition for the causation of the effect
   (d) None of the above

6. A robust causal model will minimise the gap. The gap will still remain because of the following:
   (a) There is a basic randomness in the behaviour of the variables under study
   (b) There is systematic error in the data
   (c) The explained variables are not related to explanatory variables
   (d) None of the above
7. A case of customer profiling falls in which of the following research designs?
   (a) Causal research
   (b) Descriptive study
   (c) Exploratory study
   (d) None of the above
8. While setting the research design, the practitioner might:
   (a) Combine exploratory design with causal design and not with descriptive design
   (b) Combine descriptive design with causal design and not with exploratory design
   (c) Combine all the designs
   (d) No combination is to be allowed
9. The double-log transformation is commonly employed because the assumption is:
   (a) Different elasticity between X and Y
   (b) Constant elasticity between X and Y
   (c) Increasing elasticity in X and inelastic Y
   (d) None of the above
10. A probabilistic causal study model contains:
   (a) Chances of occurrence of explanatory variables, given the occurrence of one or more explained variables
   (b) Chances of occurrence of explained variable, given the occurrence of one or more explanatory variables
   (c) Chances of explained and explanatory variables not being defined
   (d) None of the above

Answers

1. (c), 2. (c), 3. (b), 4. (b), 5. (b), 6. (a), 7. (b), 8. (c), 9. (b), 10. (b)

Q2 Answer the following

1. What are the factors that have to be taken into consideration by a researcher while choosing the type of research design?

2. What are the purposes of exploratory design? State the stages involved in an exploratory design. What are the advantages and disadvantages of using secondary data?
3. State the role of a descriptive study design along with a hypothetical example.
4. A soft drink company wants to launch a carbonated soft drink in an island inhabited by tribal people who have never tasted such a drink. As a consultant to the firm, you have been assigned the task of finding out the possibility of success of such a drink and the possible mode of operation for a 'product launch'. What is the type of research design you are likely to adopt and why?
5. A market research agency has appointed you as a consultant, to offer advice on an image makeover for one of its clients—an airline with domestic operations which has been in operation for forty years in a non-competitive environment. Over the last five years, it has had to face competition from newer airlines in the market. These airlines are acting as competitors to the ageing airline. The agency is trying to give the ageing airline an up-market image. You have been asked to develop a research design and advocate for such a design. State the secondary sources that you have to take into consideration, in the Indian context.

Sources of Data

LEARNING OBJECTIVES

After going through this chapter you will understand

- Types and sources of data
- Mechanism of data generation
- Alternative settings under which data might be collected
- Nature of data under various settings
- Issues related to the techniques of data collection under different settings

Key words: Stimuli, formal structured setting, formal unstructured setting, informal setting, verbal and non-verbal communication, participant observation, systematic observation, structured and unstructured interview, questionnaire—structured

3.1 INTRODUCTION

The basic ingredient of empirical research is 'data'. The generic source of the word 'data' is Greek. 'Data' is plural; its singular form is 'datum'. In normal usage, the word data is often taken as singular—a collective singular term which indicates information captured in precise terms. Data could be qualitative as well as quantitative. However, in most cases, the information that comes under 'data' is in the quantitative form.

In empirical research, the quality of research depends very much on the quality of data. Even if the researcher has a good deal of exposure to quantitative techniques and is proficient in handling computer software packages, he could fail to achieve a desirable quality in his research output if the quality of data is inferior. A researcher should therefore be careful while handling data. A researcher will get a better deal if he is aware of this problem and considers the issue of collecting the data carefully.

For this, one must know the origin of data. A researcher uses two kinds of data—primary and secondary. *Primary data* are data that have been generated by the researcher himself. *Secondary data* refers to data collected by the researcher from a source—the data have not been generated by the researcher himself. This is a broad division. However, as one looks deeper into the issue, one understands that in the final analysis there is nothing like secondary data. Such data which are secondary data to a particular researcher, must have been generated by other researchers to whom these were primary data. We will, however, define primary data as data generated by the researcher himself (and not collected from the outcome of research by others), without undermining the fact that all data, in the final analysis, is primary with respect to the researcher who generated that data (see Section 3.4). While using secondary data and also while generating primary data, a researcher would benefit if he takes this point into consideration and tries to understand the mechanism by which a particular data set is generated.

3.2 STIMULUS–RESPONSE RELATIONSHIP

What we observe as data is basically an outcome of the interaction between the researcher via a stimulus and the object on which the stimulus is being imparted. The mechanism by which stimulus or stimuli (plural of stimulus) generate data by working on the object may be described in the form of a flow chart (Fig. 3.1).

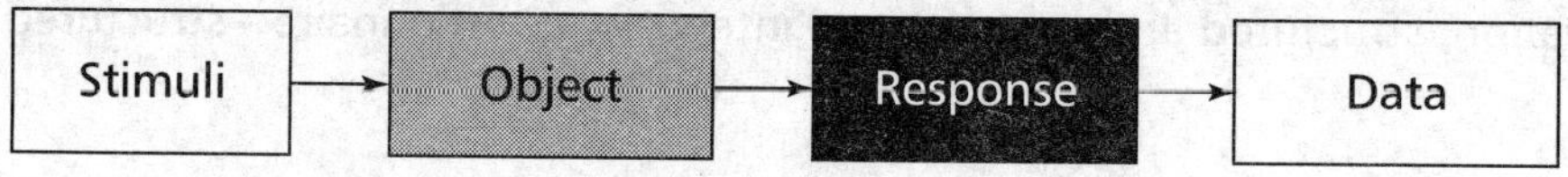

Fig. 3.1 Mechanism of data generation

In elaborating on this theme, we would state that the nature and the quality of the data depend, to a large extent, on the nature of stimuli applied to the respondent and the nature of response that the researcher receives from the respondent. Stimuli may be classified as *systematic* and *unsystematic* stimuli. What do we mean by systematic stimuli? In social research, we often collect data with respect to a set of respondents ('object' in Fig. 3.1). Under systematic stimuli, we communicate the issue to each respondent through a predetermined

EXAMPLES OF UNSYSTEMATIC STIMULI

On an income related issue, the three respondents were asked the following questions:

Respondent A: Which income range do you belong to?
Respondent B: How much did you earn in the last month?
Respondent C: Would you consult your pay slip and let me know what was the gross salary that you were paid in the last month?

The examples stated above are cases where we have altered the questions, for no two respondents are the questions the same. Hence, the stimuli will not be systematic even if the ordering of the questions remains the same.

In this reference, we must also state situations where the questions might have been standardised, but the sequencing has been changed. Suppose we are conducting a rural survey of households regarding the consumption pattern of edible oils among two groups of respondents. The question sequencing for each member of the first group is: (i) name (ii) family size (iii) income and (iv) information regarding the product. The questions regarding all four issues are worded in a standardised form and the sequence of questions remains the same for each respondent, so the stimuli in this case will be considered systematic.

In the case of the second group, the sequence is changed. For some, it is information regarding the product, which comes first, this is followed by a query on family size, and then comes the question on income, and finally, the name of the respondent is asked. For another person, the sequencing of information is changed. We would conclude that the stimuli in case of the first group followed a given pattern (systematic), but with respect to the second group no pattern was maintained (unsystematic).

set of questions. The wording of each question is carefully decided before meeting the respondents, and if stimuli are to be systematic, the requirement is that the same wording has to be used for each respondent. In systematic stimuli, the second necessary requirement is that stimuli are imparted following a given pattern. This implies that the ordering of the questions should remain the same for each respondent. Under unsystematic stimuli, the rigidity in pattern is not maintained. Again, the questions may not be predetermined, neither is it necessary that the wording would remain the same for each respondent.

Depending on the nature of stimuli, the researcher would expect two types of responses from the respondents. A respondent might behave systematically while meeting the query of the researcher. There is a possibility that the respondent would behave unsystematically while answering the questions even if the stimuli are imparted in a systematic manner. Logically speaking, there are four alternative possibilities of which three would describe the alternative formats of data collection. These alternative formats could be described as below:

3.3 ALTERNATIVE FORMATS OF DATA COLLECTION

The interaction between stimuli and response can take place in three different ways. The possible alternatives are described below.

Table 3.1 Stimulus–response interaction and alternative formats of data collection

		Response	
Stimuli	Systematic	Systematic	Unsystematic
		Formal structured setting	Formal unstructured setting
	Unsystematic	Impossible setting	Informal setting

The first is the *formal structured setting*. As one can see from Table 3.1, the data collection setting is called formal structured, because systematic stimuli are being coupled with systematic responses under this setting. This is expected to be the most preferred setting, because both the stimulus and the response being systematic, it is likely that the non-sampling errors would be relatively less in the data collected according to this format. However, the researcher may sometimes find that the nature of his research is such that the data collected through a formal structured setting would contain less information than one would have found if the structural rigidity were done away with and the data were collected under an alternative, say 'informal' setting. In such a situation, the researcher may not opt for the formal structured setting. The other point is that the formal structured setting may not be attainable for the researcher. It should be kept in mind that the formal structured setting is the outcome of *systematic behaviour on the part of the respondents as well.* It may so happen that in spite of his effort, the selected group of respondents that the researcher faces behaves in an unsystematic way while responding to the stimuli. In that case, the setting for data collection would be *formal unstructured* in nature, even though the researcher may have wanted to have a formal structured setting.

Formal unstructured, as the name suggests, is a format of data collection where systematic stimulus is coupled with unsystematic response. In many cases, the researcher may confront a situation where the responses are not systematic even though the stimuli are being imparted systematically. The researcher may decide that he will stick to systematic stimuli even though the responses are not systematic. Since the responses are not systematic, the data would then be collected under the *formal unstructured setting*. Alternatively, the researcher may decide to switch over to the technique of imparting unsystematic stimuli. The researcher will do so if in his judgement, he could get more (and better) information if the structural rigidity were done away with. The format for data collection under such a setting is called the '*informal setting*'. Since unsystematic stimuli cannot be coupled with systematic responses, we get only three alternative formats of data collection as shown in Table 3.1.

3.4 FORMS OF COMMUNICATION AND MODES OF DATA COLLECTION

Table 3.2 Alternative modes of data collection

Settings	Responses		
	Non-verbal	**Oral–verbal**	**Written–verbal**
Informal settings	Participant observation	Conversations, use of informants	Articles, letters, editorials, comments, biographies
Formal unstructured settings	Systematic observation	Interview unstructured	Questionnaire open-ended
Formal structured settings	Experimental techniques	Interview structured	Questionnaire structured

As discussed earlier, there are three alternative settings under which primary data can be generated. We did not, however, consider the form of response that the researcher obtains while collecting the data in any of the three settings. The form of response is important because it describes the *form* in which the data appears. There could be two basic forms in which the data set appears as the outcome of stimuli–response interaction. One is called *non-verbal* and the other is called *verbal.* The verbal mode of communication is again described in one of the following forms—*oral–verbal* and *written–verbal.* Non-verbal response is indirect response, often expressed through body language. A person, while seeing an advertisement, may spontaneously jump, as an expression through body language. This is an example of non-verbal communication. The advertisement is the stimulus in this case and the expression through body language is the response. The point to be noted is that the communication here is indirect.

Since there are three modes of communication and there are three different settings under which the stimuli–response interaction takes place, there are nine alternative forms in which the primary data can be generated. The possibilities are described in Table 3.2. While reading the table, a researcher will observe that each individual form of data generation has its roots in *the setting* in which the data set is generated and *the mode of communication* used by the respondent. For example, if we say that the data set has been generated by administering a structured questionnaire, the researcher will note that the primary data generated by this method is the outcome of a formal structured setting in which the stimuli were systematic and the responses were also systematic. A structured questionnaire would also imply that the response was communicated in the written–verbal form (an example of a structured questionnaire is given in Appendix 6.1). Again, if the data set is generated by an experimental technique, the researcher will understand that the mode of communication was non-verbal in this case, and the data collection setting was formal structured, that is, systematic stimuli were coupled with systematic responses for generating the data set.

3.5 NATURE OF DATA UNDER VARIOUS SETTINGS

As we have observed in the last section, primary data can be generated in nine diferent ways. Each method of data generation has its own advantages and disadvantages. Again, no particular method can be singled out as the best among the alternatives. A specific scenario has its own method of data generation which dictates the best possible method and the researcher will have to take his particular method into consideration. Thus, an anthropologist taking up research on the rituals of a particular tribe located in a remote place may find it necessary to collect data by observing the behaviour of the tribe, as a participant in their social life. Canvassing a structured questionnaire in such a situation is not expected to generate a data set which might be as good in terms of quality as that under the participant observation method. Again, a market research organisation will find that canvassing a structured questionnaire is most rewarding for a study on consumer psyche. A participant observation method is not likely to provide as rich a set as the questionnaire method is likely to generate.

We will now discuss the various methods of data collection that are available with respect to a particular data collection setting.

Informal setting

Participant observation: This method is widely used in social anthropology. The method of communication here is non-verbal. The researcher gathers information from the body-language, the reaction communicated to others by various gestures. There is no direct communication to the researcher in this case, although the stimulus is imparted by the researcher himself (or his agent). The researcher generates communication by imparting stimuli. However, the stimuli are not systematic in this case. The idea is that a systematic set of stimuli would make the respondent conscious, so that the spontaneity in their reactions would be arrested. A researcher cannot afford to arrest the spontaneity in behaviour in this case, because the spontaneity is the key to deriving the required response from the respondents.

Conversation: This is the most popular method of data collection, when the chosen setting is informal. As in the case of participant observation, the stimuli are unsystematic, the responses are also unsystematic. However, unlike what happens under participant observation, the mode of communication here is verbal; more specifically oral–verbal. Usually, the researcher has a specific topic in mind when he begins the dialogue, but the conversation follows its own sequence. The researcher monitors the discussion only to the extent necessary to keep the conversation on the right track. This method of data collection can also be done by appointing investigators when the researcher finds that it is not necessary to collect the information by a personal visit or when he does not have access to the target group of respondents. In social research, we also confront certain situations wherein direct interaction with the respondents could be counter productive (this is often the case with gender related issues). Conversation by proxy (appointing informant) becomes important in such a situation. We would add that the identification of proper informants is essential, in such a situation.

Newspapers, articles, biographies: These methods of data collection use the written–verbal mode of communication and the data collection setting is informal. The researcher cannot apply any stimuli in this case, because the process has not been engineered by him. However, he collects the information *as primary,* as no researcher has previously performed this exercise. To the researcher, the information is the outcome of stimuli imparted by others (it may be based on the volition of the respondent himself). What matters is that the outcome is consistent with what the researcher wants to use in his pursuit of research.

The reliability of such data might often be suspect. While using such data, the researcher will have to take this into account. The issue of bias being present in these data has been discussed at length by various scholars.

Formal unstructured setting

Systematic observation: The difference between participant observation and systematic observation is that in the latter case, the researcher tries to impart stimuli systematically, even though the research issue is such that the respondent may communicate his feeling in an unsystematic manner. The mode of communication in both cases is, however, non-verbal. Unlike what happens in the case of participant observation, the researcher here does not depend on spontaneity. In order to make the respondent act, the researcher himself imparts some stimuli. An example of systematic stimuli can be given from the example of a marketing campaign. While campaigning for a product, the market research organisation may display an advertisement or the product itself in a prominent place (thus imparting a stimulus), and watch or observe the reactions of people. The impact may be recorded by noting the percentage of passers-by who ignore the advertisement for the product, the percentage that try to get the message of the advertisement and so on. The mode of communication is non-verbal and what the researcher does can be described as systematic observation.

Unstructured interview: When the mode of communication is oral–verbal and the researcher imparts the stimuli systematically, it may so happen that the respondent prefers to communicate his response in an unsystematic manner. We would categorise such a data collection setting as an unstructured interview. In social research, we often find that the respondent does not behave as anticipated by the researcher. The reason could be that the researcher had been unaware of the manner in which respondents would respond to his query.

Since the researcher cannot insist on the respondent behaving the way the researcher desires, it would be rewarding for the researcher to follow the sequence in which the respondent wants to meet his query. Unstructured interview is the method used for data collection in such a situation.

Open-ended questionnaire: The setting under the open-ended questionnaire is the same as in the unstructured interview, except that the mode of communication here is written–verbal. Such a setting may suffer from ambiguity in terms of answers. Thus, one should not advocate such a setting for data collection. One may argue that the researcher would benefit by adopting a close-ended questionnaire. This is not necessarily true. We shall discuss this issue in detail in Chapter 6.

Formal structured setting

The mode of communication here might be non-verbal, when the technique for data collection is described as an experimental technique. Experimental technique is a widely used technique of data generation, particularly in some research issues related to market research. This technique is described in detail in the next chapter. The other two modes of communication under a formal structured setting are the structured interview and the structured questionnaire. Under structured interview, the mode of communication is oral–verbal, while the mode of communication is written–verbal. The method used in a structured questionnaire is often distinguished from that followed in the open-ended questionnaire by the fact that the structured questionnaire often remains closed-ended. This issue will be discussed in detail in Chapter 4, when we consider the methodological issues related to questionnaires.

3.6 CONCLUDING OBSERVATIONS

The generation of data under various settings should be studied so that the researcher understands how the problem of maintaining data quality should be handled. This is important because only after being satisfied that the quality of the data is reasonably good, should the researcher take up empirical research with a view to unveiling the truth that the data contains. For empirical analysis, there are again certain other steps that the researcher should follow. The first of these steps involve the measurement and scaling of the data. After studying the data generation process and solving the problem of measurement and scale related issues, in the next step, one would scrutinise the data for minimising the non-sampling error. After this, the data set is considered to be ready for statistical analysis. The initial step here is to summarise the information contained in the data by applying the tools of descriptive statistics. More sophisticated statistical tools are then used to study the information that can further be gathered from the data set. The methodological issues related to each of these steps will be taken up in a chronological order in the remaining part of this book.

SUMMARY

- The outcome of stimuli–response interaction gives rise to information which constitutes the basis of qualitative and quantitative data.
- There are three different settings under which such interactions can take place—formal structured setting, formal unstructured setting and informal setting.
- There are three different methods of communication that might be utilised for data collection under these three different settings. There would thus be nine methods of data collection. The main features of each of these methods have been discussed.
- Some of the methods of data collection that are often utilised in social research in general and business research in particular, have been highlighted in the last part of this chapter. Some of these techniques should be discussed in further detail. This has been taken up in the next chapter.

ASSIGNMENTS

Q1 Choose the right answers

1. In empirical research, the quality of research primarily depends on:
   (a) Quantitative techniques used in the research
   (b) Methods of handling of data
   (c) Quality of data
   (d) None of the above
2. The two important control elements in calibrating the data are:
   (a) Object and response
   (b) Stimuli and object
   (c) Stimuli and response
   (d) None of the above
3. Stimuli is said to be systematic when:
   (a) There exist predetermined questions with predetermined sequencing
   (b) There exist predetermined questions without designed sequencing
   (c) There exist non-predesigned questions with predetermined sequencing
   (d) None of the above
4. Under alternative settings, the primary data can be generated by:
   (a) One specific alternative
   (b) Two specific alternatives
   (c) Three specific alternatives
   (d) None of the above

5. Systematic stimuli that give systematic response are referred to as:
   (a) Formal structured setting
   (b) Informal setting
   (c) Formal unstructured setting
   (d) None of the above
6. 'Impossible setting' is said to occur when:
   (a) Unsystematic stimuli are matched by unsystematic response
   (b) Systematic stimuli are matched by systematic response
   (c) Unsystematic stimuli are matched by systematic response
   (d) None of the above
7. There are three types of setting in data collection method:
   (a) Unpatterned setting, formal unstructured setting, formal structured setting
   (b) Formal unstructured setting, formal patterned setting, impossible setting
   (c) Informal setting, formal unstructured setting, formal structured setting
   (d) None of the above
8. The modes of communication are stated as:
   (a) Oral, verbal, written
   (b) Verbal and written
   (c) Non-verbal, oral–verbal, written–verbal
   (d) None of the above
9. In a formal unstructured setting, the data collection method under the non-verbal response is referred to as:
   (a) Participant observation
   (b) Systematic observation
   (c) Experimental technique
   (d) None of the above
10. 'Structured questionnaire' as a method of data collection is used when:
   (a) Informal setting of data collection is matched by written–verbal communication
   (b) Formal unstructured setting is matched by written–verbal communication
   (c) Formal structured setting is matched by written–verbal communication
   (d) None of the above

Answers

1. (c), 2. (c), 3. (a), 4. (c), 5. (a), 6. (c), 7. (c), 8. (c), 9. (b), 10. (c)

Q2 Answer the following

1. What is data and what are the types of data? Give examples and explain the types of data.
2. Explain stimulus–response interaction in the process of data generation. What are the alternative formats for collecting data?
3. State how data is generated under three alternative settings.
4. Describe in detail the methods of data collection under an informal setting in the case of non-verbal, oral–verbal and verbal–written communications.
5. In a formal unstructured setting under the non-verbal form of communication, we have 'systematic observation', how is it different from 'participant observation'? Under what circumstances should one opt for participant observation?

CHAPTER 4

MAINTAINING DATA QUALITY UNDER VARIOUS SETTINGS

LEARNING OBJECTIVES

After going through this chapter you will understand

- Data quality and the relation between the data collection format and the stimuli–response interactions
- Data collection formats under oral-verbal communication
- Advantages and disadvantages of verbal communication
- Non-verbal communication and observation technique
- Content analysis and methods to improve the reliability of data
- No single method of data collection has the unique property of ensuring data quality
- The issues that a researcher should take care of by developing a simple check list
- Secondary data
- Sources of secondary data
- Official statistics

Key words: Structured interview, unstructured interview, observation, clinical interview, focussed interview, biographies, content analysis, secondary data

4.1 INTRODUCTION

In order to ensure quality of the data, it is not enough for the researcher to know how the data set is generated. The researcher must intervene in the process of data generation so that the stimuli–response interaction can assume a form which would describe the outcome in the best possible way. This can be done by checking the outcome and filtering the information in some cases, and by creating a conducive atmosphere for data generation in other cases. We shall discuss some such techniques in this chapter. The next two chapters will discuss other techniques which are widely used for ensuring data quality.

4.2 DATA QUALITY UNDER VERBAL MODE OF COMMUNICATION

As discussed in Chapter 3, the information that a researcher collects under an informal setting can be communicated by the oral-verbal, written-verbal or non-verbal mode. Communication can also be non-verbal. Communication through the non-verbal mode under an informal setting is done by a method known as the participant observation method. Whatever be the method, it is often found the quality of such information has to be improved before the researcher can use them in his area of research. The issue of improving the data quality under oral-verbal and written-verbal mode with reference to such a setting is discussed under *Content Analysis* (Section 4.5). Content analysis might be necessary even when the data generation setting is not informal. For example, the information generated by unstructured interviews (Chapter 3) might also need a content analysis.

Before one takes up content analysis, one must know how the content has been formed. As we have discussed, the information might be gathered from informal discussions, biographies or essays or, in a different setting, from an unstructured interview (Chapter 3). One may view them as the instruments of data collection. Each of these instruments have their points of strength and weakness. The quality of a particular data set that the researcher generates should be assessed taking into consideration the nature of the instrument that generated it. The researcher must be aware of this point before taking up content analysis for improving the data quality. In this section, the salient features of these instruments are discussed so that the users of these instruments remain aware of the nature of the contents that might be gathered by using them.

4.2.1 Discussion and Interview

The verbal stimulus elicits a certain verbal response. This is referred to as conversations, discussions and interviews depending on the settings which may include an informal setting, a formal unstructured setting or a formal structured setting.

Under oral-verbal communication, the responses have been classified as discussion, unstructured interview and structured interview corresponding to an informal setting, a formal unstructured setting and a formal structured setting respectively. A researcher must be aware that each of these data collection methods have certain advantages and can produce the best results under specific settings.

An informal setting is one in which the stimulus is not structured and it takes shape as the oral conversation grows. A lot of freewheeling is allowed; thus, the researcher may be in a position to understand the views of the respondents. Let us suppose a market researcher was unable to understand, through both the formal unstructured setting and the formal structured setting, why there is resistance among housewives (who are first generation entrants to the urban way of life) in adopting hygienic machine-made breads as a regular item in their breakfast. A questionnaire including alternative reasons that an urban dweller can identify with would fail to resonate with the psyche of these housewives. A researcher would get a better insight into the reasons behind problem if he visited the housewives without a questionnaire and discussed the issue in an informal setting. He would thus get varied answers till he is able to crystallise a suitable response. This process of using an informal setting yields oral-verbal response, labelled *Discussion*.

There is another situation when the interviewer administers the stimuli using a predetermined set of questions in the oral-verbal form to the respondents. The questions are standardised and the stimuli follow a given pattern. The oral interaction may reach a point when the respondent refuses to follow the pattern that the researcher wants him to. In other words, the response may not be systematic. This is referred to as an *Unstructured Interview*. A situation may exist where the researcher cannot afford to spend much time, yet the cooperation of the interviewee is essential in order to bring his views to light. It may be a situation of exploring the level of knowledge about the subject in question. For example, let us suppose a person is being interviewed on his perception regarding use of a plant's extract as a cure. This is a likely situation where the interviewer will plan to give systematic stimuli (that is, a certain set of questions in a certain sequence). The response may sometimes be off the required track. The researcher would still try to come closer and closer to the issue by stressing on the sequence. This is a typical situation where the unstructured interview is more rewarding than the structured one.

In the third case, there may be systematic stimuli and systematic response but the communication is done by oral presentation. The questions are close-ended and the answers, as expected by the interviewer, will be any one option of the multiple choice answers—'yes', 'no', 'not aware' and so on. This is referred as a *Structured Interview*.

In this regard it is worth noting that at certain times the terms *Interviews* and *Discussions* have been used interchangeably. Nonetheless, whether they are interviews or discussions, they own their genesis to oral-verbal communication. It depends on the type of approach the interviewer adopts.

(a) *Structured interview:* When interviews involve a set pattern of questioning and questions which are uniformly administered to all the respondents with hardly any exception, the interview is called a structured interview. The questions are fixed in number and alternative questions are also stipulated. The openness of such interviews is only limited to the conditions mentioned above. The sequence of questions may sometimes be changed to elicit a response to a question that might not have been answered. The waiver of a question by the interviewer is often not acceptable. The fixed questions require a response of either 'Yes' or 'No', or exercising options among the given alternative answers. Such questions are often described as close-ended questions.

EXAMPLE

While surveying the market for disposable contact lenses, the tele-interview method was adopted. The specific questions included were: whether there were members in the families who used spectacles, whether they had ever used contact lenses, either regularly or occasionally, and finally whether they had heard of disposable contact lenses. The questioning followed the same sequence for every respondent.

(b) *Unstructured interview:* Unstructured interviews are flexible and less systematic than structured interviews. The objective of such interviews is to understand the motivation and perception of the respondents. The respondents are therefore encouraged to respond with openness. The success of such interviews depends on the maturity of the respondents in reference to the issue concerned. Similarly, the interview is not structured into a sequence, pattern or fixed number of queries and alternatives. The interviewer is free to ask questions according to the situation and to the best of his wisdom.

The following are the major types of unstructured interviews.

(i) *Focussed interview:* The main function of the focussed interview is to focus on the views of the respondent regarding the topic of study. The interviewer suggests a hypothesis or a problem topic that he wants the interviewee to explore and present his views on. In other words, the interviewer has his focus on a topic which he wants the interviewee to explore. The interviewer has the liberty to make the topic lively, enriching and a worthwhile discussion by controlling the direction of flow of thoughts. It has to be kept in mind that the more knowledgeable the interviewer is about the topic and hypothesis, the better will be the focus of the interview.

(ii) *Clinical interview:* While the focussed interview concentrates on a specific experience of the respondent, the clinical interview is concerned with the broad feeling, which incidentally often reflects the motivation of the respondent or his general experience. The most common of clinical interviews are observed in psychiatric clinics, interviews in criminal cases involving the prisoners; case studies in various social groups are other areas in which the clinical interview takes place. The interviewer knows in advance the aspect of feeling or experience he wants the respondents to communicate but the method adopted would be flexible, and is therefore often left to the discretion of the respondent.

(iii) *The non-directive interview:* The term 'non-directive' owes its origin to the field of psychotherapy. In this kind of interview, the respondent is encouraged to express his feelings freely without directive questions or intervention by the therapist. Normally this is what one is expected to do under an unstructured interview. But, the difference is that in the non-directive interview, the role of the interviewer is limited to the bare minimum, at times only suggesting some guidelines so that the initiative again shifts to the respondent. The art of conducting a non-directive interview involves creating an atmosphere in which the respondent feels free to communicate. Disapproval, admonition or advice from the interviewer might hinder this process.

4.2.2 Biographies

A professional biographer usually chooses a famous person's life and plans his biography. It is also true that in doing so, one keeps the saleability in mind and makes the biography sensational, shocking or dramatic. As a result, biographies may often misinform the researcher who would therefore have to crosscheck the information that is obtained from the biographies.

Historical documents deal with events of the past and try to relate the sequence of the events and process such data. But, how far can documentary evidence be treated as authentic? It should be borne in mind that documentary materials do provide insight into the event and for this reason they are indispensable but it is true as well, that motives and interest do also play a part in such documentary evidence. What is therefore essential is proper choice of facts and sequence of events while the investigator works on the documentary evidence.

While we are discussing the modes of settings, one core fact on the whole issue is whether the disclosures are correct or not. Gottschalk (1945) states five kinds of circumstances, which may make the attitude of the investigators favourable towards the personal documents.

(a) When the truth of the statement is a matter of indifference to the writer, he is likely to be unbiased.
(b) When the statement is prejudicial to the interest of the informant, it is likely to be true.
(c) The facts of the issue are matter of common knowledge and are so proven that the scope of misrepresenting is remote.
(d) The part of the statement of primary interest is both incidentally and intrinsically probable.
(e) At times when the informant's statements are contrary to the expectation and anticipation of the investigator's knowledge.

4.3 THE ADVANTAGES AND DISADVANTAGES OF THE ORAL-VERBAL METHOD OF COMMUNICATIONS

4.3.1 Advantages

(a) The response to this method is often very encouraging as the respondent is not involved in a written discourse which is often very difficult to enforce. More people can be contacted in such a method in comparison to any other method.

(b) An interview is more revealing as it allows the respondent to give vent to his emotions and ideas in comparison to communication in the written-verbal form when he takes recourse to more guarded statements.

(c) Interviews can be more flexible as they could be customised towards the attitude of the person.

(d) Controlling of the environment is possible in this method, that is, the euthenics (especially when it has to be done in situations of surveys for selling personal products that suits both the interviewer and the respondents). This whole process could ultimately lead to a success in securing the required information.

(e) An interview could involve the informant much more and make him look deeper into his own and even leave the informant with a feeling of self-discovery rather than being superficial.

(f) Sometimes the interviewer gets hold of the informant absolutely off-guard leaving no scope for the informant but to oblige.

(g) In the interview method, the interviewer has the scope to tune the language to the ability or cultural and educational level of the informant.

4.3.2 Disadvantages

(a) Interviews are time consuming as the interviewer has to make arrangements for face to face contact for a long time which the interviewee may find difficult to accommodate.

(b) Interviewers need special training which involves cost.

(c) Bias in the oral-verbal communication cannot be ruled out as the informant and the interviewers are human beings with subjective understanding about the reality.

Personal interview requires rapport to be built before a response finally comes from the informant. In order to get a response, the interviewer may commit a *systematic error*. For example, an interview regarding the factors that determine the buying decision of a consumer durable might require the joint opinion of the wife and the husband since the buying decision involves a considerable amount of money. But, if the interview is conducted only when the housewife is present, a systematic error might occur. One must be careful to make sure that he is locating a right person(s) while organising the interview. Otherwise, systematic errors will exist in the data.

4.4 OBSERVATION

The *observation technique* for collection of data is applied under the formal unstructured setting and also under the informal setting. As we have already observed (in Section 3.4), the observation technique under the informal setting is called *participant observation.* Under the formal unstructured setting, the observation technique is known as *systematic observation.* The basic characteristics of the observation technique of data collection is that the researcher either does not impart stimuli *directly* to the respondent, or even if the stimuli are imparted directly to the respondents, the researcher does not collect the data on the basis of what has been communicated directly to the respondent. The stimuli however are imparted and the quality of the data could depend on the quality of the stimuli.

EXAMPLE

Under the participant observation method a female researcher may meet the women members of a community to collect information on their attitude towards rituals, by participating in a ritual and observing the behaviour of the individual members with respect to that ritual. The ritual in which the respondent gets involved serves as the source of stimuli, since such rituals are expressed through various rites.

In market research, a researcher often finds it necessary to apply the observation technique. For example, while launching a new product the market research organisation may find it advisable to first launch the new product in only one marketing segment of a city. The impact on the potential customers is assessed by observing their buying behaviour and comparing this with the other segments in which the product is yet to be launched. The respondents in the first segment will be noted as the *experimental group* and the respondents in the other segment of the city will be noted as the *control group.* The information can then be collected under 'before–after' or 'after-only' settings (to be explained in Chapter 5).

The advantages of the observation technique are:

- It involves recording of data as and when the event occurs. It does not follow any of the retrospective methods that are used in other research techniques.
- Many of our reactions are so predictable that they are not written down or are casually overlooked; through the observation method these are spotted and could be noted. Suppose the reaction of a consumer is to be studied and more particularly, the negative response has to be noted. The surest method would be to observe the body language

which is not usually revealed when the researcher meets the respondent directly with a structured questionnaire.

- At certain times, the respondents are not capable of giving a verbal report. A small child, a few months old, cannot state how comfortable he is with the design of the feeding bottle. To understand the comfort level, one has to use the observation technique.
- The respondent may not be interested in communicating with the investigators. For example, customers at times are very uncooperative in giving verbal or written responses. Under such circumstances it may be helpful to use the observation method.

The limitations of the observation techniques are:

- The occurrence of events might be irregular and often, the process could be time consuming. Suppose the movement of a product in a grocery is slow and the purchase pattern in reference to such product is being studied by the observation technique, the observer may have to wait for a long time to find a buyer (who is the respondent in this case).
- The method is also costly and at times the market research budget may not permit the cost.
- The investigator should have adequate expertise to understand the phenomenon and the points to observe, as the stimuli are imparted.

4.4.1 Basic Rules for Ensuring Quality under the Observation Technique

(a) It requires proper training of the observer who should be able to relate the observations with a certain structure. Untrained personnel must not be deployed.

(b) The role of the observer should be objective. He has to understand that situations or activities or observations should not get affected because of his role.

(c) If documentation is done during observations, it is necessary to keep the use of any instrument minimum. Overuse of such instruments might blur the reality. One should be competent in the use of instruments in non-participative observation as well as in participative observation.

4.5 CONTENT ANALYSIS

Content analysis is a research technique for the objective and systematic presentation of the content for communication. The following are the major purposes for undertaking content analysis.

(a) Understanding the orientation with respect to the research issue as contained in the communication content.

(b) Understanding the elements of subjectivism in the description.

(c) Understanding the psychological bent of mind of the person.
(d) To find the focus of attention in the material in the study.

Content analysis of a report or personal observation can be done by collecting and analysing the information from alternative sources. The researcher makes a thorough study on the related materials in order to have a cross-check on the information. Consistency, chronology and the absence of counter evidence in some other related reports often help one to understand the quality of the material under study.

The information under informal and formal unstructured settings, generated by the three modes of communication, should always pass through content analysis before the researcher utilises this information for his own research. Since the responses were unsystematic, objective and systematic presentation of the content for communication might be missing, at least to some extent. While taking up content analysis, the researcher should remain aware of both the strengths and the weaknesses of the instrument through which the information was collected. For example, if the mode of communication is written-verbal and the setting is informal, it is likely that the description would be unbiased if the truth of the statement is a matter of indifference to the respondent.

One cannot provide a check-list to be followed for content analysis. However, the following points must be noted while taking up content analysis.

(a) To what extent the information is relevant for the research issue.
(b) To what extent the information is logically valid.
(c) To what extent the information appears to be robust under cross-check.

Finally, one may point out that the researcher shall have to apply his own judgement in accepting or rejecting information while analysing the content.

4.6 SECONDARY DATA

A researcher does not always search for primary data. After considering the research issue and the data requirement, he makes a list of available data that he may use for his own research. A researcher would try to avoid primary data as far as practicable because of two reasons. In the first place, the comparative cost of primary data is higher and secondly the quality of the data collected from secondary sources is often better than what the researcher himself can secure. There are various agencies, particularly the governmental agencies that are better equipped to collect the data they have been entrusted with. These are called the official data. The official data are taken to be more authentic than the data provided by private agencies. In fact there are some issues on which the quantitative information is largely taken from the secondary sources. In this section, some official data which the researcher can collect while pursuing his empirical research is discussed. The list is not exhaustive. However the listing might help one understand the coverage of secondary data in India.

The official document

The following are the official documents, which are used occasionally.

(a) *Newspapers:* Newspapers often serve as a source of secondary information. The reports, the news analysis and articles published in the newspapers often contain information that the researcher may utilise in his research on a particular subject. With regard to the research in the area of marketing, the features appearing in the economic dailies often serve as very good source material. For example, the 'Brand Equity' supplement of a well-known newspaper often provides information to the researcher regarding the upcoming issues in marketing.

There are however problems with newspaper articles. Individual bias that distorts the objectivity often exists in the features, stories or even the analyses published in the newspapers. The issues are often dramatised, they are placed in an eye-catching manner, so much so that the objectivity that is necessary for good research is seriously undermined in such presentations.

(b) *Public records and statistics:* A major source of secondary information is the public records and the quantitative information (statistics published by various governmental and non-governmental agencies). These records are kept for the specific purpose for which the collection of data was organised but the researcher often finds that the information from these sources suit his purpose very well. For example, the researcher working on the nature of the rural market in India would learn a lot by consulting the results of the survey on consumption expenditure undertaken periodically by the National Sample Survey Organisation under the CSO (Central Statistical Organisation), Government of India. The researcher may also refer to the decennial census data, which are published by the Government of India. No individual researcher can even imagine collecting such a huge set of data from the field even in the course of an entire lifetime! The parliamentary papers, the departmental surveys and the legal notes and judgements passed in various courts often contain a rich set of data that the researcher can utilise if and when necessary.

In order to utilise such data, the researcher must be aware of the sources from where they can be obtained. In fact, a major problem in this regard is that the researcher may often fail to get access to the information because he does not know the exact source of the data that can be collected from the institutions. Access is also often denied even if the researcher is able to locate such sources. The third problem is that the researcher does not have a proper understanding on how such data could be retrieved and utilised to suit his own research.

In recent times, the published data that are prepared regularly by governmental agencies are being edited to suit the purpose of the general researchers by a non-governmental agency called the Centre for Monitoring Indian Economy (CMIE). The CMIE publishes such data in the printed form as well as in the softcopy form. The CMIE updates the data regularly, so much so, that it has become a major source of official data for individual researchers. One difficulty with the CMIE data, however, is that sources from which the data have been collected are not mentioned and the individual researcher is unable to check the authenticity of the data unless the sources are obvious.

The researcher should however be aware of the fact that there are limitations with respect to secondary data. A few of the limitations particularly applicable for public records and statistics are:

(a) The method of collection followed by the original collector may or may not suit the purpose of the research.

(b) The method of collection of such data is at times not accurate and consists of gross approximations.

(c) Micro-level data might often not be available.

SUMMARY

- To get quality data, proper judgement on the appropriate process of data generation for the concerned research is necessary. Such a judgement helps one freeze the data collection format in such a way that the stimuli–response interactions can assume a form which would describe the outcome in the best possible way.
- There are three different settings under which the data can be collected. The focus is mainly on the informal setting.
- Data under the informal setting can be communicated by the non-verbal, oral-verbal and written-verbal modes.
- Observation is an important data collection technique under the non-verbal mode. The issues related to the observation technique, along with its use in supplementing data collection, have been discussed in detail.
- The use of informal discussion and information in the form of biographies, essays for supplementing data gaps in a research under informal setting are also important for the generation of quality data.
- Content analysis is necessary if the responses are unsystematic and thus objective, and systematic presentation of the content for communication might be missing.

ASSIGNMENTS

Q1 Choose the right answers

1. In the informal setting, oral-verbal communication is stated as:
   (a) Discussion
   (b) Unstructured interview
   (c) Structured interview
   (d) None of the above
2. In case the response is confined to 'Yes' or 'No' the stimuli and response is:
   (a) Systematic stimuli and systematic response
   (b) Systematic stimuli and unsystematic response
   (c) Unsystematic stimuli and systematic response
   (d) Unsystematic stimuli and unsystematic response
3. The clinical interview is undertaken when:
   (a) A specific experience from the respondent is sought
   (b) General experience is the issue of the interview
   (c) The interview is in the area of psychotherapy
   (d) None of the above
4. The attitude of the investigator is favourable towards historical documents or biographies when:
   (a) The truth of the statement is not a matter of indifference to the writer
   (b) The statement is not prejudicial to the interest of the informant
   (c) The facts of the issue are a matter of common knowledge and are so proven, that the scope of misrepresenting is remote
   (d) None of the above
5. The merit in the case of the oral-verbal method is that:
   (a) Interviews involve the informant less and there is no in-depth probe
   (b) The interviewer does not have the scope to tune the language to the ability or cultural and educational level of the informant
   (c) Interviews can be more flexible as this could be more customised.
   (d) None of the above
6. 'Content analysis' is a research technique with the purpose of:
   (a) Adding subjectivism to the issue involved
   (b) Systematic presentation of the content of communication
   (c) Understanding the motivation of the author
   (d) None of the above

7. In case of 'observation':
   (a) The researcher collects the data on the basis of what has been directly communicated to the respondent
   (b) The researcher does not collect the data on the basis of what has been directly communicated to the respondent
   (c) Quality stimuli is not a factor
   (d) None of the above
8. The merit of the observation technique is:
   (a) It is the recording of data after the event has occurred
   (b) The respondent is interested in communicating to the investigator
   (c) It can unravel behaviour that is generally overlooked
   (d) None of the above
9. The limitation of the observation technique is:
   (a) The occurrence of the event is regular and therefore it may not be easy to study
   (b) The occurrence of the event is irregular and therefore it may not be easy to study
   (c) The limited market research budget is just for the cost as the cost is less
   (d) None of the above
10. For ensuring quality under the observation technique:
   (a) The role of the observer should be subjective
   (b) Very less use of mechanical instruments should be ensured
   (c) Only trained personnel should be used
   (d) None of the above

Answers

1. (a), 2. (a), 3. (b), 4. (c), 5. (c), 6. (b), 7. (b), 8. (c), 9. (b), 10. (c)

Q2 Answer the questions

1. (a) What is the role of 'discussion' in case of an informal setting?
   (b) What are the major types of unstructured interviews? Give examples for each.
2. What are the advantages and disadvantages of the oral-verbal method of communication?
   (a) What are the advantages and disadvantages of the observation technique?
   (b) How can one ensure quality under the observation technique?
4. (a) What is the importance of secondary data in research?
   (b) What are the different important types of secondary data?

APPENDIX 4.1

Type	Sources	Data
Census report (published every 10 years)	Registrar General of India	Size of population distribution, sex, age, literacy, occupation
White paper on national income	Central Statistical Organisation	Estimated national income, rate of savings and consumption
Statistical abstract, India	Central Statistical Organisation	Statistics on various sectors of the Indian economy
Statistical abstract (other states)	Bureau of Applied Economics and Statistics, specific State Governments	Data regarding area and population, environment, public health, education, agriculture and related subjects, manufacturing industries, employment and labour, trade and commerce, transport and communication, social statistics, national comparison
Annual survey of industries	Central Statistical Organisation	Number of units, persons employed and capital output ratio
Foreign trade of India (monthly statistics)	Director General of Commercial Intelligence	Export and import from India and different countries to India
Economic survey, annual publication	Department of Economic Affairs, marketing of finance	Balance of trade, spending in various sector
All India consumer price index	Ministry of Commerce and Industry	Products like food grains, food articles, petroleum, power, chemicals and others
National sample survey	Ministry of Planning	Economic, social, demographic statistics, industry and agricultural statistics
Report on industry	Ministry of that specific industry	Growth pattern in industry, budget, plans and changes in policy
RBI bulletins (monthly)	Reserve Bank of India	Expenses in various sector as indicated
Stock exchange directory	Bombay Stock Exchange	All companies enrolled with stock exchange, the range of products, shareholders basic type of business
Status report by various boards	Commodity Boards of jute, tea, spices, cardamom, coir, fertilisers and others	The growth of that industry, the new trend and making situation

Appendix 4.1 (*Contd*)

Type	Sources	Data
Industry association reports	FICCI, AIMA, ASSOCHAM, Indo–American Chamber of Commerce	The major and minor shooters against the private sectors, disbursing communications to member industries
Crop survey annual report	Operations Research Group	Cultivation, yield figures regarding commercial crops such as cotton, groundnut, mustard and rapeseed
Retail store audits on veterinary, consumer products and pharmaceuticals	Operations Research Sales Group	Veterinary formulations of over 500 chemists monitored, common goods of over 50 product types covered in a panel of 2500 retail outlets, purchase pattern of over 10,000 pharmaceutical products
Survey of agriculture, annual publication	The Hindu	Focusses on specific trends, growth and problems in agricultural industry and crops
National Readership Survey (NRS)	IMRB	Covering 55,000 households, gives information about 300 publications and the reading habits
Export related data commodity wise	Specific Export Promotion Council, that is, apparel export, promotion council, handicraft promotion council, spices, tea export promotion council	Details of export in general, the products and specific companies for such export
IENS handbook	Indian Eastern Newspaper Society, Delhi	Data regarding advertising agency-specific information
Thompson indices	Hindustan Thomson Associates	Urban market index, rural market index

CHAPTER 5

EXPERIMENTAL TECHNIQUES

LEARNING OBJECTIVES

After going through this chapter you will understand

- Types of experiments
- Settings for experiments
- Field experiments
- Errors in experimentation
- Design of experiments
- Notations used in experimental design
- Design without control group
- Design with control group
- Applications of experimental design
- Limitations of techniques
- Safeguards to be developed to overcome limitations
- The concept of *natural experiments* and use of panel data

Key words: Laboratory experiments, natural experiments, history, maturation, experimental design, notation, designs of experiments, testing effect, inter-temporal design, cross-sectional design, panel data

5.1 INTRODUCTION

The experimental technique, as we have pointed out earlier, is used when both the stimuli and the responses are systematic and communication is in the non-verbal form. Such a technique is widely used in social research when the researcher tries to impart stimuli systematically to a group which is known as the experimental group. The motivation for following the experimental technique can be described as follows.

In a causal research, we try to develop a cause and effect relation among the variables. Before developing the mathematical model, either in a deterministic or in a probabilistic framework, the researcher must understand whether there is any reason to believe that the cause and effect relationship might exist among the variables. But how would one guess whether there is such a relationship? A correlation matrix involving the specified variables might be constructed to assess the extent of correlation between any two variables in the set; a more sophisticated approach is the Granger causality test. Whatever be the method, the initial issue is to identify the variables on which such exercises would be performed. Theory is a dependable guide here, but often the researcher benefits in identifying the relationship by taking recourse to experimenting with the phenomena under study. Needless to say, such a technique cannot be used in all cases because the researcher might not have the opportunity to get an experimental group on whom the experiment can be carried out. In some cases, such an exercise may be unnecessary especially when the theory provides a strong rationale to conclude that the cause and effect relation does (or does not) exist.

5.2 TYPES OF EXPERIMENTS

In order to understand the cause and effect relation through experimental techniques, two types of research design are envisaged:

- Natural experiment
- Controlled experiment

An experiment is considered to be a natural experiment when it does not require any intervention by the researcher. For example, in a study related to the cause and effect relation between the level of income and the level of the expenditure, the researcher may decide to take up a natural study in which he plays the role of an observer. He only records the information on the level of expenditure and income without intervening in the process of data generation and makes a primary assessment, on the basis of the recorded evidence. He decides whether a further, more sophisticated investigation with regard to the existence of any relation between the variables would be rewarding. The nature of the relationship, namely, which one is the cause and which one is the effect, cannot be ascertained as such by this exercise.

In a controlled experiment, on the other hand, the researcher intervenes by manipulating the probable causal variables. We shall discuss these two processes – the process of natural experiments and controlled experiments – more elaborately after we discuss the settings and instruments required for the experiments.

5.3 SETTINGS FOR EXPERIMENTS

Two types of environmental settings for experimental techniques can be used—laboratory experiments and field experiments. The degree of realism and control on the setting are the two basic factors, based on which the research agency would decide the kind of experiments to be undertaken. Each of the above settings will be briefly discussed for better understanding of the issues.

5.3.1 Laboratory Experiments

In an artificially contrived environment, the researcher administers or observes the effects of the stimuli on the desired sample group. This sort of setting has the advantage of minimising the unwanted effects of extraneous variables. The artificially contrived environment is referred to as the laboratory. Further, such laboratories should be equipped with the required instruments such as cameras, temperature controllers, necessary lighting panels, one-way mirrors and computers.

The study of one such laboratory experiment will make things more explicit. A research agency conducted a blind test (a blind test is one in which the brands or variables are not disclosed) on a panel of coffee drinkers to understand the impact of equity on taste. The agency conducted the whole study in one of their own laboratories that had the ambience of a coffee pub equipped with the latest of computers to evaluate the results. At first the branded and unbranded coffees were displayed in different jars without the brands being disclosed. In physical appearance, the jars looked alike. 'Taste' was the treatment variable. The target group was asked to taste the coffee from every jar and each one was asked to rate the coffee. This is an example of a laboratory experiment. Incidentally, the unbranded coffees were rated high in this test. In the subsequent test, in the same laboratory, the brands were disclosed and the unbranded coffees were also allowed to be identified by the coffee drinkers. The experiments were replicated. The outcome was that the branded coffees were now rated much higher than the unbranded ones on the parameter of taste by the same group of respondents. The experiment showed that branded coffee had better equity than unbranded coffee and therefore the conclusion was that it is brand equity that matters much in the marketing of coffee.

Two important concepts are taken into consideration while assessing the results of the laboratory setting—internal validity and external validity. Internal validity is validity within the setting where there is no other plausible cause for the observed results except those that were tested. Generally, laboratory experiments offer a high degree of internal validity because the environment is within the control of the researcher. Thus, the changes in the results of the experiment can be considered as dependant only on the treatment variable and not on any other extraneous variable.

External validity is validity outside the created ambience (laboratory). The experiment would satisfy the criterion of external validity only by projecting the environment of the experiment that practically or realistically exists in a real-world situation. It could be true that a study is good only in terms of the criterion of internal validity and the results so obtained might not be valid in a real-world situation. This implies that the environment or setting of the study does not match the actual/real-world setting. There could be several reasons: the primary reason in most cases of market research where this technique is widely used is that the sample or the experimental group of customers (that is, the group on which the experiment is conducted) does not match the profile of the typical customers (sample is not representative). Then again, there could be a possibility that the combination of marketing mixes used as stimuli (treatment variables) on the target or sample group may be quite different from the real marketing mix. Results of experiments derived from such defective settings usually fail to meet external validity.

5.3.1.1 Advantages

The advantages of laboratory experiments are enumerated below.

- Laboratory experiments are conducted in an artificial environment that is within the control of the researcher. Thus it has a higher level of internal validity.
- As the laboratory is an artificial physical environment, the control elements are pre-planned and easily manageable. This makes such an experiment cost effective compared to that set in a real-world situation.
- The laboratory experiment is less time consuming; thus, it is likely to be less costly compared to the field experiment on this count also.

5.3.1.2 Disadvantages

- It is often difficult to replicate the external environment when we are setting up a laboratory experiment. Consequently there exists the possibility of having low external validity in laboratory experiments. In other words, laboratory experiments often suffer from a low level of realism.
- The selection of the target group may often be problematic. The researcher may face refusal from many quarters as this experiment takes more time than in the case of a field experiment with respect to an individual respondent. Providing a monetary incentive may often distort the sample in such a way that the very purpose of study is defeated.

5.3.2 Field Experiments

The second type of setting for experiments is referred to as the field experiment. These field experiments are conducted in the real-world environment. Therefore, in contrast to laboratory experiments, this setting has a higher degree of external validity. Then again, field experiments suffer in internal validity because extraneous factors are less controllable under such situations. In the case of field experiments, apart from the treatment variable, other extraneous variables are also active on the group of respondents. However, some of these extraneous variables can be controlled, but to a lesser extent than in the case of laboratory experiments. Field experiments are generally more expensive than laboratory experiments. In case one wants to test a new product in a certain region or market, he has to incur expenses in getting the permission of the middlemen in test marketing. Such expenses might be higher than what is usually spent on the involvement of panel customers in the agency outlet (laboratory experiment).

Test marketing is a kind of field experiment which is widely used in marketing research. Test marketing has two purposes:

- securing responses from individuals towards a new product, and
- assessing the impact of different marketing mixes or marketing plans for the product.

Test marketing is usually done in markets which could be demographically representative of the target market which the marketing personnel plan to reach. It is an experiment because the firm is replicating what it intends to use in the real-world situation. Let us suppose that a baby-milk product company wants to find out the shelf life of a new baby cereal it proposes to launch in place of an existing brand which for some reason the company is planning to withdraw. A field experiment would be done in a target market segment where the new brand would be introduced and its shelf life studied. A comparative analysis of the shelf life of both the new and the old products in the test market would help the organisation to take a decision with regard to whether promoting the new product would be rewarding or not.

5.3.2.1 Advantages of field experiments

- Unlike a laboratory experiment, it works in the natural environment. As a result, it is more close to reality.
- External validity of a field experiment is high as the experiment is carried out in a 'real-world situation'.

5.3.2.2 Disadvantages

- It is much costlier to conduct a field experiment than a laboratory experiment.
- The time involved in a field experiment is much more than that in a laboratory experiment.

5.4 ERRORS IN EXPERIMENTATION

We need to be aware of some sources of error that affect the internal and external validity of experiments. The more we understand these sources, the better will be our insight into the validity or invalidity of the experimental design for a particular situation. Most of the factors that affect the validity of research can be categorised as extraneous factors. These factors are discussed below.

History

It refers to events that are non-recurring and are coincidental to the timing of experiment. These events affect the experiment but they are not due to the effect of the experiment. Let us suppose an automobile giant is undertaking the test marketing of an air-conditioned car. The regional transport authority decides during the same period of time that higher taxes will be levied on air-conditioned cars. This decision will definitely have an impact on the test marketing of the car but the field experiment definitely has nothing to do with the increase in taxes. It has to be understood that little can be done to control such a factor.

Maturation

Maturation refers to a gradual change in the respondent over time. Let us suppose one is involved in observing the eating pattern among the respondents in restaurants between 6 pm and 10 pm in a certain locality. This data is gathered each day over six months. Over this period, fast food joints came up in the locality. Initially there was no perceptible impact but by the fourth month, it was observed that the respondents now preferred food from the fast-food joints instead of the restaurants on weekdays. When the experiment was conceived, this was not anticipated and it was thought that the pattern of flow of respondents to the restaurants would remain as usual.

Mortality

There could be occasions where the respondent in one unit suddenly dies. Under such circumstances, one will not know whether the lost test unit would have produced the same result as the other units in the experiment. Sometimes even if it is not a case of death, some units of the panel may opt to drop out owing to a change in circumstances. It has to be noted that these dropped units could have changed the results of the test. The cases of mortality and drop out do influence the results, but good panel management may at times ensure that the cases of drop outs are reduced.

Testing effect

When respondents agree to participate, they become part of the experimental group and agree to be interviewed or to fill questionnaires. There could be situations when as part of the experimental group, one may have to fill in a series of questionnaires. Under such a circumstance, prior measurement can affect the subsequent measurement within the same experiment. In other words, in completing the first questionnaire or interview, the respondent may have developed a certain attitude or focus to the issue under study. This will affect the filling of subsequent questionnaires or interviews in the same experiment. Again, the fact that they have been chosen may itself affect the approach to the test that is being undertaken by them. Let us suppose, on a survey regarding opinion on environmental friendliness, a respondent has come to know that he is being considered as part of the group because he is an environmentalist. The respondent may exhibit a more favourable attitude towards environmental issues than one would normally expect from him.

Instruments

Data are collected through various instruments ranging from questionnaires to laboratory instruments. The basic purpose of these instruments is to measure changes on the test unit. A lot depends on how the instrument, say the questionnaire, has been designed. A questionnaire probing into attitude may have questions phrased in positive language. This may unduly affect the attitude of the respondents. Sometimes the interviewers affect the outcome by their presentation of the treatment variables.

Selection bias

Sometimes the samples could have been so chosen that they do not represent the true population. However, this can be avoided and the methods for avoiding such problems have been discussed in Chapter 9.

5.5 EXPERIMENTAL DESIGN NOTATION

The literature on experimental design uses some special notations. It is necessary to understand the notational system which is used to represent the respondents and the treatment variables in the experimental technique.

Let *X* represent a treatment variable and *O* the outcome in the form of an observation or measurement. The observation or measurement can be recorded before or after administering the treatment variable. In other words, the outcome can be considered with or without a treatment variable on the test units (a unit in an experimental group can include an individual, group or object). Let *R* indicate the experimental group. In case more than one outcome is taken, then the order of these outcomes will be noted by subscripts to *O*, namely, O_1, O_2, O_3 and so on.

With the help of such notations, it is possible to discuss the types of experiments in a more elaborate manner. Let us first discuss the following relations using the notations that we have developed above.

- The sequence of events that constitute the experiment is written left-to-right. For example, the notation

$$R\,O_1\,X\,O_2$$

indicates that the experimental group *R* was considered with respect to the event where the outcome is recorded as O_1. Since there is no treatment variable between *R* and O_1, it is implied that the measure or the outcome is achieved before a treatment variable was administered. O_1 is thus a *before measure*, that is, a measure taken before administering a treatment variable. Next in sequence is *X* which is a treatment variable. This indicates that the treatment variable was administered on *R* after the *before measure* was taken. O_2 indicates that after administering the treatment variable on *R*, the outcome is O_2. The difference in outcome due to administering the treatment variable on *R* is thus captured by $O_2 - O_1$.
- All the notations being represented in one line indicates that all the test units belong to that specific treatment group.
- Notations in various lines indicate that the events occur simultaneously. For example,

$$R_1\,O_1\,X\,O_2$$
$$R_2\,X\,O_3$$

indicates that two different experimental groups were exposed to the same treatment variable *X*. In the first case, pre-test and post-test measures were taken as O_1 and O_2. In the second case only the post-test measure O_3 was taken.

5.6 DESIGNS OF EXPERIMENT

With the notations described above, let us discuss the designs that the researcher can envisage under this setting. We have already observed that a treatment (*X*) is administered on a group known as the experimental group (*R*). In an experimental design we consider the universe of the target population to be divided into two groups. The group on which the treatment is administered is the treatment group or the experimental group (*R*); the other part of the universe consists of the elements of the population on which the treatment variable (*X*) has not been administered. This group is usually described as the control group (*C*). The results of the experiments can be analysed with respect to these two groups. For example, a researcher might study the effect of an advertisement campaign (treatment variable in this case) on the housewives in the locality (which constitutes the universe in this case). In order to study the effect of the treatment, the researcher may divide the population into two groups—the members of the group which have been exposed to the advertisement campaign and the members of the group which have been excluded from the campaign. The first group in this case is the experimental group and the second one is the control group. The effect of the campaign can be assessed by considering the buying behaviour of these two groups after the campaign has covered the members of the experimental group. Alternative designs covering only the members of the experimental group can be drawn; other alternatives are also possible. The discussion on experimental design considers all these possibilities. Such possibilities are discussed below.

5.6.1 After-only Without Control Group

It is the simplest form of experimental design, in which the treatment variable is administered to the experimental group and the results are captured without any reference to the control group. In its simplest form, the design is 'after-only' in the sense that the effect of the treatment is measured by measuring the impact of the treatment on the experimental group alone. The outcome *O* can be written as *R X O*. Since there is no control group and because no measurement was taken before administering the treatment, the design is be described as 'after-only without control group'.

5.6.2 Before–after Without Control Group

Before–after without control group is the same as the above, with the only difference being that before-measurement has been included. Symbolically it is represented as $R\ O_1\ X\ O_2$.

If O_1 is the measurement in one quarter and the *X* (treatment, for example, introducing gifts for a purchase) is administered in next quarter, we get O_2. The difference, $O_2 - O_1$, will reflect the change due to the treatment over time.

A variation of the above could symbolically be stated as $R\ O_1\ O_2\ O_3\ O_4\ X\ O_5\ O_6\ O_7\ O_8$.

The experimental group was studied for four quarters (periods) before administering the treatment variable *X*. Following the administering of treatment, the behaviour was studied for another four quarters (periods). This was done on the basis of the understanding that the measurement of effect is better as a larger number of time periods are available. The outcome of this design is the difference between before and after, as in the previous case, but the outcome is measured in terms of the average of the differences in each time period. We find that the above two designs are devoid of a control group and are taken with respect to non-randomly chosen sample units.

There are two other broad settings under experimental design. The researcher may try to measure the effect of a treatment (*X*) on the experimental group by contrasting the outcome vis-à-vis a group on which the treatment was not administered. Ideally the frame of the experiment in this case would be such that the researcher takes a sample on which the treatment is administered and along with this he takes another sample on which the treatment was not administered. In other words, the researcher would select an experimental group (*R*) and a control group (*C*) from his field of study and would observe the difference that the treatment (*X*) makes by measuring the difference between the behaviour of *R* and *C*. Ideally this will capture the effect of the treatment because, *ceteris paribus* the only factor added to the experimental group is the treatment *X* and therefore the difference in outcome with respect to *R* and *C* would give the effect of the treatment *X*.

There could be two ways of measuring the effect under this setting. We will discuss them presently.

5.6.3 After-only With One Control Group

It requires only one treatment and after-measurement of both the experimental and control group. The design could be illustrated as follows:

$$R_1 X O_1$$
$$C - O_2$$

The experimental and control group might be chosen randomly. The researcher might often opt for a purposive selection. One fact that definitely stands out in this design is the absence of before-measurement. The experimental group has not been exposed to measurement before the treatment was administered. The idea is that the measurement for the group before the treatment would correspond to the behaviour of control group which was not exposed to the treatment, even though the measure with respect to the control group is taken after the experimental group is exposed to the treatment. Needless to say, the behaviour of the control group may not fully capture the behaviour of the experimental group before the group was exposed to the treatment because the assumption of 'other things remaining the same' (*ceteris paribus*) may not work out.

Despite the above disadvantage it should be borne in mind that sometimes in agriculture crop research and in marketing (the direct marketing) cases, we use this design. The most popular method of data collection with respect to this design is to send direct mail coupons to the members of the experimental group and to take another group to which no such mail coupons are sent. The after-measurement of sales is taken with respect to each group and the effect of the experiment is measured by the difference between O_2 and O_1 $(O_2 - O_1)$.

5.6.4 Before–after With One Control Group

Adding a before-measurement for the experimental group in the above design we get the following

$$R_1 O_1 X O_2$$
$$C \quad - O_3$$

The experimental group is now exposed to the treatment variable (X) and the control group is not (because a control group, by definition, is not exposed to treatment). Measurement with respect to the experimental group (R_1) was taken before imparting the treatment when it is expected to behave as the control group does. This is denoted by (O_1). A measurement after the treatment (O_2) was also taken. The effect of the treatment on the experimental group is $O_2 - O_1$. Apparently, the effect of the treatment should be captured by this difference. But an intricate issue comes in. The difference might be the product of the treatment *and also the other factors that might be working on it during this period as in the case of the control group (because the other factors would be working on non-experimental group as well)*. [For example, an increase in sales during a particular period may not be entirely due to the promotional effort (treatment), the other contributing factors might as well be working as incentive for the purchase]. If this is so, how can we isolate the effect of the treatment variable *per se*?

The design that we develop here might be used for addressing this issue. Suppose we take another sample from the same population which is not exposed to the treatment variable (the control group). This group is exposed to the other factors just as the experimental group is. Conceptually therefore, the difference in behaviour, after the treatment has been imparted, with respect to the experimental group and the control group, if at all, would be due to the effect of the treatment variable, per se. The effectiveness of the treatment can thus be measured by taking the difference $O_3 - O_2$ where O_3 is the measure with respect to the control group *at a time when the effect of the treatment was measured with respect to the experimental group.* The difference between the before and after-measure with respect to the experimental group $O_2 - O_1$ can also be compared with O_3 to make an assessment of the impact of a treatment. Ideally, O_1 should be the same as O_3 if the samples (constituting the experimental group and the control group) are drawn from the same population and the other contributing factors were same as O_1 so that $O_2 - O_1$ would be the same as $O_3 - O_2$. If the other contributing factors were not same as O_1, the measure would be different. In summary, in a before–after setting, the effect of the treatment may be studied in three ways: $O_2 - O_1$, $O_3 - O_1$ and $O_3 - O_2$. As discussed above, $O_2 - O_1$ would be sufficient if O_1 remains the same as O_3, that is, if no other factor operated on the population during the period when the treatment was being administered on the sample.

Such a design for the experiment is widely used in market research. An example could be one in a simulated marketing situation when both the experimental and control groups are randomly chosen from the same population of potential buyers and only the experimental group is subjected to an advertisement campaign. The researcher then observes the buying behaviour of both the groups. If some other factor that might change the buying behaviour of the consumers was present at the time the treatment was being administered, the researcher would measure $O_3 - O_2$ in order to assess the impact of the advertisement campaign.

5.6.5 Four Group, Six-study Design

The design will look like the following:

$$R_1\,O_1\,X\,O_2$$
$$R_2\,O_3 - O_4$$
$$X\,O_5$$
$$-\,O_6$$

The treatment could be evaluated in a number of ways, these being $O_2 - O_1$, $O_2 - O_4$, $O_4 - O_3$, $O_5 - O_6$, $O_4 - O_5$ and $(O_2 - O_1) - (O_4 - O_3)$.

It may now be necessary to find the effect of the testing. In order to do so, we could frame the design in the following manner.

	No treatment	Treatment
Before-measurement taken	O_4	O_2
Before-measurement not taken	O_6	O_5

The difference between the means in the row will provide the basis for estimating the effect of testing. The difference between the means in the column will provide the basis for estimating the effect of treatment. Analysis of the variance could be used for analysing these results.

5.6.6 Multi Time Series

In using a time series design, the possibility of establishing a control group could be helpful. It may be possible to find a matching sample as the control group and compare it with the treatment group. Symbolically this can be presented as:

$$R\,O_1\,O_2\,O_3\,X\,O_4\,O_5\,O_6$$
$$C\,O'_1\,O'_2\,O'_3 - O'_4\,O'_5\,O'_6$$

The superscripts on *O* indicate the outcomes specific to the control group. Multiple series will give us an opportunity to measure the difference, the measured difference in the experimental group and the control group and thereby the degree of effect due to the treatment (*X*) could be measured between both.

5.6.7 Cross Sectional Design

It involves measuring the effect of the treatment variable on different groups with differing treatment levels. Let us suppose that different price levels are introduced in a sample of differing populations of the nation. Symbolically this can be shown as:

$$R_1\,X_1\,O_1$$
$$R_2\,X_2\,O_2$$
$$R_3\,X_3\,O_3$$
$$R_4\,X_4\,O_4$$

This may be the case where price sensitivity is being studied across various sections of the society. The differences – $(O_2 - O_1)$, $(O_3 - O_2)$ and $(O_4 - O_3)$ – will show the degree of sensitivity in pricing across different population groups.

5.6.8 Cross Sectional and Time Series Design

Such a design is used when the treatment has been imparted to a target group and the effect is recorded over a time period in a cross section of the target group. One such commonly used design is the *Ex-post facto test control group design*. In this design, the experimental and the control group are both selected after the treatment variable has been administered. Symbolically it can be represented as:

$$R_1\,O_1\,X\,O_2$$
$$C\;O_3 - O_4$$

A practical example of this situation could be that of a new advertisement (Ad) campaign being tried on a locality. The sample units are asked that whether they have seen the Ad; then those who have seen it automatically fall into the category of the experimental group and the group that did not see the new Ad campaign is the control group. The effect is then measured by observing the behaviour of both the groups, so far as buying is concerned. The effect of the treatment variable will be visible when the difference between $O_3 - O_1$ and $O_4 - O_2$ is considered.

5.7 APPLICATION OF EXPERIMENTAL DESIGN

The experimental design is widely used in social research for generating information. The particular area in which such a design is applied is market research where the researcher has to study the effect of certain *treatment* on a target group. Now-a-days, such a design is also used in a branch of economics known as *experimental economics.* Such experiments are carried out on two broad classes of experimental settings—natural and controlled. We shall discuss the use of experimental design under both these settings.

5.7.1 Natural Experiments

As we have already pointed out, the broad class of experiments known as *natural experiments* is characterised by the fact that the researcher does not intervene (or keeps it at the minimum) in the process of the generation of information pertaining to the issue under consideration.

There could be two broad scenarios under which the research is performed. The first one is a situation where the study is spread over time. The other one is a situation where the study is spread over space. A combination of these two is also a possibility.

There are thus three types of designs among the natural experiments

- Inter-temporal design,
- Cross sectional design, and
- Combination of the two.

(i) *Inter-temporal design:* A study spread over time is called *inter-temporal.* The design is often described as a *time series* or a *trend design.* While both of them indicate that the study involves collecting data over time with respect to the object of study, there is some difference between the two. The time series design involves obtaining data from the *same sample* with some interval of time. *These are often stated as panel data.* In the case of trend design, the sampled units are not the same; these are obtained from statistically matched samples drawn from the same population at different points in time. Both the time series and trend analysis, however, aim at finding out the nature of behaviour of the sample units.

In a natural experiment with respect to a group of objects over time, it is desirable that the units of study remain the same. In other words, in an inter-temporal study, the researcher should aim at gathering information with respect to a panel of units, that is, the researcher should aim at getting the panel data. However, in certain cases, the researcher may fail in obtaining the panel data.

Let us elaborate on this point. Let us suppose the researcher wants to know whether a particular type of commodity is being adopted by the residents in a locality. A panel of shops may be selected and the researcher might collect the information from the same set of shops at certain time intervals in a given period of time. The problem is that, over time the scenario might change. After a time interval, on a visit to the locality, the researcher might find that some shops which used to sell the product might have discontinued the sales; on the other hand, some new shops might have come up which sell the product in a big way. Collecting information from the panel data would not be the right choice in this case because the panel itself has been distorted—some of the old members of the panel no longer exist. According to the terminology we have used, time series analysis is no longer possible in this case. Trend analysis might be the proper way of performing research in this context. The researcher cannot concentrate on the same set of units (shops) for this study because some of the sampled units might not exist or might not be selling the commodity at certain point in time; which means the researcher has to include new units as their replacements for getting the relevant information.

Why is this design called an *Experimental Design*? In the case of the time series or trend analysis there is an experimental group *R* on which no treatment is performed by the researcher except that the data were collected over time. If the time, *T*, is taken as the treatment variable, the design can be described in the following way:

$$R\,O_1\,T\,O_2$$

O_1 is a measure at the beginning of the event, the treatment variable (time, *T*) is administered and the measure recorded is O_2. The difference between O_2 and O_1, that is $(O_2 - O_1)$, is the measure of the treatment variable *T*.

Multi time series: In using a time series design, the possibility of establishing a control group from a different population but with same characteristics could be helpful. It may be possible to find a matching sample as the control group and compare it with the experimental group. Symbolically this can be represented as:

$$R_1\,R_2\,R_3\,T\,R_4\,R_5\,R_6$$
$$R'_1\,R'_2\,R'_3 - R'_4\,R'_5\,R'_6$$

Multiple series will give us an opportunity to measure the difference, the measured difference in the experimental group and the control group and thereby the degree of affect of the *T* (treatment) could be measured between both.

(ii) *Cross sectional design:* It involves measuring the effect of the treatment variable on different groups with differing treatment level. Let us suppose that different price levels are introduced in a sample of differing populations of the nation. Symbolically this can be shown as:

$$\begin{matrix} T_1 & R_1 \\ T_2 & R_2 \\ T_3 & R_3 \\ T_4 & R_4 \end{matrix}$$

This may be the case where over a period of time, price sensitivity is being studied. The differences, $R_2 - R_1$, $R_3 - R_2$ and $R_4 - R_3$ will study the degree of sensitivity in pricing and different population groups.

(iii) *Cross sectional and time series design:* One such commonly used design is the *Ex-post facto test control group* under a natural experiment. In this design, the experimental and the control group are both selected after the treatment variable (not imparted by the researcher) has been administered. Symbolically it is shown as:

$$R_1\,T\,R_2$$
$$R_3 - R_4$$

A practical example of this situation could be as follows. A new environmental awareness campaign is being taken up by the local authority in a locality. The researcher is conducting a market research on the prospect of a pest control service in that locality. He divides the target group in two sub-groups—those who have (negative) impact of the campaign and those who remain unaware of it. The effect is then measured by observing the behaviour of both the groups, as far as buying of the service is concerned.

5.7.2 Continuous Panel and Experimental Design

In market research, the term *panel* has been used to signify the consumer jury—a sample of people who act as experts on a certain action. These consumer jurists help in deciding on new products, new advertising campaigns, product concept testing.

The other types of panels are samples of individual households and firms who provide information over successive time intervals. These are referred to as *continuous panels.* Continuous panel is used in many areas of social science including economics and sociology. Continuous panels consist of the sample units through which collection of data over successive periods of time is carried out to measure the inter-temporal behaviour of the group with respect to the object of study.

The continuous panels in use in marketing are in the following types:

(a) Consumer purchaser panels, which are used to record purchases in a consumer 'diary' at regular intervals.
(b) Advertising audience panels, which are used to records programmes viewed and listened to.
(c) Dealers' panels, which are used to gather information regarding inventory levels, sales and prices.

5.6.3 Use of Panel Data in Market Research

Market research organisations often use the *panel data* in order to study the impact of a treatment. The members of the panel are carefully chosen so that the effect of the treatment can represent a reliable set of information. We may discuss some of the famous panel data used in India by Indian Market Research Bureau (IMRB). The widely used panel data of the IMRB is its household panel data. The IMRB household panel gathers data of the consumer's purchase behaviour. It aims at providing information on the purchase pattern of different consumer segments and the effect of external stimuli that are more controllable, such as product, place, price, promotion, public opinion and politics.

The occupants of the panels are usually the housewives who are selected from a house to house survey. This also involves random selection from the listing. The panel has representations from lower, middle and higher income groups. The panel takes into consideration a matrix of age and household income.

The housewives are provided with a diary in which they could note down the following:-

(a) Date of purchase, (b) Type of produce, (c) Brand name, (d) Colour variant,
(e) Package size, (f) The quality and (g) The schemes if availed or promotion drives.

The diary is given to the members at the start of the month and is collected back in the first week of the next month.

Television Rating Point (TRP): The TRP is a panel-based television audience measurement system. This system was introduced by IMRB in 1996. This system enables continuous monitoring of viewership. It is a means of evaluating the relative cost efficiencies of advertising through alternative TV media. The TRP system comes from at least 9 centres including Bombay (Mumbai), Madras (Chennai), Ahmedabad and Delhi.

It consists of a panel of individuals selected from households owning TVs as well as those not owning TVs. It therefore involves both primary audience and secondary audience. From each metropolitan city, it considered 406 respondents and from the five other cities the total respondent population was around 300. The pattern of selecting a sample unit was done in two stages. At first, a certain number of respondents in each city were contacted. In the second stage the panel was finally selected using the criteria of age, income and sex.

The Television Rating Point panel is also a diary record-keeping group. The television audience is requested to record the programmes they see in half-hour time slots. It should be noted that the IMRB household panel and TRP study are referred to as scanner panels in American marketing research jargon.

Limitations of panels: The following are sometimes the limitations of forming panels:

(a) Both the randomly and non-randomly selected members of the panel sometimes do not cooperate with the operators of the panel.
(b) The panel could become biased, the reason being that the members become aware of the testing effect.
(c) The panel data may show bias of instrumentation effect. The keepers of the diaries have been found to include inaccurate information, as sometimes, they may have forgotten to make a note.
(d) The major weakness is that the sample might not be a representative sample.

SUMMARY

- The experimental technique is used when stimuli are systematic, the responses are also systematic and the mode of communication is non-verbal.

- The experiments are conducted under two different environments at the field level—laboratory environment and natural environment.
- There is a treatment variable which is designed by the researcher according to the need of his research.
- The experiment needs to have a group of elements (respondents) on which the treatment would be administered. The group on which the treatment variable is administered is called the experimental group and the rest on which the treatment is not administered is called the control group. Various designs of experiment can be developed.
- A researcher often needs to work with a set of data which have been generated under the same environment. Such data are called panel data. The basic issues related to culling a set of panel data out of the available set of information are discussed.

ASSIGNMENTS

Q1 Choose the right answers

1. One takes recourse to experimental techniques when:
   (a) Theory is robust to provide for the rationale of cause to effect relation
   (b) Theory is not robust enough to provide the rationale of cause to effect relation
   (c) No in-depth knowledge is required
   (d) None of the above
2. The controlled experiment involves:
   (a) Less intervention of the researcher
   (b) Intervention of researcher by manipulating the probable causal variable
   (c) No intervention of the researcher
   (d) None of the above
3. While assessing the result of laboratory experiments two important concepts are taken into consideration:
   (a) Formal factor and informal factor
   (b) Personal factor and impersonal factor
   (c) Internal validity and external validity
   (d) None of the above
4. Field experiments have:
   (a) Lower degree of external validity
   (b) Higher degree of external validity
   (c) Higher degree of internal validity
   (d) None of the above

5. Test marketing is usually done with a purpose to:
   (a) Understand which market is more prosperous
   (b) Strengthen the marketing department
   (c) Securing the responses from individuals towards a new product
   (d) None of the above
6. 'Maturation' in errors related to experimentation refers to:
   (a) Gradual change in the respondent over time
   (b) Maturity of the trained researcher
   (c) Maturity of the market
   (d) None of the above
7. 'History' in errors related to experimentation refers to:
   (a) History of the test laboratory
   (b) History of the field of work
   (c) Events that are non-recurring and occur coincidental to the timing of experiment
   (d) None of the above
8. The reason for considering *time series* or *trend analysis* in natural experiments as *experimental design* is because:
   (a) Researchers do not intervene by manipulating the probable causal variable
   (b) Researchers intervene by manipulating the probable causal variable
   (c) Time is treated as the treatment variable
   (d) None of the above
9. Television Rating Point (TRP) was introduced in India by:
   (a) Lintas in 1986
   (b) IENS in 1994
   (c) IMRB in 1996
   (d) None of the above
10. Limitation of panel data is:
   (a) It does not allow the instrumentation effect on panel
   (b) The panel could become biased due to instrumentation effect
   (c) Over dependence on the selected members
   (d) None of the above

Answers

1. (b), 2. (b), 3. (c), 4. (b), 5. (c), 6. (a), 7. (c), 8. (c), 9. (c), 10. (b)

Q2 Answer the questions

1. What are the different types of experiments? Give an example of each type.
2. What are the characteristics of a laboratory experiment? What are the advantages and disadvantages of a laboratory experiment?
3. Discuss briefly, the alternative designs of experiment with one experimental group.
4. Explain the types of errors in experimentation, in detail.
5. State the uses of panel data and the limitations of such data.

CHAPTER 6

THE QUESTIONNAIRE METHOD

LEARNING OBJECTIVES

After going through this chapter you will understand

- A questionnaire as an instrument of data generation
- Classification of questionnaires
- Types of questionnaires
- Size and content of questionnaires
- Wording, sequence and layout of questions under different settings
- Understanding the target population and determining the type of questions
- Open-ended and close-ended questions
- Framing the questions
- Sequencing the questions
- Methods of communication
- Observation techniques
- Verbal testing
- Pictorial tests
- Formal structured and formal unstructured settings
- Projective techniques

Key words: Structured undisguised questionnaire, structured disguised questionnaire, unstructured undisguised questionnaire, unstructured disguised questionnaire, ambiguity, open-ended questions, close-ended questions, dichotomous questions, cushion questions, pre-test, randomised response technique, projective techniques.

6.1 INTRODUCTION

We have understood that the data which serves as the basis of empirical analysis is the product of stimuli–response interaction. As we know, the nature of the data depends on the mode of communication. For example, a non-verbal mode of communication in a setting where both the stimuli and the response are unsystematic would produce data in the form of observations, technically known as participant observation. The most widely used mode of communication in empirical research, particularly in market research is verbal—written-verbal or oral-verbal. Verbal forms of communication coupled with three different settings for data generation give rise to six different modes (tools) of data collection (Chapter 3). When the setting is formal (systematic stimuli coupled with systematic response), the data can be generated by verbal communication in written form; the tool used in this method is known as the *structured questionnaire.* When the setting is formal unstructured and the data set is generated by verbal communication in the written form, the tool used to produce data is the *unstructured questionnaire.* The structured or unstructured questionnaires are data collection tools. Thus, *data collection tools* are defined as the tools which help in the collection of data in the intended spirit and manner. In this chapter, the advantages of these tools are discussed along with the problems that a researcher faces while using these tools.

6.2 QUESTIONNAIRE

The stimuli that are imparted while asking questions to the respondent is the essence of what constitutes the *questionnaire.* However, a questionnaire (tool) is related to imparting stimuli systematically, which is why it is expected to maintain a pattern. A questionnaire is thus the tool that serves the desire of the researcher to impart stimuli systematically. A questionnaire, as we have discussed above also refers to imparting stimuli only in the written-verbal form. However such a setting does not necessarily imply that the response has to be systematic. The questionnaire method of data collection takes care of this possibility by defining two types of questionnaires—structured (where the response is expected to be systematic) and unstructured (where the response is expected to be unsystematic).

It is difficult to ensure that the response would necessarily be systematic because the researcher cannot induce a respondent to behave in the way he (and not the respondent) desires. However, as we know, the response will be systematic if it follows the same order in which the stimulus is imparted. The researcher may take a clue from this and set the questions in such an order that they would induce the members of the target group to follow the order in which the questions are set.

In case the researcher fails to induce the respondents to follow the ordering engineered by him, the order of questions may need to the changed. Sometimes, a weak response is followed up by taking recourse to an iterative process so that the cue is improved and the response at the desired level is attained. The interview method based on the questionnaire in such a case is replaced by the *depth interview method* and the technique of questioning is referred to as the *laddering technique*. The depth interview method is widely used in market surveys, particularly when the underlying motives of the respondents (buyers) are to be unveiled. It is generally undertaken by trained specialists who are good at using laddering techniques. There could again be situations or settings of interview where *ab-initio*, no such sequence of questions is present and free-wheeling questioning is to be conducted to evoke the desired response. The method of interviewing here also could be a depth interview. In both the situations stated above, the setting is informal (questioning without preordained structure). This is similar to the questionnaire method; the difference is that in the questionnaire method the questions are ordered and the stimuli are systematic in an oral-written mode of communication while in questioning method, the setting is informal and the questions are not preordained.

6.2.1 Classification of Questionnaires

Questionnaires are classified on the following basis:

- the degree to which the questionnaire is formalised or structured[1], and
- the objectives of the questionnaires being disclosed or undisclosed.[2]

From the discussion above, we can see that questionnaires could be a list of questions structured to provide a stimulus. In questioning, the interviewers adapt the questions as the interview proceeds and thus it may not be structured at all times. The purpose of questioning may at times be explicit, at other times it is kept hidden from the respondent. In case the purpose of questioning is revealed, it is referred to as *undisguised*, in case the purpose remains hidden, it is referred to as *disguised*. In order to capture these possibilities, the questionnaire can be classified into four groups (Table 6.1).

Unstructured undisguised questionnaires and unstructured disguised questionnaires are known also as techniques for focus group interviewing and projective techniques respectively. It is found that the most common classification that we find in use is the structured undisguised questionnaire followed by the structured disguised questionnaire. Each of the classifications with their usage, advantages and disadvantages are discussed in this chapter.

6.2.2 Structured Undisguised Questionnaires

A structured undisguised questionnaire starts with the basic premise that the objective of the interview is the same as revealed in the questionnaire. At the same time, the questions are structured to provide the systematic stimuli.

---

1 Recall that a structured questionnaire assumes that the stimuli are imparted systematically and the responses also come in a systematic way.

2 The researcher may not disclose the real objective of the study (question) lest the disclosure leads to bias in response.

Table 6.1 Classification of questionnaires

Form of data collection	Kind of structuring	
	Structured	**Unstructured**
Undisguised	Structured undisguised questionnaire	Unstructured undisguised questionnaire
Disguised	Structured disguised questionnaire	Unstructured disguised questionnaire

A survey on washing powder had, among others, the following questions:

(a) What washing powder do you use?
(b) Why do you not use brand X?

The questions were placed in a systematic order, so the questionnaire is a structured questionnaire. It is *undisguised* because, although the specific purpose of questioning is not stated clearly, the objective is clear to the respondent.

Such questionnaires are appreciated in situations where the researcher perceives that disguising the purpose will not be helpful in getting the cooperation of the respondent (or where the researcher understands that disguising the purpose will not add much in ensuring the quality of the data). In many areas of market research, the questionnaire follows this pattern. For example, when some products have been around for a long period and have strong brand equity, one may use such structured undisguised questionnaires with a minimum risk of losing information from the field.

6.2.3 Structured Disguised Questionnaire

The next most common method is the *structured disguised questionnaire*. Such a questionnaire has all the positive aspects of the questionnaire method; because it is structured, the stimuli are imparted in a systematic manner and the responses are expected to be systematic. At the same time, it attempts to minimise the bias of the respondents who are expected to cooperate better when they do not know the real purpose of the survey.

The use of this method depends on the perception of the researcher regarding the issue under consideration vis-a-vis the respondents. The researcher may think that the disclosure of the real intention of the survey may affect the respondents in such a way that the truth may not be revealed. For example, it could be a situation where sensitive information has to be gathered. The problem could be envisaged to come from the competitors in a market survey on brand equity. Even the client company may have stipulated that the real purpose of the survey should remain disguised. Thus, when one of the stipulations of the survey is not to disclose its purpose, the researcher would use the structured disguised questionnaire.

6.2.4 Unstructured Undisguised Questionnaire

Researchers at times find that a structured questionnaire does not lead to the required answers. As already discussed, the researcher would then opt for *depth interviews* or *focus group interviews.* The questions would not follow a structured predetermined pattern. If the researcher thinks that the revelation of the real purpose of the survey would not affect the quality of the information, the depth interview or focus group study would follow the unstructured undisguised questionnaire pattern.

This method is widely used when the motive of the respondents has to be studied and the study is expected to generate better results if the respondents are taken into confidence while exploring the real issue. However, such a method may not produce the desired results if the issues are such that the respondent, even after long persuasion, will not air his views to the researcher. Under such a situation, the researcher would opt for the unstructured disguised questionnaire.

6.2.5 Unstructured Disguised Questionnaire

The unstructured disguised questionnaire is widely used in anthropological and psychometric studies. However, market research organisations often find it paying to take up the disguised questionnaire which is unstructured in nature, particularly when unsystematic stimuli are expected to generate better results with respect to a group of respondents who are not expected to share their views if the issues are placed in an undisguised manner. The most widely used area in market research where this method is adopted is the area of studies in the buying motives of the respondents. In situations where the buying motives are to be explored, there might be some reasons why the respondents do not intend to disclose their motives. Let us suppose we want to explore why machine-made bread could not become very popular in a conventional industrial town of southern India. Under such circumstances, the unstructured disguised questionnaire would be well suited because the real reason, which might be social in nature, might not be disclosed to the researcher.

The unstructured disguised questionnaire in this case, reduces the bias of the respondent. This could be because the respondent has no clue why he is being questioned. It is necessary in this case because the respondents may not respond properly if the issue is raised directly.

Let us consider another example. A company is taking a survey on the quality of its after-sales service by circulating a questionnaire among its employees who are engaged in this service. It is apt to take recourse to the unstructured disguised questionnaire tool in this case. If employees become aware of the purpose of questioning, they may not divulge their real perception about the quality of the service that the company provides. In their perception, it would mean going against the commitment to the objectives or promises of the organisation.

6.3 TYPES OF QUESTIONNAIRES

The questionnaire is a collection of questions. The types of questions, the sequence in which they are placed along with the choices with respect to answers that the respondent is given, are very important issues. The choice of questionnaire is largely determined by the type of information and the type of respondents from whom it is to be obtained. As we know, the information is the product of stimulus and response. The nature of the stimulus, as determined by the researcher, largely shapes the types of questions, their wording along with the sequence in which they are to be administered. However, the nature of the respondent (whether he or she would comply with the researcher's interests) would also shape the type of the questionnaire. The questionnaires can be used for personal interviews and interviews via mail or telephone. The mode of communicating the questions also plays a role in deciding the type of questions. (The sequence might also be the other way round; the type of questions often decides whether a personal, mail or telephone interview would be appropriate.) It is necessary to decide on the type of questionnaire at this stage as, the way the questions are framed and the sequence in which they are asked will make a substantial difference to the data collected.

However, there are certain issues that must be settled even before the researcher decides upon the type of questionnaire that he would use. A brief account of these factors is given below.

6.3.1 Size of Questionnaire

The size of the questionnaire depends on the research objective. The questions are set on the basis of the research objective. The researcher would collect the field data to the extent necessary to meet the requirement of the research question. It is advised that the questionnaire should not be loaded with unnecessary questions. In order to limit the 'necessary' region, the researcher would find it rewarding to start with dummy tables that would give an idea regarding the information that the project would require. The researcher would then set the questions and thus avoid putting unnecessary load on the questionnaire.

6.3.2 Content of the Questionnaire

Ambiguity is a major problem in generating information. This problem is discussed more elaborately in the latter part of this section. The questions that are framed in a questionnaire should be worded in such a way that the intention of the researcher is properly communicated to the respondent. Even if the ambiguity in questions is minimised, the possibility of getting an ambiguous answer is not ruled out.

How does ambiguity appear? We find that there are questions in questionnaires which mean different things to different respondents, sometimes not what the interviewer means. Many a time an open question leads us to such a possibility. 'What do you think about the soap of brand X?' To some respondents it means the look of the pack, to some it means other attributes of the product such as taste, to some others it means the perception about sponsors of the brand. Editing answers will require a huge amount of effort on the part of the researcher. Some filter questions can be used to help the researcher come to a conclusion: (a) Kindly rank the brand X in relation to other brands. This could be followed by (b) What are the attributes that differentiate the brand from other brands?

6.3.3 Understanding the Target Group

Sometimes the questionnaire may have questions which may not elicit proper or truthful answers, or may encourage the process of guessing. At times even if a person does not have any knowledge, or has minimal knowledge about the topic, the question may be such that he may indulge in guessing as he may not be able to resist the temptation to admit to not knowing. The problem exists primarily in the questionnaire that the respondent addresses. The respondent does the guessing not with the motive to be dishonest but because of being provoked by the question itself. Nevertheless, this process has an impact on the research data. Under such circumstances, the questionnaire must target a precise group of respondents or it should be reframed keeping the knowledge level of the respondents in mind.

Many questions asked in marketing research involve memory to varying degrees. Memory is normally influenced by: (i) the event itself, (ii) the individual's power to recollect, (iii) the length of time since the event, and (iv) the stimulus that is addressing the individual's memory.

The first two factors are less controllable factors as far as the individual is concerned. The last two factors are within the control of the individual. It has been seen that events that are part of an established pattern or events which interrupt the established pattern are remembered better than unrelated events. Hardly a few people will remember where or when they bought their brand X which is used in a routine manner; but they are more likely to remember when they bought the toothpaste Y, a herbal product. A married person generally remembers his wedding date. Again in reference to the importance of the event, we must accept that the researcher cannot change the ability of the person to remember; the golden rule is that there are certain established habits that a respondent is likely to remember.

The researcher can maintain a control on the length of time between an event and the data that they require by limiting their questions to events that have occurred recently. This means that questions on purchases are asked on what was bought recently, the use of a product recently or regarding the quantity of the product that has been procured very recently.

The fourth factor is the stimulus that is addressed to an individuals' memory. It is easier for a respondent to recall an event with the aid of a stimulus rather than to do so without a situation to recall. An unaided recall can usually locate or remember 10% of the incidents.

The advantage of added recall is that a bigger response is noticed, though it is also sometimes observed that it does bring bias to the stimuli that help in recall. This is known as *suggestion bias*.

Instead of the aided recall being restricted to that of guidance, it sometimes increases its ambit to actual happening and thereby the respondent needs to only state his accent to the incident.

6.3.4 Does the Questionnaire Require the Respondent to do a Lot of Work?

Sometimes the respondents are asked questions for which the homework is tedious. Suppose the questionnaire has asked for month-wise sales data of different detergent brands from a wholesale outlet for 30 months, region wise and branch wise. Because of the complex nature of the requirement, data may not come quickly or the respondent may not be interested in furnishing the data, particularly to a private researcher. Finally the questionnaire may end up in the waste-paper basket.

6.3.5 Is the Respondent Ready to Give Information?

The non-response error occurs while the data collection process is in progress. The non-response error is largely because the respondents in most cases do not want to participate in the response process. There are two reasons for this—the respondents find it difficult to comprehend the question or they are sensitive to the question.

The first situation is the case where the questionnaire is not easily comprehensible because it contains some phrases or the language and words are too imposing for the respondent. For example, a respondent may find that answering a question is like sitting for an examination—even if the respondent intends to comply, he may not find it easy to honour. Sometimes the respondents do not cooperate on matters which are basically private in nature (such as method of contraception, private relations, religious beliefs and expenditure on certain items and even income). This information is sensitive in nature. The best way to handle a sensitive issue is to go in for an unstructured disguised questionnaire, but even this may be counter-productive under certain circumstances. It would be better to avoid such a situation. But, if the situation is such that the response has to be obtained, the following methods are usually suggested for obtaining information.

- The questions may be hidden in a group of non-sensitive questions.
- The question may be disguised as an indirect question.
- A special ballot that may be sealed may be prepared which the respondent can complete privately and drop in a box.
- The interviewer may explain that a particular behaviour is not unusual and then he might ask the specific question on a sensitive issue.
- Another approach is the randomised response technique. When all the questions are sensitive in nature the respondent may be persuaded to select a few of them in a

random manner (by drawing lots) and give information only with respect to the selected questions.

- Sometimes, suggesting alternative answers with answer codes and allowing the respondent to put a tick mark at the desired answer code might generate a proper response.

6.3.6 Determining the Type of Question

Before the wording of the questions is decided, it is necessary to know the type of question to be used. There could be free-answer or open-ended type of questions; alternatively the questions could be closed with the possibility of having dichotomous or multiple choice questions. We shall discuss these types of questions presently. But, before we take up this exercise, we should note that in each type of question there is the possibility of an error at the transmission stage of the communication. Such a problem is known as the *problem of ambiguity*.

Ambiguity occurs not due to unwillingness of the respondents. Usually ambiguity is associated with wrong communication. Unambiguous communication requires that the question asked and the answer given, both centre around the same subject, to both the questioner and the respondent. The researcher can minimise the ambiguity by carefully wording the questions and analysing the implications before the field survey (Chapter 7). We shall discuss this issue at length in the chapter on 'Errors in Data'. At this stage, we would only mention that the questionnaire method cannot escape this problem; it has been observed that open-ended questions have the highest possibility of ambiguity in answers but the questions would have the lowest dose of ambiguity. In the case of multiple choice questions, the possibility of having ambiguity is the highest in the questions, the answers on the other hand should have an average level of ambiguity. Ambiguity in answers is the lowest in the case of dichotomous questions. In the case of questions, the possibility of ambiguity is not ruled out in the dichotomous setting also. However, the questions in this case contain an average level of ambiguity.

Let us now discuss the types of questions that a questionnaire might contain.

Open-ended questions

In open-ended questions, the researcher builds in a provision for the respondents to exercise their discretion to the maximum level in choosing the answer to the given questions. Consider the following question in a market survey: 'What is your view about the soap of brand X?' This opens up the possibility of recording a wide range of viewpoints from individuals answering the question because they are free to answer in their own words without any prejudice. The length of the answer could be small or it could be elaborate depending on the topic and the interest the individual has in the answer.

Open questions are good as first answer to a set of questions in a questionnaire. They remove inhibitions. Therefore, when the respondent's view is to be evoked, it is better to start with an open-ended question. Open questions do not influence the answering process; they may open up dimensions which have not been thought of or which have been lost sight of by the researcher. Since open questions are thought provoking and build up confidence, they open up a lot of issues. It is to be noted that in pilot surveys, the inclusion of open questions usually helps the researcher to frame the multiple choice questions in the final questionnaire. The responses to the related open-ended questions help the researcher to comprehend the range of possible answers.

The open questions have certain disadvantages. As already pointed out, the possibility of ambiguity in the answers is the highest in the case of open-ended questions. Even the questions may have ambiguity. Consider, for example, the same question mentioned above: 'What is your view about the soap of brand X?' Note the word 'view'. View about what? It has several possibilities. It might imply the respondents' view on the soap being soft on the hands, the colour, the price range, the perfume that it bears and so on. Even if such possibilities are taken care of, the answers might be ambiguous. Again, it may be difficult to standardise the answers because the respondents might have different perspectives.

Nevertheless, a questionnaire would include open-ended questions particularly when the questions are of unstructured disguised nature. There would be the requirement of introducing open-ended questions when the researcher himself or herself is not sure about the research question or the possibilities hidden in the research issue.

Close-ended questions

Unlike open-ended questions, closed questions are closed in the sense that the researcher himself has limited the possible alternatives in the answer. The idea is to minimise the ambiguity in answers. (Note that such a pattern of questions does not exclude the possibility of the question being ambiguous.) Questions of this type offer alternatives to the respondent from which he/she has to choose the one that is most apt. The following are examples of closed questions.

1. Do you buy this brand of soap (State 'yes' wherever it is applicable)

   Exclusively __________

   Quite often __________

   Occasionally __________

2. Which of the following are your reasons for using this brand of soap? (Tick whichever is applicable)

   It is easily available __________

   No other brands are available __________

   It is the cheapest __________

   It is a status symbol __________

It represents personality ________________

It has a good perfume ________________

It is economical in usage ________________

It is used by my friends/referral group ________________

All these questions are closed questions in the sense that the set of options has been suggested by the researcher and no option outside the set can be exercised by the respondent. However, the closed questions might be of different types. In some cases, the respondent is asked to exercise only one choice and in some cases, the respondent is allowed to exercise more than one option within the set of suggested alternatives. When the options are multiple, the set of questions are noted as multiple choice questions. Let us elaborate on this point.

Multiple choice questions

The multiple choice questions are by nature 'closed' because the question is closed and the options of the respondents in choosing the answer is also closed. Within the set of what we identify as multiple choice questions, there are three categories. The first is a situation where the question has many alternative answers and one has to select only one as his chosen answer. For example, in reference to a brand, the question is framed as follows:

The soap of brand X is soft on the skin primarily because:

(a) It is made of vegetable oil
(b) It is made out of water of the Ganges
(c) It is made of glycerine as the principal ingredient
(d) It is made of herbal ingredients
(e) It does not have any chemical ingredient

The above example is a closed question with closed options and one is required to tick only one of the above options. In other words, there are multiple options, and the choice has to be only one of them.

In the second category, the choice is not confined to only one among the alternatives. The respondent may tick more than one of the suggested answers. Often the respondent is requested to rank the chosen answers according to their relative level of importance. Suppose the question is such:

The glycerine soap X sells more in December because:

(a) People have a developed a behavioural pattern of using the glycerine soap X during winter.
(b) Glycerine is the principal ingredient in X that helps moisture to be retained.
(c) The soap has a perfume that is warmth-generating in the winter months.
(d) The soap X is the cheapest among the available brands.

The respondent in the above situation is often required to order the options in terms of relative importance. Questions of this nature contain the real essence of what is termed as multiple choice questions.

Dichotomous questions

It is a two-option question and is an extreme form of a multiple choice question. The idea is to offer only two choices. Examples, *Yes or No*, *Cash or Credit*, *Air or Sea*, and so on. Dichotomous questions have more or less the same advantages as multiple choice questions. They are quick and easier for the interviewer to handle. The respondent can exercise his choice; but then this choice is dichotomous in nature, that is, the options are *mutually exclusive* in nature.

Advantages and disadvantages

The most important advantage of multiple choice questions is that it simplifies the tabulation process. The options are usually codified and the codes are entered directly in the data sheet (usually) with assigned numbers. Also, the difficult and time-consuming editing process, which is often faced in case of open-ended questions, becomes remarkably smooth in this set up because it is easier to administer and control the process when the choice is reduced to a manageable number of alternatives.

One problem with the multiple choice questions is that they have the potential of being highly ambiguous if the researcher does not take sufficient care in formulating them. The problem of ambiguity might also remain in the answers unless the alternatives which are offered to the respondents are carefully drawn. Consider, for example, the following multiple choice question: 'Do you like brand X tomato juice?' The anticipated answers as formulated by the researcher are:

(a) Yes
(b) Somewhat like
(c) Strongly like
(d) Thoroughly dislike
(e) No opinion

The problems that the researcher might face while analysing the data might be rooted in the question itself. Note the word 'like'. This might communicate 'liking the colour' to a respondent; to another respondent the reference might be 'liking the packaging', and so on. The analysis is bound to suffer because of the ambiguity in the question. One should therefore be very careful in setting multiple choice questions. Unless the researcher takes sufficient care in wording the question, it might suffer from ambiguity, so much so that the analysis of the data might even lead to a wrong conclusion. Similarly, note the choice set with respect to the answers. A response such as 'Yes' might include the possibility of 'somewhat like' and 'strongly like'. If the researcher needs a precise answer he should anticipate this possibility and take adequate measures at the option-formulating stage.

Multiple choice questions may occasionally lead to biased answers owing to the order of alternatives. The respondents often have a tendency to select the first answer; sometimes they opt for the last option. Sometimes, it becomes rewarding if the ranking of the alternatives is changed when the questionnaire is canvassed.

As the extreme form of multiple choice questions, dichotomous questions have certain additional advantages. They are quick and easier for the interviewer to handle. For the respondent, the choice of one out of two is much easier. Editing and tabulation is easier and simpler. The interviewer's bias is less and can rarely creep into the final results.

The ambiguity in answer is the least in case of dichotomous questions. In fact, this is the greatest advantage in the case of the dichotomous form of close-ended questions. The problem however, is that the possibility of ambiguity in questions is the highest in the case of the dichotomous setting. The researcher must take proper care in setting the questions so that the ambiguity is kept at the minimum. Another problem with ambiguous questions is that the respondent himself or herself may find it difficult to choose one answer. In fact, the respondent might find both the alternatives acceptable rather than only one. A question such as 'Do you use branded or unbranded detergents?' To a particular respondent (may be a housewife), the question, with only two suggested alternatives in answers, may be confusing, as on certain occasions she buys branded and on certain other occasions she buys unbranded as well. The root of the problem is the ambiguity in question. A suggested alternative framing of the question which would contain less ambiguity is as follows: Do you *always* use unbranded detergents? That reduces ambiguity because the possibility of occasional use has also been taken care of by re-framing the question.

6.4. DESIGNING A QUESTIONNAIRE

6.4.1 Wording in Questions

A number of precautions should be taken in wording the questions; the important among them are enumerated below.

(a) *Define the issue*: Each question is expected to address an issue related to the research objective. A researcher must check whether a question is relevant to the issue and whether it addresses the same issue that has already been covered by another question. After checking this point, the researcher should ensure that the question has been framed in such a way that the issue is being addressed properly. A suggested thumb rule for checking this point particularly in the context of market research: usually, the pivot of a question is either of, some of or all of *who, what, when* and *where.* A common mistake in wording a question is that these four points are not given due attention.

(b) *Should the question be subjective or objective?* Basically, the questions are either subjective or objective. But then, even in a subjective question, elements of objectivity can be imparted. For example if the question is 'Is brand X better than brand Y?', the question is fully subjective. Now consider a reframed version of the same question, 'Is brand X better than brand Y with reference to the power steering?' This question, as we can gather, is much more objective even though the subjective judgement of the respondent is the major issue. The researcher must decide *a priori* whether a purely subjective judgement would serve his purpose. Otherwise, he might have to pay heavily due to elements of subjectivity while compiling the report on the basis of the results of the field survey.

(c) *Positive and negative statement*: There is no definite rule that the researcher should follow. He should apply his own judgement, depending on the nature of the issue, whether the question should be positive or negative—which would work better for getting proper answers. When the researcher thinks that his own subjective judgement may be misleading the respondent, he could take a small sub-sample and test which manner of questioning produces better results.

(d) *Use of simple words:* Words used in questionnaires should be those that are understood universally in the target group of respondents. To them the word must have only one meaning. Otherwise, the problem of ambiguity will affect the quality of research. Consider, for example, the wording, 'Are you a prospective customer?'. The term 'prospective' does not take care of the factor of the degree of willingness that might be important for a market research survey. A similar situation exists in the statement, 'The product is dynamic in nature'. The question should be reframed by dropping the term 'dynamic', as it is unusual and the meaning of the statement is different for different people.

(e) *Avoid ambiguous questions*: Since the questions mean different things to different people, the replies are also ambiguous. In questions when the terms 'usually', 'normally', 'regularly', 'frequently' are used, ambiguity creeps in.

(f) *Avoid leading questions:* It is sometimes seen that the framer of the questionnaire has included a leading question. For example, 'Don't you think that we are the leaders in market?' The question starts with a lead, which makes the answer biased towards the lead. Unwarranted bias should be avoided.

(g) *Do not ask questions that indicate generalisation:* Questions should always be in specific terms. If generalisation is required it should be backed by adequate data from the respondent. For example, a question such as 'how many sales representatives usually visit you?' would hardly help the researcher because the respondent can only give a rough estimate. A better question under such a circumstance is, 'How many sales representatives called on you last month?' The answer in this case will be largely specific.

(h) *Cushion questions:* A situation of having to answer a sensitive or difficult question should be encountered by the researcher asking different questions to meet the same objective. For example, in order to know the economic status of the respondent, a question about the income of the respondent should have a back up question that serves as a cushion because the issue is sensitive and therefore the answer might be misleading. The cushion question in this case might be on average monthly expenditure of the respondent.

(i) *Use randomised response technique:* In case the question is embarrassing or invasive, one may use the *randomised response* technique. The respondent may be persuaded to answer a few out of a set of questions, some of which are sensitive. The specific set to be answered would be selected in a random manner (by drawing lots). One will get answers to sensitive questions from a subset of the respondents if the randomisation is done scientifically. Randomised response is used mostly in interviews with respect to personal issues.

(j) *Use split ballot:* There could be situations where the questions fail to generate adequate response from the respondents (may be the questionnaire is lengthy, may be there are sensitive questions). In such cases, we use this technique. Some of the lengthy or sensitive questions are placed in one set and the rest in another set. The target group is split in two (homogenous) groups with equal number of respondents in each group. Half of the target audience is addressed with one set of questionnaires that contains some of the questions and the other half of the target audience is subjected to another set of questionnaires in which the other questions are included.

6.4.2 Sequence of Questions

A questionnaire has three major parts: (i) Basic information, (ii) Classification information and (iii) Identification information. As the information gathering process operates after sometime, the respondents' interest also declines. The basic information forms the main part of the questionnaire. The information collected needs to be analysed on the basis of certain demographic variables such as age, sex, religion, income, profession, education, nationality and family size. This comes under classification. The identification information consists of name, address, age of the respondent and also sometimes of the interviewer.

The sequencing depends on the judgement of the researcher. However, while choosing the sequence, the researcher should bear in the mind the following:

- *The opening questions must arouse the respondents' interest*: The first question must be such that the discussion should get started. The question must raise curiosity in the respondent. The question along with the openness should endeavour to be confidence building. The best way to start is 'What is your opinion?'.

- *Positioning questions that are difficult for the respondent*: Questions which might embarrass the respondent should absolutely not figure in the beginning, they should be placed well down in the questionnaire so that the momentum of answering is not affected.
- *Arrangement of questions in logical order*: Questions should follow a logical order. Sudden changes in the order of questioning are bound to lead to confusion. For example, while one is collecting information on soap, he cannot suddenly ask for the respondent's identification. While dealing with historical data, chronology must be followed. One may start from the back and move forward or one may start at the beginning and move backwards. The point to remember is that the stimuli should be systematic, as far as practicable.

Mail questionnaires are special: The mail questionnaire must sell itself. Mail questionnaires have unique characteristics. In case the opening question is not able to generate interest, the mail questionnaire will find its place in the waste paper basket. The questions must be sequenced properly so that the respondent finds relevance in information. The wording of the questions should not be ambiguous and the size of the questionnaire should be minimum.

Pre-coded questionnaire

Many telephone interviews are conducted using equipment which allows the interviewer to record the answer directly into the computer. To speed up the process, questionnaires are pre-coded, that is, the codes of the questions that the respondent has to answer will be entered into the computer.

While pre-coding is designed to speed up the tabulation process, it also has a favourable effect on the researcher. It makes him think through each question and the possible answers. If the answer that could be obtained doesn't provide the information needed for an analysis, a new or reworded question is called for.

6.4.3 Layout and Reproduction

Three major points that should be considered in planning the layout and reproduction are, (i) securing acceptance of the questionnaire from the respondent, (ii) making it easy to control the questionnaire and (iii) making it easy to handle the questionnaire.

Securing acceptance: The physical appearance of a questionnaire influences the respondent in a personal interview or mail survey. If the questionnaire is typed or mimeographed on poor quality paper, the respondent may think that the project is no good. A questionnaire on good quality paper usually gives a good impression. The name of the organisation conducting the study appears on the top of the page or on the cover if the questionnaire is in the book form. Many of the organisations give fictitious names on the questionnaire to prevent bias.

Easy to control: For the purpose of tabulation and editing, the questionnaires should be numbered serially so that the researcher, at the end of the day, can account for all the questionnaires and note the responses. The lost questionnaires can be traced when they are sequentially numbered. However, in the case of a mail survey, numbering of the questionnaires may sometimes lead to suspicion on the part of the respondents, who may feel that his identity should not be disclosed. Nevertheless, it is advisable that the questionnaires are serially numbered, as the process is likely to help in speeding up the system of editing and tabulation.

Ease of handling: The size of the paper is of relevance. Too small a size is difficult for documentation or may get lost while on field survey. The ideal size recommended is 8.5" × 11". When the questionnaire runs to a few pages, it is advisable that it is made into a booklet rather than being stapled so that pages are not lost.

6.4.4 Pre-test

Before the questionnaire is finally approved for data collection, the researcher pre-tests the questionnaire. Pre-testing is done by personal interview even if the questionnaire is meant for a telephone or mail survey. During the personal interview, the researcher will understand behavioral responses through verbal and non-verbal actions and make the necessary corrections in the questions. Once corrected, the questionnaire needs to be sent back for pre-testing. The second pre-test could be through a mail or telephone survey. Three factors are to be kept in mind while the pre-test is being carried out:

- To see that questions are clear to the respondent, that is, not only the wording but also the meaning should reflect the researcher's original thought.
- Words that are not understood should be removed or simplified so that they are understood. In the process, some questions may be eliminated and a few may be inserted.
- The sequence of questions needs to be checked so that the thought process of the respondent is not interfered with. Again one has to check whether the opening questions are able to generate interest in the respondents.

When the pre-test shows indications that no further correction is required, the questionnaire is approved for the final draft.

6.5 THE METHODS FOR COMMUNICATION

There are three methods to communicate with the respondents through the questionnaire. These methods are: (i) Personal method, (ii) Mail method and (iii) Telephone method.

In the personal method, the interviewer personally visits the respondents with the questionnaire (could be structured or non-structured). Sometimes the purpose of collection of data is revealed, at other times it may not be. In the mail method, the questionnaire is mailed to the target respondent, who fills up the questionnaire and sends it back to the researcher. It is advisable that the questionnaire be of the structured disguised or structured undisguised type. The telephone method is one in which the interviewer uses the telephone as the medium of administering the questionnaire. The response of the respondent is noted or recorded as the communication proceeds. The questionnaires advisable for such interviews are of the structured type only.

The factors that are important in deciding the method of such communications are the following:

(a) The total number of respondents to be communicated with.
(b) The type of respondent to be communicated with.
(c) The accuracy desired in the research.
(d) The cost of each such contact.
(e) The distance that separates the interviewer from the interviewee.
(f) The responses that are available with the researcher.
(g) The level of technology within which the research is to be carried out.
(h) The number of questions in the questionnaire.
(i) The nature of questions.
(j) The kind of editing and tabulation that is required.
(k) The control mechanism that is available to the researcher.

A comparison is made between the three methods focussing on the advantages and disadvantages of the system (Table 6.1).

6.6 PROJECTIVE TECHNIQUES

In all the techniques considered thus far, individuals have either reported or recorded their evidence or response. At times it may not be possible to find out why the person has not responded, or is not willing to divulge facts or is not able to respond. There could be several reasons including lack of social approval, inferiority complex and others. The researcher needs to elicit data from many such respondents especially on issues involving forgery, malpractices, tax evasions, under invoicing and politics. Certain indirect techniques could be used to explore the feelings, habits, attitudes and motivation of such respondents. One such indirect method is the projective technique.

A projective technique involves presentation of stimulus–situation, selected or devised in such a manner that it will never reveal to the subject what the experimenter or the researcher wants to seek. It should bring out the personal and private idiosyncrasies of the respondent.

Table 6.1 Advantages and disadvantages of different modes of communication

Factors of comparison	Modes of communication		
	Personal survey	**Mail method**	**Telephone method**
Reach out and time	Not many respondents can be contacted by a single investigator as time taken to contact and span of time spent on personal interview is high.	A large number of respondents can be contacted. This is conditioned by the available database of addresses.	A large number of respondents can be contacted, and time per contact is less.
Cost	The cost per contact is high because it involves conveyance cost and may require repetitive calls.	The cost per contact is not high. The only expense is the mailing cost.	The cost is not as high as in personal survey, but is higher than the mail method. Skilled telephone operators need to be employed and in case the person to be contacted is not available, a further call is necessary.
Accuracy of data	As the interviewer and interviewee are both present and they meet face to face, the data is collected in near perfect manner. The response rate is also higher and purposeful.	The response rate is low and it may at times be only 10%. The right person may not have filled the questionnaire in the right manner. The questions may not have been rightly understood.	Depends largely on the quality of telephone interviewer. The data can be more accurately collected by trained telephone interviewers. The response rate is high.
Geographical area	When the respondents are many and scattered over a large area this method will be time consuming and costly.	With respondents widely scattered, this method is the best. What is required to administer the questionnaire is a good database of prospective addresses.	If the distance is more, the cost is more and since the telephone is a technical device, there could be an interruption in the line.
Infrastructure	This method requires good infrastructure for collection of data in terms of field force and supervision staff.	Excepting secretarial service and postal service nothing much will be required.	Technological infrastructure will be required. The data from the telephone needs to be recorded.

Table 6.1 (*Contd*)

Factors of comparison	Modes of communication		
	Personal survey	**Mail method**	**Telephone method**
Type of respondent	When the literacy level is low and the respondent may not be able to fill in a questionnaire, this method will be the best.	When the respondents are able to read and write this method is found to be helpful.	As long as respondents are available over the telephone and able to communicate properly, this method is well suited.
Size of the questionnaire	When the questionnaire is lengthy, the interview approach is found to be helpful.	For lengthy questionnaires one needs time in filling up the responses. So mailing is the most suitable.	For shorter questionnaires this method is suitable as time and computation on the telephone may prove to be costly.
Availability of personnel	The availability of a skilled interviewer is an important factor, otherwise the element of bias will be more.	The requirement of trained hands is least.	The requirement of skilled/trained interviewers is a must to get information.
Nature of questions	If the questions are open type and discussion oriented, this is an advisable method. If it involves questions of a very personal nature, this method may not be helpful as embarrassment may be involved.	Personal questions and personal matters are best handled through this method.	Questions requiring spontaneous answers are well suited for this method. Questions of a personal nature need to be avoided as it might be embarrassing for the respondent.

This stimulus–situation could be a photograph or a symmetrical ink blot and the subject responds to it in his own manner. The researcher now looks into the meaning that the material has to the subject who organises the material as per his own understanding. The outcome is the individual's own world of tension, anxiety, need, personality and ideals.

At times it may be difficult to hide the purpose of testing. The subject may know that a part of the projective technique is being used to find out to what extent he supports a particular practice. Still we can say that projective techniques are good for the following reasons:

- The respondent may find it easier to express himself if he is not talking about his own feelings and attitudes explicitly.
- The respondent may be unable to describe his attitudes and projective techniques will enable him to do so.
- The projective technique test may produce more information than any other form of data collection.

In marketing, we find that projective techniques are widely in use for discerning the minds of the subjects. The methods mostly adopted are (i) verbal testing and (ii) pictorial testing. Both the techniques are based on attitude testing for the respondent.

6.4.1 Verbal Testing

(a) *Word association test*: This is a test in which a number of words are presented or stated to the respondent, one by one, and he is asked to respond to the first thought that he could associate with the word. Supposing the word is 'forgery', the thought that could be associated is 'harassment'. The speed of the response as well as the content is very important in such cases, it is a valuable indicator of the attitude of such respondents.

(b) *Sentence completion test*: In this kind of technique, incomplete sentences are presented, leading the respondent to complete them. The completion will give considerable insight into the minds of the respondent. For example, we could frame the following sentences for completion.

- The products were not as promised but traders ___________
- MNCs with their range of products are ___________

Completion of these sentences will help in revealing the respondent's attitude.

(c) *Story and argument-completion technique*: In this kind of testing, the respondent is presented with a story or an argument (it could also be a story with an inner argument) that is incomplete and the respondent may be asked to complete the story.

EXAMPLE

'A travel agency operating inter-state tourist buses, has a bus operating between Calcutta and Bodh Gaya. The buses usually carry Buddhist tourists who consist of foreign nationals of Indian origin. The agency found that 10% of the passengers failed to turn up for such trips. It instructed its over-the-counter salesmen to say 'Bon Voyage' to customers once all the formalities of booking the seat were over. In the busy month of May, one fine morning, the holder of a confirmed ticket failed to get his seat in the assigned air-conditioned coach and came to the office of the agency ________________'

The attitude of the respondent towards customer servicing can be understood by analysing the completed story.

- *Description*: It involves asking the subject to describe the kind of person who would behave in a specific way. For example, describing the type of seller he would like to handle most of the time.
- *Projective questions*: The respondent is presented with a vague question such as, 'What about quality?' This would make the respondent imagine situations and futuristic events. The respondent's response is indicative of his perception, beliefs and attitude which would have pre-disposed him to answer the question the way he has gone about it.

6.4.2 Pictorial Tests

Pictorial tests are borrowed from well-established clinical procedures and they help in attitude formation.

(a) *Thematic Apperception Test* (TAT): This consists of a series of pictures about which the subject is asked to tell stories. The pictures may deal with unusual as well as some ordinary events. From the stories told by the respondent, the researcher is able to understand the personality, stress, aggressive and expressive aspects. The stories that the respondent tells is a projection of his own internal thoughts.

(b) *The Rosenweig test:* This test uses the cartoon format. It could be two figures, one of the buyer and the other of the seller; the buyer saying, 'I want the best product at the lowest price', the seller's speech bubble being blank. The respondent is asked to fill in what the seller could be saying. This situation is likely to reveal the subconscious mind of the seller in handling such problems.

(c) *The doll play test:* The respondent may be given a set of dolls representing different sexes, age groups and ethnic backgrounds. The subject may be asked how he would handle the dolls in interactions and group meetings under different settings. Which of the dolls would he allow to speak first and lead the group? What roles will he assign to different dolls? This is likely to reveal the kind of attitude the respondent will have towards gender, age and ethnicity.

(d) *Psychodramatic technique:* This test involves role play. The respondent is asked to act out a role in a setting as he would like to see in a real-life situation. The respondent may be asked to play the role of a consumer or of a buyer in a situation where there is a complaint regarding the product. The kind of role he plays under the situation will reveal the attitude he will have towards such a happening.

Finally, one has to admit that projective techniques in marketing research or any other social research, help in revealing many hidden traits and in discovering the personal and private characteristics which would otherwise be difficult to understand. On the other hand, one has to accept that sometimes the validity of the results could be questioned. Using the same stimulus–situation two researchers may give two different interpretations. At times there will be validity of the results when the projective test result matches with the alternate results obtained from other forms of data collection techniques.

SUMMARY

- The questionnaire is the tool or instrument to collect data in the written-verbal mode. It is used under formal unstructured setting and formal structured setting.
- The four classifications of the instrument are structured undisguised questionnaire, unstructured undisguised questionnaire, structured disguised questionnaire and unstructured disguised questionnaire. These classifications have their distinct properties and therefore distinct applications and limitations.
- There are two types of questions—open ended questions and close-ended questions. Close-ended questions are of two types—multiple choice questions and dichotomous questions. Each of these types have their own advantages and disadvantages.
- Ambiguity should be avoided as far as practicable.
- The questionnaire needs to be communicated through personal survey, mail method or telephonic method. The options of the communication mode are based on the merits and demerits of the specific mode and the requirement of the researcher.
- Getting fruitful data is also conditioned by the wording of the questions. The robustness of the questionnaire is ensured by pre-testing of the questionnaire.
- Data can also be collected under the verbal mode of communication with a questionnaire under both formal unstructured setting and formal structured setting. The communication is often done through verbal testing and pictorial testing.

ASSIGNMENTS

Q1 Choose the right answers

1. The projective technique in questionnaire classification is a part of:
   (a) Structured disguised type questionnaire
   (b) Structured undisguised type questionnaire
   (c) Unstructured undisguised type questionnaire
   (d) Unstructured disguised type questionnaire
2. The term 'disguised' means:
   (a) The administrator of the questionnaire disguises himself
   (b) The purpose of the questionnaire has been disguised
   (c) Just calling the questionnaire disguised, as it may not be physically visible
   (d) None of the above
3. In the case of a mail survey, the type of questionnaire should preferably be:
   (a) Structured disguised and structured undisguised
   (b) Structured disguised and unstructured undisguised
   (c) Unstructured undisguised and unstructured disguised
   (d) None of the above
4. In the case of a telephone survey, the type of questionnaire should be:
   (a) Structured undisguised
   (b) Structured disguised
   (c) Unstructured undisguised
   (d) Unstructured disguised
5. The cheapest method of communication of the questionnaire is possible through:
   (a) Personal survey method
   (b) Mail method
   (c) Telephone method
   (d) None of the above
6. Word association testing is part of the:
   (a) Pictorial testing method of projective technique
   (b) An independent method of projective technique
   (c) A verbal testing method of projective technique
   (d) None of the above
7. Dichotomous questions are:
   (a) Uni-option questions
   (b) Multi-choice questions

(c) Multi-choice questions with only two options
(d) None of the above

8. A cushion question is one which is:
(a) A question that is used at the end of the questionnaire
(b) A question that is used to suppress facts
(c) A question that elicits difficult or sensitive data
(d) None of the above

9. The full form of TAT is:
(a) Thematic Appreciation Test
(b) Thematic Apperception Test
(c) Test After Test
(d) None of the above

10. The method to unravel the respondents' mind is:
(a) Interview method
(b) Projective technique
(c) Experimentation method
(d) None of the above

Answers

1. (d), 2. (b), 3. (a), 4. (a), 5. (b), 6. (c), 7. (c), 8. (c), 9. (b), 10. (b)

Q2 Answer the questions

1. A company has asked you to conduct a survey among jute mill owners regarding the brand of lubricants they use, usage pattern, usage behaviour, occasion and reasons for brand switching. In this regard the company has informed the agency that till last year these mills were using a brand of a nationalised oil company. You are requested to make a questionnaire to attend to the problem.
2. You are a consultant to an NGO which supports the cause of an AIDS prevention programme. The social workers want to study the adoption process of contraceptives in certain belts known for nightlife. What kind of data collection tools will you recommend and how is it different from other data collection tools?
3. Discuss the problem of ambiguity in the questionnaire method of data collection.
4. Discuss the projective technique as a method of of data collection.

APPENDIX 6.1

An example of a structured questionnaire

A survey on automobile owners' buying decision

1. Kindly state the following:
   1.1 Manufacturer's name: ______________
   1.2 Brand name: ______________
2. Rank the following attributes/factors in order of your preference in choosing the brand: (in ascending order, using numericals)
   2.1 Durability ______________
   2.2 Price ______________
   2.3 Corporate image ______________
   2.4 Brand image ______________
   2.5 availability ______________
   2.6 Aerodynamic quality ______________
   2.7 Choice of colour ______________
   2.8 Fuel efficiency ______________
   2.9 Customer service ______________
3. When did you buy the car? (Date of delivery)
4. Who might have influenced you in your decision of choosing the brand: (Tick whichever is applicable)
   4.1 Friends
   4.2 Family
   4.3 Automobile engineer
   4.4 Dealer
   4.5 Sales person
5. Which of the following source of information plays the most important role for your brand preference: (tick)
   5.1 Media/advertisement ______________
   5.2 Feedback from past usage ______________
   5.3 Feedback from peers who used this brand ______________
   5.4 Company brochures ______________

5.5 Survey data ________________

5.6 Promotion by dealers ________________

6. How long have you been buying cars from this dealer? (Tick whichever is applicable)

6.1 For the first time

6.2 Used in the past

DEMOGRAPHIC DATA

Name ________________
Address ________________
____
____
Age ________________
Sex ________________
Yearly income ________________

Signature of the investigator ________________

CHAPTER 7

ERRORS IN DATA: MEASUREMENT ERROR

LEARNING OBJECTIVES

After going through this chapter you will understand

- Non-sampling error
- Sources of non-sampling error
- Response and non-response error
- Error due to wrong questionnaire design
- Response bias
- Data processing error
- Checks on data
- Outlier labelling
- Measurement instrument bias
- Data validation and editing

Key words Total error, measurement error, experimental error, response and non-response error, ambiguity, specification error, outlier labelling, consistency check, post-survey check

7.1 INTRODUCTION

While collecting the primary data for empirical research, one of the targets of the researcher is to minimise the error in information. There are various types of errors in information. The first is *measurement error* (reporting error), that is, error that is basically rooted in wrong or ambiguous information. The other is the error due to the design by which data are collected. The researcher might decide to take information from the entire set of target population or, in order to save time, cost and depending on feasibility, he might have to concentrate on a section of the population. Such a design where a part of the universe forms the basis of research is popularly known as *experimental design*. The type of error expected to arise due to this design is called *experimental error*. The root of such error is the experiment itself—it arises because the researcher attempts to infer details about the nature of the population from a small set of representatives (known as sample) taken from the population. The fact that we try to infer information about the entire population from the information collected with respect to the sample is itself the source of this type of error. An error of this nature is therefore often referred to as *sampling error*. There is a powerful branch of statistical theory known as the *sampling theory* that helps one understand error in information.

This chapter is devoted to the analysis of measurement error. Measurement error is said to occur when there is a variation between information that describes the state of the phenomenon and the information obtained by the measurement process. There might be various reasons for the existence of such error. One point that should be highlighted here is that measurement error could exist in every type of data collection—a sample survey or a census study (a study based on complete enumeration). Experimental error, however, appears only in a sample survey. This does not however, imply that the *total error* (experimental error + measurement error) would be higher in a sample survey. The measurement error tends to increase as the size of the sample increases if the research administration remains the same. Logically, the volume of measurement error should be the highest in a census study where every member of the population is surveyed. The experimental error in this case would be zero. But, the total error could be higher than what is expected in a sample survey. This is because, in a sample survey, the measurement error would be lower if the research administration remains the same as in a census study, leading to a lower total error (in a census, where there is no experimental error, measurement error itself might be greater than total error in the sample survey).

Error due to sampling is a widely discussed area in empirical research. Experience however suggests that the quality of research is no less dependent on the extent of *non-sampling error* which may occur at the data generation stage or at the stage of processing and analysis of the data. In this chapter, we shall discuss in brief, the sources of non-sampling error in empirical research. We shall consider first the problem of non-sampling error at the stage of data generation.

7.2 RESPONSE AND NON-RESPONSE ERROR

Error that occurs when there is a variation between information that describes the state of the phenomenon and the information obtained by the measurement process, that is, measurement error may appear at various stages. The first stage of course is the stage of data generation. The primary source of error at the data generation stage, is error in response (or non-response) from the respondent. All measurement errors at the data generation stage are not response (or non-response) errors. The error might be due to wrong specification of the field; some errors might be due to wrong selection of field personnel. These are all non-sampling errors but it is quite unlikely that the researcher will start with wrong specification of the field or select a whole set of inefficient field personnel. The major problem for a researcher with regard to non-sampling error at the data generation stage is the problem associated with response or non-response errors. Common sense often fails to alert the researcher when such a problem creeps in.

A major source of non-sample errors lies in the stimulus imparted by the researcher and the response that has been received from the respondent. In most cases, the lack of quality in the empirical work is neither due to a fault in data processing, nor due to the wrong sample frame or lack of command over statistical tools. The problem basically lies in the quality of field data which, in most cases, is due to wrong or inadequate stimuli leading to bias in the response. The problem is manifested sometimes as non-response from members of the sample group. Sometimes, it is manifested in the response itself. The intensity of damage is higher if the source of such bias is response.

At the outset, it has to be understood that in checking of non-sampling error, it may be necessary at times to incur additional cost. Sometimes, it becomes difficult to estimate such cost a-priori. This is because the process is not as straight forward as in the case of sampling error. In the case of a sampling error, the only source of error is the size of the sample. If the sample is a scientifically drawn sample, we can reduce the error simply by increasing the size of the sample. But in the case of a non-sampling error, the error may not be confined to a single source because it may occur at various stages. Cost sometimes may be very high if the error had been committed at the stage of data generation. A pragmatic approach will be to invest in training the research personnel so that the non-sampling error might be kept under control.

7.2.1 Non-response Error

If we select a large sample of respondents, it is unlikely that the investigators would be able to interview all of them. The failure rate largely depends on the mode of survey. In the direct interview method, it is usually found that the failure rate for a fairly large sample of respondents is not less than 5%. The failure is due to either denials or non-availability of the respondent. In the case of the mail survey method, we find that the response rate is poorer if the interview involves building up the confidence of the respondents. It is the same in the case of the telephoning method as well. Such a problem, namely, the problem of denial or non-availability is called the problem of non-response.

The question that crops up next is whether non-response distorts the sample. The answer is yes, since the sample size has reduced due to non-availability of response from some members of the sample group. The researcher however knows that the extent of damage might not be high if the rate of denial or non-availability is low (not exceeding 5% usually). If the anticipated damage is low, the researcher would not too bothered. In case the non-response rate is high, the researcher will have to consider the issue seriously.

Non-response might be due to non-availability. Murthy has discussed this issue in his book, *Sampling Theory and Methods* (Statistical Publishing Society, Calcutta), at length and suggested that for such 'not-at-home' cases, one can follow the method outlined in Politz and Simmons (1949). According to this method, at the time of household listing, the investigator would also ascertain the chance of the respondent being at home at a particular time. Let us suppose at the time of household listing, an enquiry is made regarding the frequency of the respondent being at home during specific hours in the previous 10 days and that frequency is recorded. If a particular respondent was reported to be available two times in last ten days during those specified hours, the investigator would assign a probability value 2/10 for the person being present when the field survey would take place. The respondents might be classified according to the assigned probability values of 2/10, 3/10 and so forth. To minimise non-availability in the sample, the number of respondents would be selected from each class by weighing the required number of respondents in the class by the inverse of the probabilities. (If we need 3 respondents from a class with 3/10 probability of being at home, then we would assign 10 households to this group).

If the respondent is available but refused to respond, the researcher will have to check whether the stimuli were imparted to the respondents in the desired manner. The field staff would have to be re-trained if it was found that the stimuli were not imparted to the respondents in the desired manner. Again, it may be observed that that the failure is due to limitations in the stimuli. The questionnaire will have to be rechecked to examine if the problem lies in framing of the questions, their ordering and the length of the questionnaire. In some cases, it is often observed that the respondents have been wrongly selected. The researcher would then go back to the sample frame and seek replacements for the non-responsive cases. There are statistical methods for maintaining the representative character of the sample in case some entries are to be dropped (for example, circular systematic sampling).

7.2.2 Response Bias

This bias occurs when the reported value of a variable differs from its actual value. The apparent source of such bias is, of course, the respondent. The respondent could have misrepresented the fact; it is also possible that the problem is more deep rooted. When a respondent responds to a stimulus either by direct communication (verbal) or indirectly (non-verbal), an error might occur either due to miscommunication or due to wrong observation. In such cases, the respondent is not responsible for the bias. The responsibility lies with the researcher.

The issue should therefore be discussed in more detail. What are the stages through which the outcome of the stimulus–response interaction gets the shape of 'information' which ultimately is captured as 'data'? The information is first formulated, that is, the response is assimilated for being transmitted to the researcher. In the next stage, the information is transmitted. The error might occur in either of the two stages or in both. An error occurring in the formulation stage can be noted as *inaccuracy*; the error occurring at the transmission stage is known as *ambiguity*. We shall discuss both these types of errors.

Inaccuracy

During formulation of the answer, the respondent could suffer from three types of problems. In the first place, he might have an honest intention to answer the question but is unfortunately unable to provide the information, that is, he cannot *formulate* the answer. This type of error results from the *inability* of the respondent. Another source of inaccuracy is the *unwillingness* of the respondent to formulate the answer. The third problem is that the respondent might be dishonest and give a wrong answer. Such a problem appears mostly in market research on the willingness to buy a product. It is often found that a respondent reveals that he would buy a particular brand of durable goods within a short period. A re-survey after the period is over might reveal that the product has not been purchased by the said respondent. The reason might be that he never had any intention to buy the product; he was not honest enough to reveal his intention to the respondent. There is however, another possibility that we must not overlook. It is possible that he had the intention to buy the product when the market survey was being conducted but the prediction that he would buy the product within the stipulated time period was in fact wrong. He was not dishonest; he changed his mind during the period. In the first case, the inaccuracy is known as *concurrent inaccuracy* and the error in the second case is known as *predictive inaccuracy*. There is hardly any check on concurrent inaccuracy. The market research organisations try to select a set of respondents who are likely to take interest in the product and therefore might not have any reason to cheat the researcher. Predictive inaccuracy might be checked by collecting information on the past buying behaviour of the respondents. However, the cost of administering such a check might be high.

Market research is not the only area where concurrent inaccuracy might occur. It is often found that various sensitive issues face the same type of problem if these are administered to a target group without taking adequate pre-survey measures. Such measures include developing a rapport with the target group. Often the data are collected by an experimental technique so that the issue could be addressed in the framework of a panel data. In some cases, information on sensitive issues is collected by indirect methods; sometimes the issues are discussed by developing a surrogate questionnaire.

Experience suggests that in most cases of field survey, the sources of inaccuracy are either *inability* or *unwillingness*. In case inability is the reason, it might be rewarding to change the sample respondent. In some cases, the particular stimulus which is expected to generate information might have to be changed. Sometimes it is found that re-training the field staff produces better results.

Unwillingness of the respondents is a more complex issue. The question is unanswered, not because the respondent does not know the answer or that he wants to cheat the researcher. He has the answer, but *he does not want to transmit the answer.* There might be two reasons behind this behaviour. The first possibility is that the respondent does not have enough time to entertain the researcher or field staff. The second reason might be that the issue is sensitive; instead of cheating the researcher the person has opted for not answering the question.

Time costs

In the field survey, the researcher often finds that the respondents try to complete the interview as quickly as possible by giving abrupt answers which are often ill-considered. The consequence is inaccurate information. This is a type of response bias. The root of this bias is the time factor at the respondent's disposal. The researcher could address this problem by reconsidering the questionnaire and the time that the interview would involve. There is always a trade-off between the time involved and the quality of the answer. It would be rewarding to keep this point in mind while organising a field survey. In case an experimental technique is involved, the researcher often pays the respondent so that the time cost is taken care of. While such a method often produces good results, particularly in case of panel data, the researcher should also keep in mind that paying a respondent might often be counter-productive.

Sensitive issues

Sometimes the respondent does not transmit the correct answer—not because of time constraints, but because the issue is sensitive in nature, he is unwilling to provide accurate information. In market research, a problem of this nature is often confronted with respect to high value consumer products. A respondent would hardly reveal his mind because of a perceived loss of prestige in disclosing the real reason for not purchasing a particular product.

There are two problems involved. In the first place, the researcher must identify the sensitive issues, that is, the issues that the respondent might find sensitive. Secondly, the researcher should know the extent of inaccuracy that might occur due to wrong answers with respect to the sensitive question. With regard to the identification of the sensitive issues, it is difficult to enlist them. A researcher should apply his own judgement in some cases. Sometimes, a feedback from the pilot survey helps the researcher to identify such questions. Some market research organisations consult psychometric experts when the survey involves certain sensitive issues (for example, a survey on birth control practices among the Indian women).

The second issue is to minimise the error in the case of sensitive questions. A common sense approach is that sensitive questions should be avoided. But this is really no answer. The researcher often finds that the research issue itself is sensitive in nature. The questions, in whatever way they are formulated, remain sensitive. The researcher cannot avoid them. When such issues cannot be avoided, the researcher would find it advisable to apply various techniques—the most common of which is to ask for the information in two different ways. Both the methods try to develop such treatments that would minimise the inaccuracy without killing the problem. In fact, this is what the researcher aims at when a sensitive issue cannot be avoided in a questionnaire.

If the approach is to minimise the inaccuracy, the researcher might take recourse to what is known as *randomised responses technique.* This technique is widely used in market research when the research involves a set of sensitive questions. The questions are usually close-ended. The response comes sometimes in dichotomous setting (Yes/No), sometimes some answers are suggested and the respondent is expected to tick the correct answer. The respondent would be allowed to select a set of questions by drawing lots. The questionnaire is designed in such a way that the respondent will have to answer some sensitive questions along with some innocuous ones. The answers must not be revealed to the field staff (the answers may be given to the respondent in a sealed envelope without any mark of identification). The response is randomised because the arrival of the sensitive question is random in nature.

It is true that all the respondents will not respond to every sensitive question. But it is certain that a section of them would definitely respond to some of the sensitive questions. If the sample size is large enough, the probability that all the sensitive questions will be attempted becomes large. We may also calculate the proportion of respondents who would respond to sensitive questions.

Proportion of attending a sensitive question = (Proportion of questions attempted – Proportion of innocuous questions attempted). We may also calculate the probability of getting 'yes' to a sensitive question if we know the proportion of respondents who answer 'yes' to innocuous questions. Suppose the proportion answering 'yes' is 0.08, the proportion answering the innocuous question is 0.06 and the probability of answering each question is 0.5.

The probability of answering 'yes' to the sensitive question = $[0.08 - (0.5 \times 0.06)] / 0.5$

This technique can be used efficiently provided the researcher uses a suitable randomising device. The weakness is that the probability of answering a sensitive question is constrained by the number of innocuous questions.

In the face of sensitive questions, the major problem is that the researcher often faces a set of respondents who consider such questions an *invasion of privacy.* Questions in the areas of political belief, voting behaviour in case of exit polls or issues concerning family life are some examples. While the researcher would never purposefully invade privacy, it might be unavoidable because of the nature of the survey. In the first place, the researcher shall have to earn the confidence of the respondent by assuring anonymity in dealing with sensitive questions (as in case of exit polls). Secondly, the researcher should frame the questions carefully so that the invasion of privacy is kept to the minimum.

Ambiguity

Inaccuracy is not the only source of response error. As stated earlier, there is another kind of response error called *ambiguity.* Ambiguity occurs at the transmission stage of the answer. Ambiguity occurs not due to the unwillingness of the respondents but due to wrong communication either from the investigator or from the respondent.

Unambiguous communication requires that the question asked and answer given, each mean the same thing to both the questioner and the respondent. Often the researcher fails to communicate the questions correctly; as a result, even if the respondent tries to give a precise answer, he communicates something which is ambiguous to the researcher. Ambiguity may also occur due to the difficulty in communication faced by the respondent though he is otherwise friendly to the researcher and wants to transmit the information willingly.

Formulating the questions properly is a skill which the researcher acquires by carefully selecting the wording for the questions and analysing its implications before the field survey. Pre-testing may also help one understand the extent of ambiguity that is hidden in the question.

One way of arresting ambiguity is to select the proper form of question (see Chapter 6). As we know, there could be free-answer or open-ended type of questions; alternatively the question could be closed with the possibility of having dichotomous or multiple-choice questions. The nature of expected ambiguity associated with the questions and answers with respect to various forms of questions are given in Table 7.3.

Table 7.3 Expected levels of ambiguity

Form of questions	Nature of ambiguity	
Open-ended	Q: Lowest	A: Highest
Dichotomous	Q: Average	A: Lowest
Multiple choice	Q: Highest	A: Average

Q = Questions; A = Answers

While confronting real life issues, the researcher has to use various forms of questions. The questions are chosen according to the scope of the research. It will help the researcher if he/she remains aware of the fact that ambiguity can be arrested by formulating the questions carefully. A researcher will also gain much if even the obvious questions are sent for pre-testing and feedback is analysed carefully before launching the field survey.

7.3 OTHER SOURCES OF MEASUREMENT ERROR

Response and non-response error are not the only sources of variation between information that describes the state of the phenomenon and the information obtained by the measurement process. Such a variation may occur due to various other reasons as well. M N Murthy in his book *Sampling Theory and Methods* (Statistical Publishing Society, Calcutta, pp 451), has listed the following reasons for the existence of such errors:

1. Data specification being inadequate and inconsistent with respect to the objectives of the census or survey.
2. Omission or duplication of units due to imprecise definition of the boundaries of area units, incomplete or wrong identification particulars of units or faulty methods of enumeration.
3. Inaccurate or inappropriate methods of interview, observation or measurement with inadequate or ambiguous schedules, definition or instructions.
4. Lack of trained and experienced investigators.
5. Difficulties involved in actual data collection arising from recall error and other types of errors on the part of respondents.
6. Lack of adequate inspection and supervision of primary staff.
7. Inadequate scrutiny of the basic data.

8. Error in data processing operations such as coding, purchasing, verification, tabulation.
9. Error committed during presentation and printing of tabulated results or graphs in a census or survey.

This is a fairly exhaustive account of the sources of non-sampling error. It may be noted that response and non-response bias (already discussed) is also contained in this list (under inaccurate or inappropriate methods of interview, observation or measurement with inadequate or ambiguous schedules, definition or instructions). Following Murthy, the sources of error are classified into three categories:

- Specification errors,
- Ascertainment errors, and
- Tabulation errors.

Specification errors are the errors that occur at the planning stage. Such errors can occur for reasons (1) to (3) above. Ascertainment errors may arise in the data collection stage. As Murthy observes, such errors occur because of reasons (4) to (6). Tabulation errors occur at the data processing stage. Such errors are due to factors (7) to (9).

It should be noted that all errors under specification errors are not response errors. The researcher might commit an error due to wrong specification of the problem; some errors might be due to wrong selection of field personnel, at other times the error could occur due to wrong tabulation or carelessness at the data entry stage. These are all non-sampling errors that might exist in every type of data collection design—a sample survey or a census study (a study based on complete enumeration). The researcher must remain careful about this problem particularly in a survey with a large sample size because measurement error tends to increase as the size of the sample increases if the research administration remains the same. The issues related to some of these errors are discussed below.

7.3.1 Specification Error

An error in data specification is a non-sampling error that a researcher has to watch out for. Sometimes, the problem is specified as surrogate information error. It occurs when the researcher seeks information other than that required to directly address the issue at stake. Failure to define the problem properly could be the reason. For example, research was carried out on the reasons for low occupancy of beds in a particular hospital. The hospital belonged to a specific religious minority group. The researcher focussed on customer satisfaction whereas the actual problem lay in the attitude of the customers towards the religious group.

Omission and duplication of units, faulty or wrong identification of units, imprecision in defining the units—all these are surrogate information errors. This occurs when the researcher collects information but the information does not meet the data specifications of the research issue. A pilot survey followed by the analysis of the data in using dummy tables might provide a check against such mistakes. Large surveys take care of such problems by holding a series of discussions on data specification problems by involving experts in theoretical and empirical research.

7.3.2 Interviewer's Error

A large part of the problem at the data generation stage is due to wrong or inappropriate stimuli imparted to the respondent. The interviewer influences the interviewee through his bias or pattern of behaviour (verbal or non-verbal) and these errors are consciously or unconsciously committed. The mistake could be corrected by proper recruitment and training. Yet, there could be situations of cheating by the interviewer. This could be corrected through the process of data validation, editing and an intelligent data entry system. We would add that there is no fool proof system that might check this bias. A lot of problems arise in practical research because of the interviewer's error. The golden rule for minimising this error is to motivate the field staff properly so that there is no mistake by commission.

7.3.3 Data Validation and Editing

Another type of non-sampling error arises due to non-compliance with the method of data collection as envisaged in the research plan. The researcher could minimise the incidence of this kind of error by taking recourse to data validation. Data validation is a device by which the research organisation checks whether the data generation process has adhered to the method envisaged by the organisation or not. In other words, the issue is to check whether the stimuli were administered in the same way and with the same content as was framed by the research organisation. It could happen that the interviewer might not have adhered to it, the stimuli had not been administered at all and the data submitted for analysis had either been concocted or contained deliberate bias imparted by the interviewer. An interview is said to be valid if it was conducted in the manner and with the same content and purpose for which it was conceived.

In other words, the problem lies in the quality of the field survey. One way of checking the quality is to go through the records of the field survey, though it may not always be sufficient. Where it is an in-depth interview, records could be used but such a luxury may not exist in other kinds of data collection devices. In case the respondent can be reached by telephone, a professional researcher uses telephone validation as a technique. The query is usually done covering five dimensions:

- Whether the person was actually interviewed,
- Whether the person who was interviewed belongs to the target group,
- Whether the interview had been conducted in the required manner,
- Whether the whole process was completed, and
- A query on the performance of the interviewer so that the organisation understands the quality of the interviewer, as perceived by the respondent.

Editing is the stage when a further check on the quality of data can be done. Under normal circumstances the editing in the questionnaire is done in two stages—at the field level by the field supervisor of the survey who checks the entries and at the second stage before the data entry is performed. At the second stage, the task is usually performed by senior research personnel who would also be involved in data analysis.

The editing process is usually a manual checking process. Now-a-days there is an inbuilt checking system in the answer codes. At the data entry stage, the consistency is checked for data validation. The data entry devices need to be programmed to check whether logical consistency is maintained. This system could be used to check (i) erratic responses and (ii) violation of the skip pattern which is incorporated in the questionnaire.

7.3.4 Measurement Instrument Bias

These are errors that could occur because of the method of measurement or wrong questionnaire design. It could occur if the specific attitude measurement scale is not used but a general scale, that is a scale which is not properly calibrated to provide specific answers to the problem, is used. There could also be problems due to improper administration of proper lead questions in the questionnaire.

Let us suppose a chocolate company wants to find out the sweetness level of its éclairs. In order to understand the attitude of consumers towards the level of sweetness in the product, the researcher usually uses a general ordinal scale with ratings such as, very high sweetness, high sweetness, moderate sweetness, less sweetness, low sweetness, to elicit responses from customers. Since the difference in ordinal attitudinal levels remains vague with so many ratings, the respondent could falter in registering the right response.

One may suggest in this context that a specific attitudinal scale called the *Thurstone scale* needs to be used if the right attitudinal level towards sweetness has to be registered. Responses towards any statement (derived through the Thurstone Scaling Technique) would bring in more precision. The response would have to be registered against the following statements.

(a) It is as sweet as a sugar candy.
(b) It is as sweet as a juicy fruit.
(c) It is as sweet as synthetic commercial gelatine.
(d) It is a shallow sweetness.
(e) It is a bland (tasteless/saccharine) sweetness.
(f) A lot of sugar has to be added to bring a semblance of sweetness.
(g) It is far from being sweet.

In the above few statements (d) is the neutral position, options (a), (b), (c) are favourable and options (e), (f), (g) are unfavourable.

7.3.5 Processing Errors: The Outliers

These errors are also quite common in social research. They are usually inadvertently entered by data entry operators. Wrong responses to certain questions might also be the source of such errors. A portion of it could be checked through coding of questionnaires, coding of questions and coding of answers as well. For others, one shall have to use the technique of outlier detection.

An *outlier* is an unlikely entry in the data set. It is an observation or a subset of observations which appears to be inconsistent with the other entries of the set of data. A researcher could check at the processing level, whether there is an unlikely entry in the data sheet. The first check in this regard is to examine whether there is an unusual entry in the data set. Let us suppose the temperature record at 10 am in the morning for seven successive days in winter in a city of North India had the following output: 10°C, 12°C, 10°C, 15°C, 41°C, 13°C, 12°C, 10°C. It is obvious that a 41°C temperature on a single day in winter in a city in North India is most unlikely. It might be that the actual recording was 14°C on the fifth day and while transferring it into a document, the research assistant or the data entry operator could have inadvertently recorded it as 41°C. The researcher will guess this and label 41°C as an outlier.

Outlying observations are often seen as contaminating the data. As a result of the contamination, the information gets distorted. It is thus natural to seek a remedy when such a problem is present in a data set. A remedy is sought by finding the means of interpreting or categorising outliers. There are methods for handling these outliers so that the property of the data set is restored or at least the impact of such outliers is minimised.

How can we detect an outlier? There are various statistical tools by which an outlier can be detected. We will give a brief outline of these tools. An outlier is characterised by its impact on the observer. To the observer the data appears to be extreme and in some cases, surprisingly extreme. The researcher would check the history of the process by which the observation was recorded. In many cases, the outlier is got rid of by this method. Sometimes this thumb rule is not sufficient to meet the problem of outliers. In fact this is a process of rejection and comes with the risk of losing genuine information.

Conceptual difficulties with outliers

An observation is declared as an outlier in perspective to the assumption from a specific distribution from which it comes. The assumption might be wrong. Consequently an outlier would not have appeared unreasonable if some other distribution criterion was used as a model for explaining the data. Again the model used for explaining the data may not be a single model but the mixture of two or more distributions. As a result, putting the tag of outlier on an observation might not be rational. Statisticians therefore suggest an accommodation approach in the presence of suspected outliers. They would suggest that a statistically valid method be developed, so that valid inferences about the population from which the random sample has been obtained can be drawn even if outliers are present in the sampled observations. This is called the *method of accommodation*. This method accommodates outliers at no serious inconvenience or is robust against the presence of the outliers. Some such tools are:

(a) Median,
(b) Mid-point of shortest half sample,
(c) Trimmed mean,
(d) Median deviation, and
(e) Inter-quartile range.

The basic idea behind such tools is to avoid the arithmetic mean since it gives more weightage to higher order values. In statistical analysis of estimation, the estimator is redefined in the presence of the outlier to make it more realistic. The idea is to take a more general objective function so that the contaminated data may not affect the researcher's pursuit for the truth underlying the data.

In regression analysis, outliers are accommodated by replacing the standard procedure of minimising the least square (deviation of original values from the arithmetic mean, squared) with least median of Squares Regression or least Trimmed Squares Regression.

Outlier labelling

In a situation where we cannot live with outliers, that is, in a situation where we cannot allow any outlier in the data set, we shall have to detect the outliers and eliminate them from the data set. In other words, we shall have to identify and label a suspect observation as an outlier at the data processing level. The data set would be cleaned by removing outliers so that the tools that we outlined above need not be applied while analysing the data. The simplest procedure is to apply the *boxplot rule*. By this method, it is feasible to test any observation and determine whether the observation is an outlier or regular. The usual boxplot rules declare an observation to be an outlier if it does not fall in the interval between the following limits:

$$M_1 = Q_1 - 1.5(Q_3 - Q_1)$$

and

$$M_2 = Q_3 + 1.5(Q_3 - Q_1)$$

where Q_1 = first quartile and Q_3 = third quartile. Such a measure can take care of the extreme values, whether they are extremely low or extremely high.

Several statistical tests have been suggested to check whether a particular observation labelled as an outlier is true in the statistical sense. Dixon statistics, internally studentised Extreme Deviation from Mean (ESD) are some such statistics which have been suggested by experts for testing the hypothesis that a particular observation taken as an outlier is really so.

7.4 OTHER CHECKS ON DATA

We have discussed how a researcher can take care of the problem of measurement error. One should however remember that there is no fool proof method for mitigating the problem of errors in data. While the methods outlined above are widely used for ensuring the quality of the field data, there are some other checks which are elucidated below.

7.4.1 Consistency Check

It refers to designing of the questionnaire and checking whether the right types of people have been surveyed or not. Care has to be taken to check whether certain items of information have been included in the questionnaire or not. If the additional information is easy to obtain, the questions may be put in all the questionnaires. The profiles of the respondents and non-respondents based on some of this information when checked could reveal the pattern of answering and whether the right person has been interviewed or not. For gender data and age data, demographic data sources are helpful and it helps in checking non-sampling errors because it ultimately gives an indication of the quality of data that has been collected.

Another technique of assessing the quality of data is to arrange the observations in increasing order of some basic variable. If the consumption pattern of concentrated cattle feed is being studied, then the consumption per cattle-head could be an important variable and we will find a pattern in the per-head consumption which will provide one with information of any erratic trend (that is, probability of any error existing). Similarly, the expenditure per cattle-head will be another important variable and this will also show a trend or a pattern in a graphical representation. A value that is inconsistent and does not conform to the trend needs to be dropped.

7.4.2 Sample Check

The method to control a non-sampling error is by duplicating the assignment in miniature for a sample that is much smaller than the original sample. If the sample has been rightly designed and if the checking is properly carried out, it will be possible to detect the non-sampling error and get an idea of its magnitude. One may apply this procedure systematically by dividing the output at different stages of the survey into lots and checking samples from each lot. When the error percentage is higher than the prescribed percentage in a specific lot, then the whole lot will be re-checked and corrected.

7.4.3 Post-census and Post-survey Checks

An important type of sample check used to assess non-sampling errors consists in selecting a sample of units from the census and re-enumerating or re-surveying it by using better trained surveyors than in the previous situation. This procedure is called a post-census or a post-survey check. The requirements for such checks are:

- Re-enumeration should be done just after the census or sampling survey to avoid recall errors.
- Steps should be taken to minimise the conditioning effect that the main survey may have on the check survey.

To ensure that the check survey is carried out in a proper manner, the investigators are provided with a list of the original respondents and the questionnaires that have been filled by them earlier. Sometimes a few of the entries in the administered questionnaire will be dummy entries. After the survey, the results with the original census work or survey is checked. The knowledge that there are artificially introduced errors in the dummy entries will make the investigator cautious and alert. The entries should therefore be done carefully without arousing any suspicion among the investigators. Minimising the conditioning effect and at the same time avoiding recall error is the major challenge in a post-survey check.

When there is a discrepancy between the re-enumeration work and the original work, the analysis of this discrepancy is done at the unit (individual) level. If the discrepancies are suspected to be due to non-sampling errors, a reconciliation survey to find out the reasons and causes is necessary. This involves senior, trained and experienced staff. The unitary check process is of course costly. But in case the error appears to be severe, unit level check cannot be avoided. Resurvey is costly and therefore the approach should be to retain the original findings unless they are found to be grossly erroneous.

SUMMARY

- The total error in research is the summation of measurement error and experimental error. While experimental error has its origin in the sample survey, measurement error is rooted in wrong or ambiguous information.
- Measurement error can be minimised by developing a robust survey apparatus. Experimental error can be optimised by carefully choosing the sample size in a scientifically designed sample frame.
- Measurement error may occur at the data generation stage or at the stage of processing and analysis of data.
- A major source of error at the data generation stage is response or non-response error. Response error can again be identified as inaccuracy and ambiguity in information.
- There might be other sources of error at the stage of specification, ascertainment and tabulation of data.
- The existence of non-sampling error in the data can be ascertained by outlier labelling.

ASSIGNMENTS

Q1 Choose the right answers

1. The concept of 'total error' is:
   (a) Total of response and non-response error
   (b) Total of non-response error

(c) Total of measurement error and sampling error
(d) None of the above

2. The concept of 'measurement error' is:
(a) Present in the scaling technique
(b) Wrong or ambiguous information
(c) Present in computation of data
(d) None of the above

3. In case of 'census', the error pattern is:
(a) More of experimental error
(b) More of measurement error and less of experimental error
(c) More of measurement error and nonexistence of experimental error
(d) None of the above

4. In case of 'sampling' error, the source is:
(a) Only the sample size
(b) Only the information or ambiguity
(c) Only the computation
(d) None of the above

5. The 'randomised response technique' helps the researcher to
(a) Choose a random sample
(b) Preparing sets of sensitive questions to be administered
(c) Randomly choosing an answer
(d) None of the above

6. Predictive inaccuracy is said to exist when:
(a) The respondent has dishonestly furnished information
(b) The respondent was wrong in predicting his behaviour owing to occurrence of some event
(c) The interviewer was wrong in his prediction
(d) None of the above

7. 'Ambiguity' is said to exist when:
(a) The data is missing from records
(b) The data is inconsistent with the other data in the data set
(c) The data is merged with other data
(d) None of the above

8. In case of an open-ended question, the expected level of ambiguity is:
(a) Low in question and high in answer
(b) Average in question and low in answer
(c) Highest in question and average in answer
(d) None of the above

9. Error is composed of:
   (a) Specification error, ascertainment error and tabulation error
   (b) Measurement error and ascertainment error
   (c) Sampling error and tabulation error
   (d) None of the above
10. Specification error occurs in the stage of:
   (a) Planning of research
   (b) Data collection of research
   (c) Computation of research
   (d) None of the above

Answers

1. (c), 2. (b), 3. (c), 4. (a), 5. (b), 6. (b), 7. (b), 8. (a), 9. (a), 10. (a)

Q2 Answer the questions

1. State the sources of non-sampling error and the broad types of classification of such errors.
2. 'In a situation where we cannot live with outliers, that is, in a situation where we cannot allow any outlier in the data set, we shall have to detect the outliers and eliminate them from the data set'. Explain this statement and state the methods of handling outliers while editing the data. How does one label an outlier?
3. State how ambiguity is a source of response error and suggest the methods used to address this problem.
4. 'Response and non-response error is not the only source of variation between information that describes the state of the phenomenon and the information obtained by the measurement process'. Discuss.

Q3 Write notes on

1. Randomised responses technique
2. Sample check
3. Predictive inaccuracy
4. Measurement instrument bias

CHAPTER 8

MEASUREMENT AND SCALING TECHNIQUES

LEARNING OBJECTIVES

After going through this chapter you will understand

- Scaling problem
- Scaling techniques
- Nominal scale
- Ordinal scale
- Index rank
- Weighted index rank
- Interval scale
- Ratio scale
- Specialised scales
- Multi-dimensional scaling
- Thurstone scale
- Likert scale

Key words Weighted index rank, paired comparison, subject centred approach, stimulus centred approach, quantitative judgement method, response method, variability method, Thurstone scale, Likert scale

8.1 MEASUREMENT

We have discussed how stimulus–response interaction generates the data. We have also deliberated on the problems of errors that might crop up in the process of data generation through stimulus–response interaction. One point that was not touched upon was that the outcome of the stimulus–response interaction captured in terms of data must be measured, so that this could be analysed for unveiling the information that the data contain. It appears that measurement is not a very important problem because measuring tools have been used since very early stages of civilisation. This contention is true, but still a discussion on research methodology on this issue is warranted.

How can we conceptualise 'measurement' pertaining to data? It relates to the properties of the object of study that the researcher wants to analyse. Let us suppose the researcher wants to study the fluctuations of the price of a commodity over time. The object of study is 'price behaviour'. Measurement here would refer to a quantitative expression (rupee or dollar per ton) which is a symbol that represents the property called 'price'. Similarly, with respect to a study on 'preferred brand', the measurement would be in the form of a qualitative expression like 'Brand B is preferred to Brand A'. Here, measurement represents the property called 'preference' which is qualitative. The expression here is 'B P A', P being the symbol representing preference. Measurement can thus be defined as 'a way of obtaining symbols to represent the properties of persons, objects, events or states, which symbols have the same relevant relationship to each other as do the things they represent' (Green, P E *et al.*, page 242). Measurement helps in representing certain properties, characteristics and behavioural acts that are to be represented in the form of data. These characteristics are captured in terms of the order in which the information is collected. Measurement not only represents just the property, it also implies the *degree* or *intensity* of the presence of what is represented as property in the element that is being measured. (Say, the property is 'price' of the commodity, the symbol Rs 50 or Rs 80 also captures the degree at which 'price' is present in these elements, that is, the first and the second elements in this case).

Measurement is ideally described in terms of four properties. A measurement over elements under study should *identify* the properties of the object that the researcher wants to analyse. These are represented in terms of symbols. The degree or intensity of the presence of what is represented by symbols should follow an *order*. The *origin* from which the measurement begins should also to be specified. And finally, the *distance* between the individual symbols that represent the degree or intensity of the property of the attribute under study in each element should be measured. We can therefore state that measurement can ideally be described in terms of identification, order, distance and origin of the data. There are different scales by which these characteristics are represented; these are called *measurement scales*. The implications of having identification, order, distance and origin in a scale would be explained as we consider the specific scales. However, all scales do not possess all of these properties and therefore all of them cannot be termed ideal scales.

8.2 MEASUREMENT SCALES

Measurement scales are classified into (i) Nominal scale, (ii) Ordinal scale, (iii) Interval scale and (iv) Ratio scale.

8.2.1 Nominal Scale

It is a system of assigning numbers to the elements of the object under study. *The purpose is only to identify the elements or the objects*; the order and distance between elements are not considered in this scale. This scale does not need an origin either. A typical example here is that of assigning a number to a name (person). While assigning a number, the rule that is followed is that there must exist a one to one correspondence between a name and a number. If player Donald has the number 2 and player Asterix has the number 4, then 2 will identify Donald and 4 cannot identify anyone but Asterix. Bank account numbers are also examples of numbers in the nominal scale. Essentially, the numbers here are only identifiers. Such numbers do not require to have 0 as the starting number, the ordering of the elements need not follow the order that numbers might usually imply. For example, it does not indicate that 4 should to be positioned above 2. Again, there is no question of assigning distance between elements. One cannot say that 4 is twice as big as 2. Nominal scale has thus only one property. It can only identify the elements in terms of a measurement scale. The only requirement for measuring the data under this scale is that there must be a one to one correspondence between an element in the data set and a number or a symbol.

The scope for mathematical operations on the data under the nominal scale is very limited. Only frequency-based operations can be performed with numbers in the nominal scale. Thus, in some cases, the modal class (class or category with highest frequency) could be depicted by identifying the category of highest occurrence. Market researchers sometimes apply the nominal scale to identify the product which has the highest or the lowest occurrence. For example, market research might try to identify the category of product that has been stocked by most of the stores in a locality. Let us allocate number 3 to the food category. If the highest number of departmental stores stock the food category, then the food items under category 3 would belong to the modal class. The percentage of a particular category appearing in a set can also be ascertained.

8.2.2 Ordinal Scale

This scale possesses an additional property when compared to the nominal scale—the property of *ordering*. It identifies the elements uniquely, as in the nominal scale; it puts them in an order (which is not done in nominal scale) but does not measure the distance between the elements, nor does it need the elements to follow a particular origin. The ordering is often described in terms of ranking. As the nomenclature indicates, the order here (rank) indicates the relative positions of the elements with reference to an attribute (that is, say, brightness or happiness or performance). The measure here is a qualitative measure reflected in the position of the element in the order or rank. The order or rank might be described in terms of numbers. However, the numbers do not indicate any quantitative property of the object under study.

We shall elaborate on this point. Let us suppose that the students in a school are being ranked in terms of their performance in examinations. The first three candidates are given the numbers 1, 2 and 3 to indicate their ranks. The numbers describe the ordering of the three candidates with respect to an event—performance in the examination. The numbers do symbolise the performance of the three candidates, the numbers also measure the intensity of performance of the candidates. However, the measurement here is only in *qualitative terms* (the best, the second best and the third best).The numbers in the ordinal scale do not indicate the distance or difference in merit among the candidates in any quantitative terms. We know that 1 is the best, 2 is the second best and the third best has the rank 3, but the difference between 1 and 2, or 2 and 3 cannot be ascertained from these numbers. One cannot say that 3 – 2 is the same as 2 – 1 on the basis of the fact that both the differences are equal to 1 in quantitative terms. The numbers here just follow an ordering (1 > 2 > 3 because the candidates have been ranked from the best to the second best and the third best). The quantification of the differences could have been ascertained if the performance of the candidates were described in terms of the marks in quantitative terms as obtained in the examination (which is a measure of performance in a different scale).

With ordered data, some additional statistical work (compared to data under the nominal scale) can be performed. For this, however, the ordering should have the property of transitivity. If *A* is better than *B* and *B* is better than *C*, then *A* must be better than *C* as well, if the relation is transitive. The magnitude of difference between *A*, *B* and *C* is however not captured in this description. In terms of rank scores, the relation among *A*, *B* and *C* would be described as 1, 2 and 3 if they are ordered in a descending manner; if we put the information in the ascending order, then obviously the order will change. In the absence of quantification, the permissible statistical exercises on ordinal data are percentiles or quartiles including median and rank correlation. As we shall discuss later, ordinal data can be transformed in the interval scale under certain situations.

To sum up, in the ordinal scale the assigned numbers would identify the elements in terms of symbols with respect to an attribute; the distinction between two elements in relation to the attribute is captured here in the same way as in the case of the nominal scale. The only difference is that a description in the ordinal scale follows an ordering that might be of some help for further analysis of the data. In market research and other research on qualitative variables, the rank scores are utilised for developing various statistical measures. A widely used tool is the *Weighted Index Rank* which is discussed below.

Weighted Index Rank: The weighted index rank is a composite rank which is utilised in a situation where an event, a phenomenon or a product has various attributes and the performance of an individual element in the data set is assessed in terms of these attributes. The basic problem here is that multiple attributes of the concerned event cannot be captured in a single scale because each attribute needs a unique scale for measurement. Let us suppose, as a product, toothpaste has three attributes which are important from a marketing point of view—whiteness, foam and taste. The power of the toothpaste in terms of creating foam cannot technically be described in terms of the scale that might measure the power to create whiteness or taste. Three different attributes here need three different scales for measurement. The performance of an individual element in the data set is assessed in terms of these three scales. Since the scales are different, one cannot get a composite measure that might describe the phenomenon more comprehensively, unless one gets a method for integrating the measure in different scales. Weighted index rank under the ordinal scaling suggests such a method.

For a composite measure under the weighted index rank, the attributes are measured first in the ordinal scale where the measure is captured in terms of rank or order. The measure here is a qualitative measure reflected in the position of the element in the order or rank. Consider the example of toothpaste which has three attributes from a marketing point of view—whiteness, foam and taste. There are various brands of toothpaste and the respondents are to rank the brands according to their perception in terms of these attributes. If there are three brands which a respondent is to rank according to three attributes, each brand will get three rank scores from a respondent (Table 8.1, first three columns). The rank scores will reveal the ordering of the brands with respect to each attribute, as perceived by the respondent. For example, rank scores in Table 8.1 reveal that in the perception of the respondent, brand Kleenex performs the best (rank 1) in terms of power to provide 'whiteness', but its performance is the worst (rank 3) in terms of power to provide 'foam'. While this is a fair description of the perception of the respondent with respect to the attributes under study, one may point out that such a description does not reveal the *overall perception* of the respondent about the contesting brands (which one is the best, which one is the second best and which one is the worst among the three in terms of the three attributes, taken together). Weighted index rank technique addresses this issue. It suggests a method by which one can construct a composite rank score that would reveal the overall perception of the respondent about the phenomenon under study.

The suggested method is simple from a mathematical point of view. Assuming that the attributes belong to a homogeneous group, a composite rank score is derived which, in effect, is a linear combination of the rank scores under different measures. If rank with respect to the first attribute is X and that with respect to the second and the third are Y and Z respectively, then the measure with respect to the composite score is

$$w_1(X) + w_2(Y) + w_3(Z)$$

$$w_1 + w_2 + w_3 = 1$$

w_i is the assigned weight for the ith term (i =1, 2, 3). The weights are usually assigned according to the judgement of the researcher.

A point to be kept in mind at this stage is, when one adds these scores, one violates a basic understanding about the ordinal scores that we discussed at the very beginning of this section. The measurement in ordinal scale is valid only in *qualitative terms* (the best, the second best and the third best, and so on).The numbers in the ordinal scale do not indicate the distance or difference in measure in quantitative terms. Adding or subtracting the scores should not therefore be allowed with respect to these data. However, such exercises with ordinal data are widely carried out in various areas of social research. One may rationalise this operation on the ground that ordinarily the relative positions of the individual elements are not expected to change very much under such measures which belong to a homogeneous group (measures that try to ascertain the quality of toothpaste, for example). Technically, this is called the property of having concordance among the rank scores. To what extent the property of having concordance among the rank scores is present in a data set can be examined. For example, researchers often use the measure of Spearman's *Rank Correlation Coefficien*t or Kendall's *Coefficient of Concordance* for developing such exercises. While utilising these data for such mathematical operations which need quantitative distance among the numbers to begin with, it is strongly recommended that the researcher should first perform a test of concordance on the data set. If the hypothesis of having concordance is rejected, one should not proceed further with the ordinal data.

Let us come back to the issue of constructing a weighted index rank. In constructing the weighted index rank with the given rank scores, we need to assign weightage to each ordinal measure. Ordinarily, the weights are assigned by the researcher according to his own judgement regarding the importance of a measure. The weights are thus subjective in nature. The rank scores are multiplied by the stipulated weight of the attribute to get a composite rank score. The elements get composite rank scores and finally all the elements are ranked according to a composite rank index which is known as the *weighted index rank* for the element.

The following is an example of the use of weighted index rank with respect to the previously introduced problem of market research with toothpaste. Note that the weights of the three attributes have been given as 0.2, 0.3 and 0.5 respectively for whiteness, foam and taste (Table 8.1A, columns 4, 5, 6) making the total weight distributed over three attributes equal to 1. Note that the total weight has been distributed as 20% for whiteness, 30% for foam and 50% for taste. The weights are purely subjective. The researcher himself has given these weights. However, *a good researcher would distribute the weights on the basis of his experience and also on the basis of opinions of knowledgeable persons.*

Three brands of toothpaste – Kleenex, Anchor and Freshen – have been ranked on the basis of a set of three attributes—whiteness of foam, quantum of foam and the taste of the paste. A respondent has ranked the brands according to his perception in terms of these attributes. For example, Kleenex has a rank score of 1 when we consider the property of whiteness, as perceived by a particular respondent. This implies that Kleenex is the best among the three, so far as the property of whiteness is concerned (higher the score, the worse is the position of the brand). Needless to say, this score has nothing to do with whatever the score of Kleenex is in terms of the two other attributes. In *weighted index ranking,* we assume a property of comparability of scores in numerical terms so that we can develop a total score for a particular brand. The brands are then ranked again on the basis of these total scores. For example, we may add the rank scores of all the brands here and observe that the total score of Kleenex is 6, Anchor 4 and Freshen 8. If, we now rank the brands in terms of the total score, Freshen is the worst (rank value 3) followed by Kleenex (rank value 2) and Anchor (rank value 1). This in brief, is the method followed in composite rank score technique *with equal weights* for all the attributes.

In the previous example, all the attributes were taken to have the same importance which is why the scores were just added. In weighted index ranking, we allow the weights to be different, that is, we exercise the option of assigning a variation in importance of the factors or attributes under study. For example, consider the case described in Table 8.1. There are arbitrary weights for the three brands (arbitrary because the researcher did not follow any mathematical rule in selecting the weights), however all the weights taken together is equal to one.

Table 8.1 Computing of weighted index

Brands	Whiteness X	Foam Y	Taste Z	Weighted rank values			Weighted score
				w(X) 0.2	w(Y) 0.3	w(Z) 0.5	
Kleenex	1	3	2	0.2	0.9	1.0	2.1
Anchor	2	1	1	0.4	0.3	0.5	1.2
Freshen	3	2	3	0.6	0.6	1.5	2.7

From Table 8.1 we get the order of ranking through the weighted score—Freshen with 2.70, Kleenex with 2.10 and Anchor with 1.20. Here, Anchor is better than Kleenex and similarly Kleenex is better than Freshen. (Higher rank scores indicate a worse performance because, as we have assumed, higher the score value, worse is the position of the brand.)

One difficulty with the weighted index ranking is that the weights are subjective and therefore the results of the exercise might change as the weights are assigned differently. The other difficulty is that the composite rank positions might change even if the weights remain the same and the relative positions of the brands remain unchanged. This may happen if the survey includes some other brands and the numerical values of rank scores with respect to various attributes become different. The following example elucidates this point.

The same three brands are again considered. But the respondent has a choice among a group of 50 brands of toothpastes including Kleenex, Anchor and Freshen. The individual rank scores are now different because the brand positioning was done with respect to fifty brands. The respondent assigns the rank scores in such a way that the *relative positions* of these three brands remain unchanged with respect to the three attributes, namely whiteness, foam and taste. The weights remain the same as in Table 8.1. However, as Table 8.2 reveals, the weighted scores with respect to each brand has changed and the rank order has also changed. Freshen with 16.1 is followed by Anchor with 14.6 and Kleenex with 11.3. Kleenex is the best among the three, Anchor is now worse than Kleenex. Freshen with a score of 16.1 is the worst among the three. This shows that rank orders are not only weight dependant but are score dependant as well.

Table 8.2 Weighted index with a different set of rank values

Brands	Whiteness X	Foam Y	Taste Z	Weighted rank values			Weighted score
				w(X) 0.2	w(Y) 0.3	w(Z) 0.5	
Kleenex	2	28	5	0.4	8.4	2.5	11.3
Anchor	24	26	4	4.8	7.8	2.0	14.6
Freshen	25	27	6	5.0	8.1	3.0	16.1

The limitations notwithstanding, weighted index ranking is a widely used technique applied in various areas of social research. We should add that there are also other statistical tools that the researcher might utilise while analysing these ordinal data. For example, ranking by ordinal scores may be utilised for developing some advanced techniques like Thurstone's scale V technique. Likert's scaling is also an ordinal scaling technique which is widely used in social research. Essentially, all these techniques assume that ordinal numbers can be treated as numericals in a ratio scale. We shall discuss them in detail at the end of this chapter.

8.2.3 Interval Scale

The nominal scale does not have the property of indicating the order and the amount of difference among the data. The ordinal scale has the property of capturing the data in a given order (preference, sequence). Although index ranking and other techniques utilise the values or scores describing the order as the 'difference' among the scores, strictly speaking this is done by infringing on another branch of scaling that tries to measure the difference. These are done either by interval scale or ratio scale. We shall first discuss the properties of the interval scale.

The interval scale differs from the ordinal and nominal scales by the fact that in addition, it measures the quantitive difference among the scores that describe the data. Needless to say, the interval scale has the property of identifying the elements (as in the case of the nominal scale) and of measuring the order (as in case of ordinal scale). The added property is that it measures the difference among various elements *in quantitative terms*.

A measure of the difference should have a reference point. Ordinarily, the reference point is 0. Measures in interval scale also have 0 as the reference point. But the reference point (0) is set arbitrarily. The rationale behind taking an arbitrary reference is as follows. If we want to know the difference among various elements in the data set in quantitative terms, it is sufficient to take an arbitrary point of reference. It does not matter where we fix the point of reference. The Roman calendar starts with January 1; January 1 was fixed arbitrarily. The Chinese New Year has a different reference point as do the Bangladeshi or Indian calendars.

While measuring the differences in quantitative terms, the point of reference does not matter. But then, wherever be the point of reference, there must be a rule for measurement. Consider the case of calendar dates. A calendar that follows solar movement fixes the dates by unequal distribution of 365 days (plus about 6 hours) among 12 months. If we want to find the days needed to identify a particular date of a month from the origin (January 1) we need to follow a complicated rule of measurement associated with this calendar. With every quantitative measure, there is a rule of measurement. A measurement in interval scale can fix the point of reference arbitrarily. But it cannot escape the requirement of framing a rule for measurement; a measurement that must follow a well-defined rule.

With a well-defined rule of measurement, a measurement in the interval scale works with differences among various elements in the data set. Since the point of reference (0) is fixed arbitrarily in the interval scale, a measurement in this scale might be quantitatively different from what is obtained when the measurement is carried out from absolute 0. However, the differences among the elements will remain the same as in the case of a measure with absolute 0 as the point of reference. Since this is of much significance for a measure in the interval scale, let us elaborate on this point.

Consider a measure of temperature in the Fahrenheit scale (F). Water freezes at 32°F and it evaporates at 212°F. 0 in the Fahrenheit scale has thus been arbitrarily fixed, having no reference to a unique point vis-à-vis temperature where absolute zero could be set. Let us fix the unique or absolute point of reference at 32°F, that is, at the point where water gets solidified. Now consider two points in the Fahrenheit scale 70°F and 35°F. 70°F is not twice as hot as 35°F. The proof is simple. Introducing a new scale with absolute zero at freezing point (the Centigrade scale) and applying the formula for conversion from the Fahrenheit scale to the Centigrade scale,

$$T_c = \frac{5}{9}(T_f - 32)$$

T_c = Temperature in Centigrade

T_f = Temperature in Fahrenheit

we transform both 70°F and 35°F into the Centigrade scale. It is obvious that with respect to absolute 0 as benchmark, 70°F is not twice as hot as 35°F because 35°F is very near to freezing point (1.66°C) and 70°F is about 20 times hotter (21.11°C) than 35°F. Consider now the interval measure with arbitrary 0 at 0°F). Using the conversion rule, we get

$$70°F - 0°F = 21.11°C - (-17.77°C) = 38.88°C$$

which is roughly twice as hot as

$$35°F - 0°F = 19.43°C$$

Thus the difference in temperature between 70°F and 0°F would be twice the difference between 35°F and 0°F.

The inner logic of the interval scale becomes apparent when we realise that the variables X and Y indicating different values in an interval scale are related not as $Y = bX$ so that $Y/X = b$, but as $Y = a + bX$ so that Y is not equal to 0 when X is 0. A relation of $Y = a + bX$, with $a \neq 0$ indicates that the values are related to each other in an interval scale.

8.2.4 Ratio Scale

When the measures follow a relation such as $Y = bX$ (such that $Y/X = b$) the scale is called the *ratio scale*. Ratio scale is referred as the *Queen of scales* as it possesses all the attributes of a scale (identifying or indicating an event, giving a measure, measuring the differences among the data in quantitative terms) and at the same time having the mathematical quality of being used in all kinds of statistical analysis with quantitative measures because this measure has an absolute 0 in the scale of measurement. The data in interval scale can also be used in many areas of statistical analysis with quantitative measures. However, its usage is not as wide as in case of the ratio scale data because it does not have an absolute 0 in the scale of measurement. For example, one cannot measure the geometric mean and the harmonic mean with the data given in the interval scale. The difference between a measure in the ratio scale and a measure in the interval scale becomes apparent when we consider the following.

Consider a linear relation $Y = a + bX$. It can be observed that changes in variables by a certain constant sum do not get reflected correspondingly in a similar manner in the respective ratios generated. Suppose a is equal to 10, b is equal to 0.5 and we change the values of X by a certain specific value (interval), then the derived values of Y will also change by a specific interval value. This interval change will not get reflected in a similar manner in the ratios. To illustrate this phenomenon study Table 8.3.

In the above example (Table 8.3), the change in X (in column 3) has been by a value of 10 and the corresponding change in Y (in column 4) has been by a value of 5. It has to be noted that the ratios of X and Y as given in column 5 are different for various values of X and Y. Now, consider the ratio of differences—for ΔX it is always 10 and for ΔY it is always 5. The differences always maintain a constant ratio (in this example it is 2:1) but this is not reflected

Table 8.3 Measure in the interval scale

X	*Y*	Δ*X*	Δ*Y*	*X*:*Y*
10	15	-	-	1:1.5
20	20	10	5	1:1
30	25	10	5	3:2.5
40	30	10	5	4:3

Δ refers to changes in the value of X and Y.

in the values of *X* and *Y* which do not follow a constant ratio. This is precisely the difference between the interval scale and the ratio scale. In the interval scale, when $X = 0$, $Y = a$. It has an arbitrary origin (not absolute 0). *X* and *Y* therefore do not maintain a constant ratio. But the differences of values of *X* and *Y* do maintain a constant ratio, that is,

$$(X_2 - X_1/Y_2 - Y_1) = (X_3 - X_2/Y_3 - Y_2)$$

The numbers that maintain the pattern between *X* and *Y* are the numbers in the interval scale and the numbers that maintain the pattern between Δ*X* and Δ*Y* are in the ratio scale. Thus, in case of temperature in the Fahrenheit scale which is an interval scale, the ratio between 50°F and 25°F will not be the same as the ratio between 25°F and 0°F but the difference between 50°F and 25°F will be the same as the difference between 25°F and 0°F .

As we have pointed out, the problem arises due to the existence of an arbitrary origin. If we do away with the arbitrary 0, *X* and *Y* will maintain a constant ratio. To illustrate this point, if one considers the same linear equation $Y = a + bX$ (where the value of *a* is 0 and b is 0.5), then Table 8.3, changes as follows (Table 8.4).

Table 8.4 Measure in the ratio scale

X	*Y*	Δ*X* (col 3)	Δ*Y* (col 4)	*X*:*Y* (col 5)
10	5	-	-	2:1
20	10	10	5	2:1
30	15	10	5	2:1
40	20	10	5	2:1

Δ refers to changes in the values of X and Y.

The internal mathematics is obvious. Consider the following two pair of values (X_1, Y_1) and (X_2, Y_2). With $Y = a + bX$, we have

$$\frac{Y_2 - Y_1}{X_2 - X_1} = b$$

When $Y = bX$, that is, when $a = 0$, we have $Y/X = b$. The first one is an example of a measure in the interval scale; the second one is on the ratio scale.

From the above discussion, we can see that a conversion from the interval scale to the ratio scale is possible. Therefore, researchers often use a measure in the interval scale with the understanding that the mathematical properties of the measures in the ratio scale can be utilised even though the measure is taken in the interval scale. The Fahrenheit scale can be transformed to the Centigrade scale which is a ratio scale. The Fahrenheit scale is not the only example of the interval scale. Consumer price index, calendar dates, measures of energy are some other examples of measures in the interval scale.

8.2.5 Properties of Various scales of Measurement

We shall now summarise the discussion on measurement scales. The nominal scale has the minimum number of properties of an ideal scale. It only gives unique identification of the numerals. The order of the numerals, the distance among the numerals and the origin of the numerals cannot be assigned in the nominal scale. For the statistical tools that can be applied to the numerals in the nominal scale, the frequency and percentage of a particular numeral appearing in a set and the mode (maximum frequency) may be found. For statistical tests, a measure in the nominal scale can be utilised for the binomial and chi-square tests.

A measure in the ordinal scale does give a unique definition of the numerals as in the case of the nominal scale. The added property is that it maintains an order of the numerals. The difference of distance among the numerals and the origin of the numerals are not given in the ordinal scale. Among the statistical properties, the additional tools that one may utilise in this scale are percentiles, median and rank correlation. The interval scale has the added property of measuring the distance or difference among the numerals. The numerals also follow an origin—defined in arbitrary way (absolute 0 is not taken as the origin). The statistical tools that can be applied on the data set in the interval scale (in addition to those that are applicable in the nominal and ordinal scales) are range and standard deviation as measures of dispersion and arithmetic mean as a measure of central tendency. Correlation and regression analysis are also done on this type of data set.

The queen of scales is the ratio scale. Most of the data that we handle are in the ratio scale. The numerals in the ratio scale have all the properties of an ideal scale. The numerals uniquely define an attribute, the numerals maintain an order, the distance or difference among the numerals can be measured in quantitative terms and all the numerals in the ratio scale refer to absolute 0 as the origin. All the statistical tools can be applied to the data set in the ratio scale (Table 8.5).

Table 8.5 Characteristics of the four scales of measurement

Scale	Number system	Example	Statistical tools*
Nominal	Unique definition of numerals (2.0.9 and so on)	Brands, regions, population type	Percentages, frequency, mode, binomial test, chi-square test
Ordinal	Order of numerals 0 < 1 < 2 < 3....	Attitude, preference, quality	Percentiles, median, rank correlation
Interval	Equality of differences 2 – 1 = 7 – 6	Index number, temperature, intensity of preference (Thurstone scale)	Range, AM, standard deviation, correlation regression
Ratio	Equality of ratio 2/4 = 4/8	Age, price, cost, revenue profit	GM, HM, coefficient of variation

* All statistical tools applicable to lower order measurement are appropriate for higher order as well.

8.3 SCALING TECHNIQUES FOR MEASUREMENT OF ATTITUDE

The data in the ratio scale and in the interval scale are measured in quantitative terms so that the difference between any two events is expressed in terms of quantitative differences. Thus a profit margin of 5% on cost given as Rs 100.00 would imply a measure of profit by Rs 5.00 when the measure is in the ratio scale. A profit margin by 10% on cost gives a measure of profit as Rs 10.00. The difference between the two is measured as Rs 5.00. Similarly, quantitative data on the interval scale can also be expressed in terms of quantity.

A measure in the ordinal scale lacks this property. What it can at best suggest is that the profit scenario is better in the second case. We have already observed that the information in the ordinal scale cannot be used for further analysis unless we add the property of addition, subtraction, multiplication and division followed by further mathematical operations on the data. Basically, this implies that we need to know the distance among the data—a property that exists only if the measure is taken in interval or ratio scale. The numbers in ordinal scale do not indicate the distance or difference in measure in any quantitative terms. Adding or subtracting the scores, as done under ratio scale or interval scale should not therefore be allowed with respect to these data. However, as we have pointed out earlier, such exercises with ordinal data are widely performed in various areas of social research. One may rationalise this operation only on the assumption that there is concordance among the rank scores and therefore assigning the property of distance in ordinal numbers would not distort the truth.

There is a vast area of social research where the researcher needs to measure the attitude of the respondent. Information comes as preference for a product or approval of some kind of intervention (such as, preferring a particular brand of detergent, approving a particular government action, and so on). The researcher tries to use this information for further statistical analysis. Typically, the information is compiled in the ordinal scale and therefore the attitude is captured in terms of ordinal numbers only. In the absence of quantification, the permissible statistical exercises on such ordinal data are percentiles or quartiles including median and rank correlation. What we would point out now is that this is not the only option before a researcher while measuring the attitude of the respondent.

When the attitude is measured in terms of ordinal numbers, that is, no distance or difference is assumed in the property of the numbers, the researcher might still plan to use the data for further analysis in quantitative terms by designing a scaling technique so that some statistical technique can be applied to transform the ordinal data into an interval scale. Again, the researcher might himself plan to assign the property of distance in ordinal numbers at the time of collecting the data by adopting a scale of measurement in which direct numerical judgements are made by the respondents. In other words, in measuring attitude, the researcher may plan to develop a technique in which the attitude is captured directly in ratio scale or interval scale; he might as well stick to pure ordinal numbers with the provision of utilising the numbers for further statistical analysis in quantitative terms. There are a few scaling techniques by which such exercises can be performed. In this section, we will discuss some of these techniques.

Ordinal data that we usually utilise are basically related to the measurement of attitude of the respondents. A set of stimuli are imparted and the responses are captured. The information related to ordinal data in such studies reflect the opinion, approval or disapproval, and so on, which are expressions of attitude or other psychological behaviour of the respondents. While collecting the information, the researcher should be careful about the emphasis of the set of stimuli. When the researcher examines systematic variation across respondents the approach is known as *subject centred approach*. The approach is known as *stimulus centred approach* when systematic variations across stimuli, if any, are studied. Usually, the researcher examines both the subject and the stimulus variation, which is noted as *response approach*.

Whatever be the approach, the researcher must know how the basic data that he is going to collect would be measured (which scale of measurement would be used). If the basic data are to be used in the ratio or interval scale, the method to be followed in case of the measurement of attitude should be the *quantitative judgement method* which assigns direct numerical values to the responses. If the response is measured on the ordinal scale, the method to be followed for collecting the basic data is called the *variability method*. Ranking the brands according to an order, paired comparison and ordered category sorting as also various rating techniques are examples of data collection through the variability method. The data collected through the variability method can sometimes be translated into the interval or ratio scale. How this can be done will be discussed at length when we consider the methods of utilising the ordinal data for further statistical analysis.

8.3.1 The Quantitative Judgement Method

For measuring attitude, the researcher need not necessarily follow an ordinal scale. The researcher may apply a ratio scale or interval scale. This is what is done for measuring attitude by *quantitative judgement method.* The respondent is requested to assign a quantity according to his subjective perception in the suggested scale with respect to an attribute. Suggesting the scale depends on the a-priori judgement of the researcher according to the way he wants to quantify the information.

The following are some examples of the quantitative judgement approach.

(a) The researcher assigns a scale having numerical values as in the ratio scale. Suppose it is a 5 point scale with 0 as its origin. The respondent is requested to assign a number in this scale with respect to an attribute which is usually expressed in qualitative terms (such as, it tastes better, it smells better, and so on). The quality is now expressed in numbers which are placed in a ratio scale. The data collected in this way could be utilised for further analysis with the provision that it retains all the mathematical properties associated with the data described in ratio scale. The advantage is that we now have qualitative information directly transformed into quantitative data. The approach is a *subject centred approach* because the systematic variation across respondents is the key issue here.

(b) Here is another example to show how preconceived scales matter in the quantitative judgement approach. Let us suppose there are five competing brands and the rating regarding the quality of perfume is to be done following the quantitative judgement approach. The researcher would put the issue in the following way. If brand A is a valued perfume and is given a rating of 10, how do you rate B, C, D and E with reference to perfume as an attribute? In the perception of the respondent, it works as follows. Brand A is assigned 10. My perception is that B is a better brand and the quality of being better might be captured by assigning 12 to B. This implies that quantitatively speaking, B is rated 20% higher than A in terms of the given attribute. Here, the researcher examines both the subject and the stimulus variation; the approach therefore is *response approach* in this case.

Pre-assigning a scale can be done in various other ways as well. The researcher selects the scale according to his own perception on the utility of the scale in analysing qualitative information in quantitative terms.

8.3.2 Variability Method

In variability method, the response is measured in ordinal scale. The stimuli response interface is usually captured by the *response method*. As we have pointed out, the response method is used when we consider both the stimuli-centric and the respondent-centric measures of attitude. It therefore deals with inter-respondent and inter-stimuli differences. Scaling is required here for the respondent as well as for the stimuli. The first step is to use a scale to know whether the respondent agrees or disagrees to the stimulus and to ask for ordering his response in terms of a set of stimuli. Usually, the response method is used for ascertaining the preference of one stimulus to another, that is, one statement to another. Ranking is one such method. There are many other methods by which the response can be recorded. One technique under the variability method that is widely used is the technique of paired comparison.

8.3.2.1 Paired Comparison

A consumer is exposed to six brands of detergents and the requirement of the market survey organisation is to find out the consumers' order of preference with respect to these detergents. The simplest way would be to ask the consumer to make an ordering among the six detergents. But the consumer may not like to perform the exercise which involves applying a judgement on the order of preference among six detergents. Even if the consumer is induced to make such an ordering, the quality of the revealed preference might be poor since he will have to rank six brands at a time. A better way to get at the psyche of the consumer is to induce him to reveal his preference in a pair wise comparison among the brands which would be easier for him. The paired comparison requires the respondent to state which is dominant between two brands, or which one precedes, wins-over or exceeds over the other in response to an attribute, property, feature, benefits or subjects. The only requirement is that the order of preference would be transitive in nature. If A is preferred to B and B is preferred to C, then we infer that

Table 8.6 Pairwise comparison among the brands

Brand	**Score in pairwise comparison**					
	A	B	C	D	E	F
A	-	0	1	1	1	1
B	1	-	1	1	1	1
C	0	0	-	0	0	0
D	0	0	1	-	0	0
E	0	0	1	1	-	1
F	0	0	1	1	0	-

A is preferred over C as well. Let us suppose six brands of toothpaste are being compared in terms of a certain attribute such as taste. If the consumer reveals his preference of brand A over B, and brand D over A, the implication when the relation is transitive is that since D is preferred over A, D would be preferred to B as well.

Table 8.7 Permuted rows and columns

From	To brands						
	B	A	E	F	D	C	Sum
B	-	1	1	1	1	1	5
A	0	-	1	1	1	1	4
E	0	0	-	1	1	1	3
F	0	0	0	-	1	1	2
D	0	0	0	0	-	1	1
C	0	0	0	0	0	-	0

Given this rule of ordering, the researcher would apply this technique by requesting the respondent X to reveal his preference pattern pairwise. The results in a hypothetical case are given below.

B is preferred to A
A is preferred to C
D is preferred to C
E is preferred to D
E is preferred to F

From this, following the law of transitivity, relation of a brand with respect to the competing five brands may be inferred. The results of this exercise are given in Table 8.7. 0 indicates not preferred and 1 indicates preferred. Since B is preferred to A, A is not preferred to B. This is indicated by 0 in the table in the cell (A, B). Since B is preferred to A the cell (B, A) gets 1. These are binary numbers indicating a measure in ordinal scale. Every cell has a number based on the five statements from consumer X.

We then rearrange the table to describe the preference pattern in a descending order of pairwise scores. The table that is formed is referred to as *permuted rows and columns*. Brand B dominates over the other brands A, E, F, D, C. Hence the cells (B,A), (B,E), (B, F), (B,D), and (B, C) each have a score of 1. The total of the scores has been shown as 5 in the last column of Table 8.7. In the case of brand A, we observe it is not preferred to B but is preferred to C, D, E and F, when compared pairwise. A similar exercise has been carried out for other brands as well and the total scores against each brand have been recorded in the last column. The table forms a block triangular matrix for obvious reasons. It may be noted that C is not preferred to either A, B, D, E or F, and therefore the total score for C is 0. Finally arranging the scores in *diminishing order* we find that B gets the highest rank, followed by A, E, F, D and C. Hence we get B > A > E > F > D > C in terms of preference pertaining to the attribute taste, as revealed by consumer X.

The same exercise, namely, placing the brands in the order of preference could be done by consumer X without going in for pairwise comparison (the researcher might ask the consumer to rank the brands in terms of preference by considering all the brands together; the results would have been the rank scores as well). A pairwise comparison would also end up with the rank scores as perceived by the respondent. But the respondent now exercises the options in a more focussed manner because he applies his judgement with respect to two brands at a time and not by considering 6 brands at a time. It is expected that the pairwise comparison would capture the judgement of the consumer in a better way. The only requirement is that his preference pattern should honour the rule of transitivity. If transitivity is violated, the researcher might have to inform the respondent that he is becoming inconsistent (if you prefer A to B and if you prefer D to A, you cannot say that you prefer B to D).

The rank scores are pure numbers, but they are ordinal numbers. If B scores 5, it implies that B has been preferred in 5 pairs of comparison. If we use these numbers as the numbers in a ratio scale we violate the basic premise that 1 implies not a number; it only communicates the fact that a brand is preferred over the other. The preference is indicated by 1. The rules of addition, subtraction, multiplication and division should not be permitted if the implication of 1 as ordinal number is strictly honoured. What would the column indicating 'Sum' in Table 8.7 then imply? It implies the extent by which a brand is preferred in pairwise comparison. Brand B in this exercise, for example, has been preferred 5 times in the pairwise comparison. A variation of this measure has been suggested by Thurstone in his exercise on comparative judgement. We shall discuss his method presently.

Paired comparison requires that the order of preference is transitive in nature. What would the researcher do if the judgement of the respondent is not transitive? If A is preferred to B and B is preferred to C, then A has to be preferred to C as well if the relation is transitive. If in the respondent's perception, A is not preferred to C, instead C is preferred to A in this case, there is a situation which is called the *circular triad.* If the problem is detected at the field level, the researcher might inform the respondent that he is becoming inconsistent; the respondent might change the statement accordingly and thus transitivity may be restored. What happens if such rectification or revision is not done and the circular triad is present in the data set? Nothing can be done if the presence of circular triad is very serious. If it is not very serious in nature, the researcher would try to make the paired comparisons transitive by making minimum number of alterations in the original data set. But then, how to judge whether the problem is too serious or not? One may apply Kendall's method of testing tolerable levels of intransitivity in a data set by computing Kendall's *Coefficient of Consistency* and testing the null hypothesis that the respondent has responded randomly (Kendall M G, *Rank Correlation Methods*, 1962).

8.3.3 Specialised Scales

Let us also consider a few scales related to measurement of attitude. Some of the scales are stimuli centric, some are respondent centric and many of them consider both the stimuli and the response while considering qualitative information. Some of the scales follow the variability method, some follow the quantitative method. A combination of both the methods is also observed in some cases.

The scales that are discussed here are:

(a) Rating scale,
(b) Constant sum scale,
(c) Semantic differential scale, and
(d) Multi-dimensional scale.

Rating scale: In social research with qualitative data, this is the most widely used scale. It is primarily based on the variability method where the response is measured in ordinal scale. However, the rating scales also include quantitative judgement method, implicitly or explicitly, in many cases. It is better to understand the method by starting with *ordered category sorting*, a scale in which the responses are captured in terms of categories. The categories are ordered in ascending or descending order of an attribute. Let us suppose we want to study user habits in reference to certain food items.

Table 8.8 Stimuli in a consumer based survey

	Use regularly	Use occasionally	Might use	Probably never use	Would never use
Milk					
Butter					
Cheese					
Dessert					

The scale shown above is in fact based on identifying a category where the attitude depends on usage of a certain product. If the product is most popular or most near to usual habit it is placed under 'Use regularly', which, from a scaling point of view is just a point—a point marked by an ordinal number, say, 1. If popularity or habit is the issue of concern, then the categories can be sorted in an order with numbers identifying the rating. The ordering implies rank scores as well, as in the case of ordinal ranking. Each product gets a rank score in this exercise. The scale here has an odd number of points, at other times it could have an even number of points as well. The favourable points in the scale could be positively numbered and the unfavourable points in the scale could be negatively numbered. It should be kept in mind that having an odd scale always helps as the middle point stands for neutrality. The scale should be so chosen that the discrimination between the positive and negative is clearly identified in cases where such identification is necessary.

Let us proceed further. In the variability method, we assume only an ordering of the category boundaries. The interval separating the boundaries is not a concern here. As in the above example, the interval separating the boundary between 'Use occasionally' and 'Use regularly' is not as distinct as that between 'Use occasionally' and 'Might use.' The ordering can still be done because, as we have pointed out, the interval is not a point of concern here. In a consumer based survey, the respondent in this case would clearly distinguish one stimulus from the other. This serves the purpose of scaling under ordered category sorting. The ratings here will indicate certain ordinal numbers that can be used for permissible statistical analyses.

The interval separating the boundaries can be an important issue in scaling attitude. Consider the following description (Table 8.9).

Table 8.9 Stimuli in an opinion poll

	Strongly disagree	Disagree	Undecided	Agree	Strongly agree
Statement 1					+2
Statement 2	−2				
Statement 3				1	
Statement 4					+2
Statement 5		−1			

There were five statements on which the opinion of the respondent was sought. The response was captured in terms of five alternative statements. The interval separating the boundaries is a concern here because not only the direction but the intensity of the respondent's attitude is also a point of concern (to what extent does 'disagree' differ from 'strongly disagree'). A measure by variability method cannot meet this requirement. One needs quantitative judgement method as well to supplement it. Rating methods can provide the scaling techniques that may serve this purpose. Rating allows a respondent to communicate a degree or even an amount of the characteristic or attribute which is being captured in the study. The measures can be captured in ordinal scale (when the interval separating the boundaries is not required), ratio scale or interval scale. The data can be gathered in numerical, graphic or verbal form. As we apply the quantitative judgement method and capture the intensity of the respondent's attitude in a ratio scale, we place the points in equal intervals, as in the ratio scale. The attitude can then be measured with the intensity of the respondent's attitude registered in numbers in ratio scale. If 'undecided' is placed at 0 in ratio scale and the other points are places at equal intervals, then a score 1.8 will imply that the opinion is mere inclined to 'Strongly agree' with 'Strongly agree' having a score of 2.

The ratio scale that we describe here is a subjective ratio scale. The respondent knows that he is using a continuous scale defined in a range of –2 to +2. He chooses his own subjective score here when he is allowed to exercise the option of placing his intensity of attitude in a numeric way, but not necessarily in the form of integers only. The range may be suitably designed to capture direct judgment (see 8.3.1). One may organise the rating scale in such a way that all the scores taken together will equal a constant sum. This is often referred to as constant sum scale. Since this scale is widely used in various branches of social sciences including market research, we shall discuss this scale in detail.

Constant sum scale: This scale is used in measurement of the relative importance of factors or issues. A respondent is usually given a sum of 10 or 100 and is requested to distribute it among the various objects indicating their weightages or importance. The average response of all respondents could indicate the average position of various attributes and objects.

Example: Let us suppose that the respondent is to divide 100 points on attributes that are important while considering the purchase of a car. The following attributes are considered.

- Company name,
- Price,
- Mileage,
- Maintenance, and
- Comfort.

The response of a particular respondent is given below:

Factors/Attributes	Points
Company name	40
Price	20
Mileage	25
Maintenance	10
Comfort	5

One may record the responses of a sampled set of respondents in this scale and use the numeric values for further analysis, as in case of the ratio scale. This scale is a type of rating scale which is widely used in market research especially for surveys on consumer durables and services.

Semantic differential scale: One may intend to use the quantitative scores as interval scaled raw data that may be used in various multivariate models. The initial scaling for such a purpose is done by collecting the data using the *semantic differential method.* We shall discuss the method presently. At the outset, it should be kept in mind that adequacy of the scaling model itself is not the issue for consideration here. In other words, when we apply the semantic differential method, it is assumed that the raw data are interval scaled.

Semantic differential scale is usually used for comparison of messages, items, brands and corporate image in reference to certain attributes or topics. Collecting the data in semantic differential scale is aimed at probing into both the direction and the intensity of the respondent's attitude. For this, the scaling has to be properly designed. Bipolar scaling is one such design. For example, when we compare four brands of car over a number of characteristics by a scale which has two poles, the best in one pole (extreme) and worst in the other pole (extreme), we get the description in terms of both intensity and direction of the psychological behaviour of the respondent. A typical description in this context might come as follows.

Table 8.10 Measuring car profile by semantic differential

Colourful	x					Non- colourful
Good mileage			x			Bad mileage
Sturdy body	x					Weak body
Comfortable			x			Not comfortable

The unique characteristic of this scale is the use of numbers in bipolar scales as above to rate the four brands of cars. In the above example, each scale consists of two opposing adjectives which are separated by a continuum of five distinct points; with scale values moving step-by-step from one side of the adjective to the other.

Semantic differential can be used to work out total attitude scores. Let the scales be numbered, the most favourable being 1 and the least favourable being 5. After all the scales are completed, these values are summed up for each brand to obtain an attitude score. The total score obtained in this manner is an indication of the overall attitude towards a brand. It assumes that all the important factors that determine consumer attitude towards the brand have been included and that *they are relatively equal in weightage.* The method is easy to implement and control. At times, the semantic differential could be done in a reverse process by using mean values of the scores of each attribute with respect to each brand, and then plotting it on the bipolar scale. Consider the following example. A total of twenty people were asked to rank the three brands on the four attributes – sturdy body, colour, mileage and comfort – on a scale of 1 to 5, where 1 is the most favourable and 5 is the least favourable. Each brand will get twenty scores with respect to each attribute. A table can be constructed that describes the mean score of these twenty respondents with reference to each attribute for each of the comparative brands (Table 8.11). The average scores can then be utilised to find the rating of the brands in the perception of the respondents.

Table 8.11 Brands and their attributes

Brands	Colour	Mileage	Sturdy body	Comfort
Brand A	1.6	1.8	1.8	2.8
Brand B	2.7	2.5	2.4	2.2
Brand C	2.3	2.5	2.9	2.6

From Table 8.11 we find that A is more favourable on colour, mileage and sturdy body in comparison to B and C and it is only less favourable with reference to comfort. Brand B and C are more or less equally preferred with the mileage, being rated the same.

Multi-dimensional scaling (MDS): All scales discussed so far consider one attribute at a time which implies that the stimuli are points with only one dimension. Consider now a situation where a stimulus is expected to capture the respondent's behaviour in more than one dimension. If one dimension is uniquely related to one attribute, the stimulus here refers to more than one attribute. The scale value would therefore capture the data in the multi-attribute space. This is what MDS is expected to do. The implication is that the integrated picture on a few common attributes can be gathered through MDS. More precisely, MDS helps the researcher to compare the relative importance of various characteristics; how these characteristics relate to each other in reference to the various objects of study (such as brands in a market survey) may also be analysed with the help of the data in MDS.

In market research, multi-dimensional scaling is a term used to describe a group of analytical techniques used to study consumer attitudes particularly relating to perceptions and preferences. It helps in finding answers to the following questions.

(a) What are the major attributes of a given class of product that are important in discriminating between brands?
(b) Which brands are similar to one another and which are dissimilar?
(c) What would be the consumer's ideal combination of product attributes?

There are many possible uses of multi-dimensional scaling in market research. Some of the uses are the following:

(a) Market segmentation: If brands are located on a preference space we get clusters of consumers who have similar preferences in a particular market.
(b) Product life cycle: By analysing the perception of respondents at different times, researchers might be able to relate movement along certain characteristics and identify the stages in product life cycle for different brands.
(c) Vendor evaluation: The purchasing managers could choose among vendors on factors such as price, delivery, reliability, technical service and quality. The cluster of vendors as required could be located.
(d) Selection of advertising media: Depending on factors such as reading habits, cost of media, type of product and message delivery abilities (attributes), media vehicles could be tabulated and chosen.

In MDS, when the input data are ratio scaled or interval scaled, the corresponding scaling methods are called metric scaling. When the data are measured at nominal or ordinal scale level, the scaling techniques are called non-metric scaling. Ordinal scaled input data are often transformed in interval scale at the level of output. Since metric MDS methods ordinarily produce results that are close to what non-metric methods would have produced, metric methods are usually recommended for practical computations because the metric methods have the advantage of having more computational efficiency.

Limitations of multi-dimensional scaling: The limitations of multi-dimensional scaling can be classified into three categories:

(a) Conceptual: The concept of *similarity* and *preference* are not very clear or cannot be made explicit to the respondent. The criteria for similarity are quite different from those for preference. Preference is behavioural and therefore many other factors need to be included.
(b) Empirical problem: In the use of multi-dimensional scaling process, it is pointed out that the levelling of dimensions is not very objective. Lots of discussions could be triggered on these issues. The existence of bias cannot be ruled out; one should admit that subjective bias remains very much within the process.
(c) Computational problem: Most multi-dimensional scales require the use of computers. Several different computer tabulations are used based on the type of input. The computer applications generally address the measurement in straight lines or linear distances. Such calculations are often very expensive particularly when the scaling is non-metric. Calculations with non-metric data set might lead to degeneracy.

(d) Now-a-days, hybrid models of categorical-dimensional structure are replacing the pure MDS models (cluster analysis and MDS hybrids for example).

We shall now discuss two specialised scales which can utilise qualitative data for developing a quantitative analysis. These scales are very powerful scales that can introduce quantitative rigour into qualitative data that describe attitude, preference, and so on which otherwise can never be quantified. These are known as the Thurstone scale and the Likert scale.

8.4.1 Thurstone Scale

The data on an ordinal scale may further be refined to unveil more information if we include certain mathematical properties in the data collected in the ordinal scale. Thurstone discussed the issue and developed a technique based on his law of *Comparative Judgement*. The basic approach is to construct a uni-dimensional interval scale on the ordinal data collected by the variability method. One may develop a class of methods out of the basic model. However, the most widely used one is known as the 'Thurstone Scale V' method which will be discussed here in detail. The data collected through the variability method can also be analysed by methods other than Thurstone's method. Researchers often use a method which was developed by Rensis Likert which will be discussed subsequently.

The method may be described though an example. Consider a scenario in which there are three brands of detergents—A, B and C. Members of a set of respondents are asked to do a comparative judgement regarding brand preference in a pairwise manner (which do you prefer between A and B, which do you prefer between B and C, and so on). Let us suppose there are 500 respondents and 480 out of them opined that A is preferred to B, a comparison between B and C showed that 260 respondents are in favour of B and 240 are in favour of C. Comparative judgement, as the description indicates, is a judgement based on pairwise comparison.

What do we get from such a comparative judgement? The comparative judgement definitely indicates that there is a strong case in favour of A when compared with B but the case in favour of B vis-à-vis C is not quite strong—definitely not as strong as in the previous case. Based on the observation of this phenomenon, a new scale was developed by Thurstone that can capture the *intensity of difference* by further refinement that would not have been possible had we followed the method of paired comparison only.

When 500 respondents perform a pairwise comparison between A and B, they work under a stimulus. The stimulus here generates a process of discrimination between brands in the perception of the respondents. When the comparison is between A and B, respondents under this stimulus would discriminate against either A or B by revealing their preferences (in the above example, 480 respondents preferred A and 20 respondents preferring B to A). This process is known as the *discrimination process*. The discrimination process may reveal different results under different scenarios with respect to the same stimulus. One would however assume that there is likely to be a situation which corresponds to the highest number of occurrences (mode of a distribution). According to Thurstone, the difference between modal discriminations among various pairs would be noted as *discriminal difference*.

How would the discriminal differences behave in a population? Thurstone assumes that each discriminal process follows a normal distribution, that is, the distribution will be bell shaped if a very large number of respondents exercise their judgement in any paired comparison. This is not surprising if we understand the law of large numbers. Thurstone adds that the discriminal differences will also follow the law of large numbers, i.e., , the *discriminal differences will also follow normal distribution*. This is also quite logical. If two variables have a normal distribution, the difference between the variables would also follow a normal distribution.

Thurstone uses these concepts for developing a new scale for handling the ordinal data. Consider two pairs of discriminal processes the results of which are measured in a psychological scale (captured as S_i and S_j where S_i and S_j are the mean values of two discriminal processes *i* and *j*). What the researcher would like to measure is the distance between the outcomes of these two pairs of stimuli. Thurstone considers the linear distance and suggests a measure of the difference in comparative judgement that can be described as below:

$$S_i - S_j = Z_{ij}\sqrt{\sigma_i^2 + \sigma_j^2 - 2\rho_{ij}\sigma_1\sigma_j}$$

where

$S_i - S_j$ = a linear distance between the psychological scale between stimulus *i* and stimulus *j* described in terms of mean values of two normal distributions describing the discriminal processes *i* and *j*,

Z_{ij} = standard normal variate associated with the discriminal difference captured in terms of the observed proportion in which stimulus *i* is preferred to stimulus *j*,

σ_i^2, σ_j^2 = discriminal dispersion (variance) of stimulus *i* and stimulus *j* respectively,

ρ_{ij} = coefficient of correlation between the discriminal processes associated with stimulus *i* versus stimulus *j* judgements.

The statement mentioned above is based on the understanding that the discriminal difference can be measured in terms of a standard normal value. But the difference between two discriminal processes will also depend on the dispersion of outcomes of both the stimuli and also the correlation between the stimulus *i* and stimulus *j*. *If the stimuli are mutually independent and each discriminal process has the same dispersion (but with different mean) the discriminal difference will follow a standard normal distribution.*

The rationale of Thurstone's proposed measure can be understood easily if we consider the extreme case where $S_i = S_j$, that is, when there is no distance between the pairwise measures in the psyche of the consumer. Let $\rho_{ij} = 1$ and let $\sigma_i = \sigma_j$. As we get $S_i = S_j$, there is no discriminal difference. *The absence of discriminal difference is possible if and when there is perfect correlation between two discriminal processes and the variances of both the distributions are equal. In fact, the second discriminal process is now the replica of the first.*

In the same way, we can get a scenario in which (*i*) the discriminal dispersions are equal and (ii) the correlation between S_i and S_j is equal to zero. By setting $\sigma_i^2 = \sigma_j^2$ for all stimuli and letting $\rho = 0$, we obtain the following simplification $S_i - S_j = Z_{ij}\sqrt{2\sigma^2(1-\rho)}$

With $\rho = 0$, we get

$$S_i - S_j = Z_{ij}\sqrt{2\sigma^2}$$

$$\text{or, } Z_{ij} = (S_i - S_j) / \sqrt{2\sigma^2}$$

The standard normal variate now has a value which is the ratio between mean values of two discriminal processes and $\sqrt{2\sigma^2}$, that is, $\sqrt{2}\,\sigma$.

If we take $\sigma_i = \sigma_j = 1$ then $Z_{ij} = (S_i - S_j) / \sqrt{2}$

For any two stimuli S_i and S_j, Thurstone's most general model for comparative judgement can be reduced to

$$Z_{ij} = S_i - S_j$$

as Thurstone's case V model by noting that with equal dispersion ($\sigma_i = \sigma_j$) and a common correlation ρ,

$$Z_{ij} = (S_i - S_j) / \sqrt{2\sigma^2(1-\rho)}$$

Taking the interval scale with $\sqrt{2\sigma^2(1-\rho)} = 1$ we get $S_i - S_j = Z_{ij}$ which is a standard normal variate.

Thurstone's Scale V Model is widely used because the assumption of equal dispersion and a common correlation is supposed to be consistent with most real life scenarios with varied stimuli on a set of respondents.

Thurstone's Scale V Model can be utilised for analysing the ordinal data collected by the comparative judgement method and is the most widely used technique in market research. Basically, it records the mean associated with the discriminal processes; it assumes equal variance in each discriminal process and the absence of correlation between the stimuli, it transforms the mean differences to *Z* values in a corresponding standard normal table. The *Z* scores are used as the values that can be described in an interval scale with the lowest

Z value serving as the arbitrary origin of the data set. Operationalisation of this method will be explained with the help of an example.

Example: Let us assume that 100 respondents were asked to compare four brands of cars—A, B, C, D. The preference of one brand to another is tested with reference to the attribute 'engine'. The observed proportion‡ for each comparison is presented in the Table 8.12.

Table 8.12 Observed proportions showing brand preferences

Brands	Preferred brands			
	A	B	C	D
A	0.50*	0.60	0.70	0.80
B	0.40	0.50*	0.90	0.40
C	0.30	0.10	0.50*	0.30
D	0.20	0.60	0.70	0.50*

* The diagonal entries in the table represent self comparison and are shown as 0.5; to indicate the mean of the corresponding *Z* values which would be 0. The diagonal entries of Table 8.12 have no effect on the resulting scale values.

From Table 8.12, we find that 60% of respondents have favoured brand B to A and 40% have preferred A to B (if we arbitrarily allow columns to dominate rows). From the data of Table 8.12 we prepare Table 8.13, which summarises the *Z* values appropriate for each proportion (the *Z* values are in the Appendix, Table 1). If the proportion is less than 0.5, the *Z* value carries a negative sign. If the proportion is greater than 0.5, the Z values carry a positive sign, because Z is a standard normal variate which has 0 as the mean with half of the values lying on the left of 0, that is, having negative values. Again while tabulating Table 8.13, where the *Z* values of the above proportions have been computed, the positive values of the column dominance in reference to preference of one brand over another is reflected in the row value of less preference of one brand to another merely by prefixing a negative sign to the *Z* value ascribed [that is, *Z* value in the cell (B,A), where column dominates row, is 0.26 is reflected in the cell (A,B) as –0.26)]. The *Z* values are standard unit variates that are associated with a given proportion of total area under the normal curve. Thus, all entries in Table 8.13 are obtained in a similar manner, a minus sign being prefixed to the *Z* value when the proportion is less than 0.5.

‡ The observed proportions approximate the mean of a discriminal process. It is calculated directly from the data on pairwise comparison. If C_X is the total number of cases favouring *X* in a set of data on pairwise comparison among *n* number of brands of cars with *N* as the number of respondents, then $M_X = (C_X + N/2)/\, nN$ is the mean proportion associated with brand *X*.

Table 8.13 *Z* values related to prefered proportions

Brands	Preferred brands			
	A	B	C	D
A	0	0.26	0.53	0.85
B	−0.26	0	1.29	−0.26
C	−0.53	−1.29	0	−0.53
D	−0.85	0.26	0.53	0
TOTAL ($\sum Z$)	−1.64	−0.77	2.35	0.06
$\overline{Z}$ (mean)	−0.41	−0.19	0.59	0.015
R*	0	0.22	1.00	0.425

R is the scale value*

The column totals are stated in Table 8.13. The scale values are obtained from the column sums by taking the simple average of each column's *Z* values. For example, from Table 8.13, we note that the sum of *Z*s in the first column (A) is –1.64.

$$\text{The average } \overline{Z_A} = -\frac{1.64}{4} = -0.41$$

This scale value expresses A as a deviation from the mean of all four scale values. The means of the four values computed from the full row of $\overline{Z}$ s will always be 0 (zero) under this process. Similarly, one finds the average *Z* value for each of the remaining three columns.

Since the 0 point of an interval scale is arbitrary, we can let the scale value of A ($R_A = \overline{Z_A} = -0.41$) be the reference point (or origin) of zero. We then add +0.41 to each of the other $\overline{Z}$ values to obtain the case V scale values of the other brands. The scale values of brands A through D indicate the preference as:

$$C > D > B > A$$

We have seen that using Thurstone scale V and shifting the base to the largest negative amount (that is, making it 0 in the scale) we get the data in the interval scale (interval scale because 0 has been chosen arbitrarily). The position of each brand in an interval scale with its origin at A can be illustrated diagrammatically (Fig. 8.1).

The interval scale is proven through the equation where we get an equation of the nature

$$(C - B) = 1.835 (D - A)$$

$$0.78 = 1.835(0.425) \text{ (approx)}$$

It is nearly equal and substantiates that the interval scale has been rightly formulated.

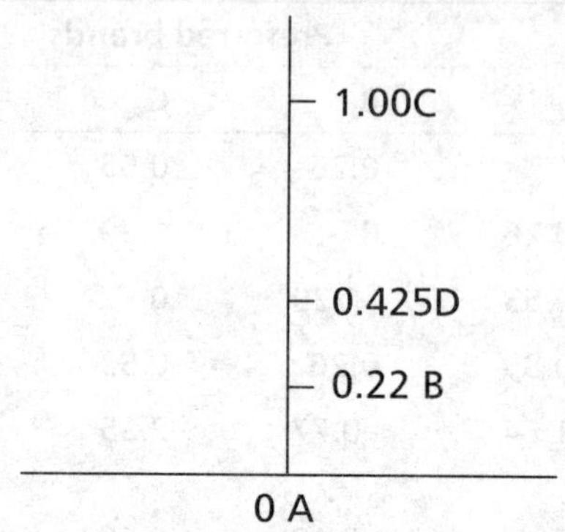

Fig. 8.1 Positioning of four engine brands in Thurstone's scale

8.4.2 Likert Scale

The Thurstone scale has the drawback of not categorically stating what the degree of agreement/disagreement of the respondent is. The purpose there was to scale stimuli (brands of motor engine, as in the above example) and not the respondents. One may, however, like to measure inter-respondent differences in intensity of agreement or disagreement. In an ordinal scale, we could develop a measure by which the intensity of difference among the qualitative measures can be ascertained. In pschycometry, a measure of the intensity of difference was developed by Professor Rensis Likert. The measure suggested by Likert is basically a summated scale in which the scaling is done by a specially designed method. The method involves constructing a set of statements centring on a particular attribute. Some of the statements are favourable to the said attribute and some are not. The respondent is exposed to these statements and his reaction is captured in terms of certain ordinal numbers, the numbers capturing the intensity of the reaction. Let us suppose a rating scale of +2, +1, 0, –1, –2 is used in describing the intensity respectively as strongly agree, agree, undecided, disagree and strongly disagree. The implication of this rating is that +2 is the most favourable, +1 is favourable, 0 is neutral, –1 is unfavourable and –2 is strongly unfavourable. This rating with the help of the *summated scale* will help us understand the degree to which the respondent agrees or disagrees. The example given below will make the interpretation of the scale more explicit.

Let us suppose a marketing agency is entrusted with conducting a survey on consumers' perception on 'holding a credit card'. If a set of respondents is exposed to certain statements related to the issue with respect to a specific statement, each specific respondent has a reaction or comment which can be captured in terms of 'agree', 'disagree', 'strongly disagree' or 'strongly agree'. The other option is that the respondent has no opinion. The Likert scale tries to capture these statements in terms of ordinal numbers. Suppose the statement is 'One should not buy a credit card because it leads to a debt trap'. The statement might get a reaction such as 'I do not agree'. For rating the corresponding score in the Likert scale, it will be noted as –1. The scale is usually based on a three point scoring system or a five point scoring system (always odd, having 0 as the starting point indicating indifference). A statement like 'I strongly disagree that a credit card drives one to a debt trap' would get a score of –2. The logic of putting a plus or a minus sign in Likert scale has further complications which will be explained shortly.

There are three important points that a researcher should know while utilising the Likert scale:

- There should be some statements favouring the issue under debate, some statements should intrinsically be unfavourable to the issue.
- The statements should be prepared after a pilot run among a select set of respondents. The purpose is to check the viability of a question in unfolding the psyche of the respondents so that the intensity of the reaction is properly communicated. *The number of statements to be selected depends on the extent of reach out of the field survey* but there should be sufficient number of such statements so that the intensity of the reaction of the respondents is adequately captured.
- Answers to unfavourable statements should be multiplied with –1 in order to calculate the total score that a respondent has to be assigned. This is so because we want to know the respondent's perception about the issue under consideration. If a respondent strongly agrees to a statement he will be assigned a score of +2, But the nature of the statement, whether it is favourable to the issue under consideration (buying a credit card provides safety in transaction) or unfavourable (credit cards make one extravagant), is important in analysing the perception of the respondent. If he strongly agrees to the statement that 'credit cards make one extravagant', he will initially get a score of +2 in the Likert scale, as he should for strongly agreeing with a favourable statement such as 'buying a credit card provides safety in transaction'. But, as one would appreciate, *strongly agreeing with an unfavourable statement is in effect, strongly disagreeing with the proposition that 'buying a credit card is good'*. In the Likert scale, this is captured by assigning a minus sign to every score which is unfavourable to the event or the issue.

The technique of using the Likert scale is rather simple. After setting the statements with respect to which the researcher would ascertain the perception of the respondents, the questionnaire would be canvassed among the sample households (respondents) and an ordinal number against the response with respect to each of the statements would be assigned. The numbers would vary between –2 and +2 if the response is captured in a five point Likert scale; the variation will be between –1 and +1 if the scale of measuring the response is a three point

Likert scale. The individual scores will be added to get an average score for a respondent. Applying this technique for all the respondents, a frequency distribution in a five point (or three point) scale is obtained that may be utilised for further statistical analysis.

Let us illustrate this technique with the help of a hypothetical case. Let us suppose there are one hundred respondents exposed to a study on their perception regarding holding a credit card. Suppose, following a pilot study 10 statements have been selected for ascertaining the perception of the respondents and the perception is being captured on a five point Likert scale. An individual A has the following response pattern:

Table 8.14 The response pattern of individual A in a five point scale

	Strongly disagree −2	Disagree −1	Undecided 0	Agree +1	Strongly agree +2	Score
Statement 1 (F)					+2	2
Statement 2 (UF)	−2					(−2)(−1) = 2
Statement 3 (UF)				1		(+1)(−1) = −1
Statement 4 (F)					+2	2
Statement 5 (UF)		−1				(−1)(−1) = 1
Statement 6 (F)					+2	2
Statement 7 (F)				+1		1
Statement 8 (UF)		−1				(−1)(−1) = 1
Statement 9 (F)					+2	2
Statement 10 (UF)				+1		(+1)(−1) = −1
					Total score	11

The total score of individual A is 11. Needless to say, the total score indicates the overall position of the respondent and not what he thinks about a particular statement. But, how should we interpret the total score? In reference to 10 statements, the maximum possible score in a five point scale is (+)20 and the minimum is (−)20. The respondent is placed at 11 *which implies that his overall position is in favour of the issue under consideration.* If he is strongly in favour of the issue, his total score should be nearer to (+)20. [It cannot exceed (+)20 for obvious reasons, it is again unlikely that the total score would be exactly equal to (+)20]. If the respondent is undecided or indifferent, his total score should be somewhere near 0. For an unfavourable position, the scores should have negative values with higher magnitude.

What transpires is that the average score for a respondent has a range between (–)2 and (+)2 on a five point scale. [Averaged over 10 statements, the total score has a range between (–)20 and (+)20; the average would thus vary from (–)2.0 to (+)2.0]. With respect to the individual A the average score is 1.1, which indicates that he is just above the bench mark score of 1, that is, favourable. If his total score is found to be(–)17, (–)1.7 on an average, he is more inclined towards being strongly against buying a credit card. Figure 8.2 depicts the scenario.

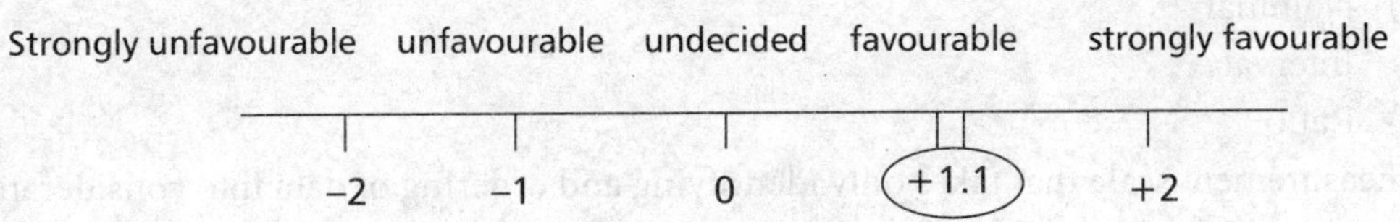

Fig. 8.2 Positioning of the respondent in Likert scale

The individual A is placed slightly above the position of being just favourable to buying a credit card. All the individuals under consideration will have such average scores. Arranging them in ascending or descending ranking can be done to get the individual rating of a respondent as potential buyer of a credit card. Permissible statistical exercises can be performed on these rank scores. Thus distribution of the respondents among various quartiles can be observed. Also the dispersion in average scores can be measured. If we are allowed to use ordinal numbers as numbers in the ratio scale, respondent-specific scores can be used for further statistical analysis.

SUMMARY

- Measurement aims at unfolding a certain property, characteristic or behavioural trait that might be hidden in the data set. For measurement, one needs a scale.
- The generic measurement scales are four, namely, nominal, ordinal, interval and ratio. All these scales have their specific characteristics and statistical usage. For example, the data in nominal scale aims at providing information in terms of frequency without any other measure of central tendency except mode. The permissible statistical tests are binomial test and chi-square test.
- The added statistical tools that data in the ordinal scale might use are percentiles, median and rank correlation. Similarly, data in the interval scale have some added statistical properties but data in the ratio scale can utilise all statistical tools which is why it is called the queen of all scales.
- The methods by which data in the ordinal scale can be best utilised for further statistical analysis is discussed. Weighted index ranking and paired comparison as a follow up are the ways in which data in the ordinal scale can be transferred in the interval scale.
- Various specialised scales widely used in social research have also been discussed.

ASSIGNMENTS

Q1 Answer the questions

1. A measurement scale to just identify the data is referred to as:
   (a) Ordinal
   (b) Nominal
   (c) Interval
   (d) Ratio
2. A measurement scale that takes only identifying and ordering of data into consideration is:
   (a) Interval
   (b) Ordinal
   (c) Nominal
   (d) Ratio
3. All the scales lack the concept of absolute 0 except:
   (a) Interval
   (b) Nominal
   (c) Ratio
   (d) Ordinal
4. Pre-assigning attributes in a continuum is known as:
   (a) Judgement approach
   (b) Qualitative approach
   (c) Variability approach
   (d) Response approach
5. Maximum number of statistical activities is carried out with data in:
   (a) Nominal scale
   (b) Ordinal scale
   (c) Interval scale
   (d) None of these
6. The graphic rating scale is one of the following scales:
   (a) Nominal
   (b) Ordinal
   (c) Interval
   (d) Ratio

7. The scale that permits a change of ordinal data to cardinal is:
   (a) Thurstone scale V
   (b) Semantic differential scale
   (c) Graphic rating scale
   (d) None of the above
8. The scale that primarily serves the purpose of scaling the respondents' attitude is:
   (a) Constant sum scale
   (b) Thurstone scale
   (c) Graphic rating scale
   (d) Likert scale
9. In multi-dimensional scaling, the input data might be:
   (a) Ratio scaled
   (b) Interval scaled
   (c) None of the above
   (d) (a) and/or (b)
10. A scale that is bipolar with two opposite adjectives are:
   (a) Likert scale
   (b) Thurstone scale
   (c) Semantic differential scale
   (d) Ordinal scale

Answers

1. (b), 2. (b), 3. (c), 4. (a), 5. (c), 6. (b), 7. (a), 8. (d), 9. (d), 10. (c)

Q2 Answer the questions

1. Discuss the difference between ratio scale and interval scale.
2. Describe the statistical properties of four generic measurement scales.
3. 'When the attitude is measured in terms of ordinal numbers, that is, no distance or difference is assumed in the property of the numbers, the researcher might still plan to use the data for further analysis in quantitative terms by designing a scaling technique so the ordinal data are transformed to data an interval scale'. Describe an appropriate scale that conforms to this starement.

4. 'The measure suggested by Likert is basically a summated scale in which the scaling is done by a specially designed method'. Discuss the method.

Case assignment: In the comparison of four brands of foam, let us suppose a market analyst considers the attribute of comfort. The brands are known as Monafoam, Lightfoam, Coirfoam and Deluxfoam. The preference is tested on a sample in reference to the attribute comfort and the observed proportion matrix is stated below.

Observed proportion preferences

From	To Monafoam	Lightfoam	Coirfoam	Deluxfoam
Monofoam	-	75	80	60
Lightfoam	25	-	60	70
Coirfoam	20	40	-	40
Deluxfoam	40	30	60	-

The ordinal scale needs to be transformed to cardinal and needs to be interpreted.

CHAPTER 9

METHODS OF DATA COLLECTION

LEARNING OBJECTIVES

After going through this chapter you will understand

- The difference between census and sample
- Optimum sample size
- Methods of sampling
- Random sampling
- Systematic sampling
- Stratified random sampling
- Multi-stage sampling
- Sequential sampling
- Cluster sampling
- Convenience sampling
- Snowball sampling

Key words Population, precision, sample frame, random sampling, purposive sampling, sequential sampling, multi-stage sampling, snowball sampling

9.1 INTRODUCTION

In this chapter, some of the basic problems associated with the concept of sampling are discussed. A sample survey is usually taken to make inferences about an aggregate, which is known as the population. The method involves the logic of induction, to infer from the *part* about the *whole*. A sample survey is taken up more often due to the fact that it costs less compared to the cost involved in getting information from the whole, that is, through a process of complete enumeration. What we get from a sample survey is not expected to exactly match what one may get from a study of the whole set, that is, the entire population. There will exist errors in sample estimates which could have been eliminated, had there been a complete enumeration[1]. But this would involve an increase in the cost of the survey. Naturally, there exists a trade-off between efficiency (degree of accuracy) and the cost. The researcher has to apply the '*Principle of Optimisation*' that ensures the maximum level of efficiency at a given cost. Again, the researcher has to understand the '*Principle of Random Sampling*'—the sampling procedure that ensures the validity of statistical inferences based on the sampled observations. We shall consider these issues in this chapter. How the robustness of the estimates is tested is also an important issue; this will be discussed in a separate chapter.

9.2 SAMPLE VERSUS CENSUS

Census refers to complete enumeration for collecting the information on an attribute, by ascertaining the issue under study with respect to each unit of the whole set. The set is defined to be the *population*. Thus, population is a collection of objects comprising all members of the set. The people residing in the territorial jurisdiction of India constitute a set which can be denoted as the set of demographic population of India. The members of a cricket team, the workers organised under the banner of a particular trade union, the executives of multinationals, the packets of a particular brand of detergent produced in a day may describe a population in the statistical sense of the term. The idea is that the units must constitute the whole set of a group, thereby implying that the number of units outside the group is zero.

A sample, on the other hand, is a sub-set of the set that constitutes the population. If someone decides to test the quality 'gentleness on the hands' with respect to the packets of detergents produced in a particular day, one may select 10 detergent packets from the whole set (say, one thousand packets) and test these packets with respect to that attribute (gentleness). The set of 10 packets chosen for this experiment is a part, a sub-set, of the set of detergent packets. If the whole set is noted as the population the part will be denoted as the sample.

A sample is selected in order to make an inference about the characteristics of the population. This is an inductive process, that is, inference about the whole from the knowledge of a part of

1 Reporting error will exist even in the case of complete enumeration. This problem will also be taken up in this chapter.

the whole set of elements. The validity of such inference depends on the validity of the logic of induction. The whole process fails to generate a valid inference if the logic of induction fails. Even if the induction is considered to be valid, a sample cannot generate valid inference about the population unless the sample itself is representative. The heterogeneity involved in the population should be adequately represented in the sample. The statistician takes care of this problem by taking recourse to what is known as random sampling (see Sec. 9.5.1).

If one can make a valid inference about the population from the sample, why should one then go for a complete enumeration? For example, if a valid estimate can be made of the number of people residing within the territorial jurisdiction of India by making estimates on the basis of a sample, then why is a door-to-door survey necessary for ascertaining the number of people residing in India? The answer is that there exists error *due to* sampling. If someone estimates the population of India even on the basis of a statistically valid design of sampling, an error will exist in the estimated value (called the estimator). The root of the error is that we tried to infer about the whole from knowledge of a part.

Let us elaborate on this point. If we try to estimate the average height of 1000 school children by measuring the actual heights of 100 representative school children (taken randomly), the estimated mean height is likely to be different from what a complete enumeration would give. This difference is the error occurring due to the fact that we tried to infer the average height of 1000 school children from what was found by considering the heights of 100 children—the set of children who represented the whole set of 1000 children. *An error which is due to the fact that we tried to estimate the average height of a set of 1000 children from a sample of 100 children is called sampling error.* This error has arisen due to the very fact that we tried to estimate the heights of 1000 school children by taking a shortcut that reduces both cost and time.

But then, one may ask a pertinent question. Admittedly, when we take up a sample survey, we lose precision (accuracy), but at the same time we gain in terms of time and cost when we take up a sample survey. If this is so, why should we always not follow the method of sampling? Why should we not always *sacrifice* some of the precision and save both time and money by abandoning census study and always prefer a sample survey? The answer is that sometimes we require the actual value of the variate in the population. In estimating the height of 1000 school children from the information on 100 children, the issue that the researcher must settle is the extent of accuracy that can be sacrificed. If the opinion is that, precision (accuracy) can be sacrificed to some extent, we can possibly go for a sample survey. If precision is to be maintained at cent per cent level (which is called accuracy), then sample survey cannot be adopted.[2]

2 Maintaining cent per cent accuracy is again a theoretical proposition. No measure is error free; the spirit here is to maintain the maximum possible accuracy.

A researcher should also know that in some cases, the cost might be prohibitive and the results might be of no practical use if complete enumeration or census study is undertaken. Sample survey is the only option in such a situation. For example, consider the suitability of the method of complete enumeration when the issue is to ascertain the endurance of a set of electric bulbs. Such a problem is a practical problem often faced by the quality control department that issues certificates on the strength of electric bulbs produced by a company. A census study in such a situation would entail testing the endurance of each of the entire set of electric bulbs by burning them until the endurance is over, that is, until the bulbs go out of service. The findings of the tests of the experiment would of course be most reliable, but the cost would be prohibitive and the findings would be of no use for the company. The quality control department shall have to take up sample survey for ascertaining the endurance of electric bulbs produced by the company and settle for an estimated value of endurance which will not be accurate. One should also note that precision at cent per cent level may remain unachievable in some cases even though the exercise does not involve a destructive test, as in the above case. One may face a situation where complete enumeration is not feasible because the population is unknown. Statisticians would suggest a sample survey in such a situation. The estimated results here cannot be compared with actual values in the population and therefore the extent of deviation from accuracy cannot be ascertained under such a situation.

Thus, if accuracy is the target, one should note that the degree of accuracy of the sample results cannot always be measured because the population often remains unknown. But then, whenever one takes a sample survey, one must know how far the results of the sample survey are reliable. The term '*precision*' is used in sample based studies to serve this purpose. *Precision* refers to population, but the link is established through the laws of probability. The larger the sample size, the smaller is the standard error and therefore, the estimated value is more precise. In sample based studies, one can therefore always measure the *degree* of precision.

9.3 COST EFFECTIVENESS AND OPTIMUM SAMPLE SIZE

When the researcher decides to take up a sample survey, the first issue that he has to settle is regarding the size of the sample that he would draw from the population. In a sample survey, we need to study a section of the units that constitute the population. Thus the number of units to be surveyed is reduced in the sample survey. As the number of units to be surveyed is reduced, less time is required and logistics become less complex. As a result, the cost is reduced. But, as discussed earlier, accuracy will also be lost, there will be some error in the findings. In other words, there will be a loss in information/precision as the cost is reduced. Under the circumstance, what should be the optimal trade-off between the cost and error? In this discussion, it should be noted that sampling is not the only kind of error that we face in a sample survey. Errors arising at the ascertainment and data processing stages may also exist. Technically, these are termed as non-sampling errors. This type of error is common both in census and sample surveys because errors may be commited at the stages of collecting information as well as processing of data.

There are thus two types of errors—sampling and non-sampling. If the trade-off is between cost and error, one must know how the errors behave with change in the sample size.

The non-sampling error, that is, the error due to ascertainment and processing of data increases with the sample size assuming that the quality of logistics remains the same. With increase in the sample size, the work load increases. If the quality of the logistics declines as the sample size increases (some sort of an internal diseconomy) then one understands that the cost increases along with increase in the sample size and the error also goes on increasing. (There are methods for reducing non-sampling errors. This issue is discussed in Chapter 7.)

It should be noted that sampling error usually decreases with the increase in sampling size. Theoretically, it can be established that the degree of sampling error is inversely proportional to the square root of the sample size. The implication is that at the initial stage, with increase in the sample size, the reduction in sampling error is substantial, but after a certain stage it becomes marginal. If we go on increasing the sample size after this stage, the marginal cost increases substantially but the gain in terms of precision is rather poor.

The statistician or the researcher could take a clue from this theoretical description—non-sampling error is likely to increase with the sample size but sampling error is reduced with the increase in the sample size. The cost however, goes on increasing with the increase in the sample size. If we now assume that the non-sampling error maintains a constant proportion to the sample size and sampling error decreases with the increase in the sample size and the decrease is inversely proportional to the square root of the sample size, then with the increase in the sample size the error per unit (that is. loss of information per unit) would decline at the initial stage. This is so because the reduction in sampling error is higher at the initial stage than the increase in error due to factors related to non-sampling (the decrease in error due to sampling counter-balances the increase in error due to non-sampling at a higher rate). The cost increases but the error also decreases.

If the sampling error decreases at a slower rate than an increase in the sample size, which takes place at a later stage, then obviously a further increase in the sample size increases the cost but causes the total error to decline only marginally. In other words, the benefit due to increase in sample size is lower than the enhanced cost involved in taking the sample survey with the increase in sample size. Naturally the researcher would go on increasing the sample size, so long as the benefit (B) due to gain in terms of precision is higher than the increase in cost (C), that is, ($B > C$). The researcher will not opt for a sample for which the cost is greater than the benefit ($B < C$).

The optimum sample size is one for which the benefit equals the cost ($B = C$). The researcher should opt for a sample size which is optimum in the sense that, a further increase in the sample size does not contribute to achieving more precision in information, than what it implies in terms of an enhancement in the cost.

9.4 SAMPLING: THE BASIC FRAMEWORK

In order to draw a sample we must know what constitutes a sampling unit. Elementary units or a group of such units – besides being clearly defined are identifiable and observable – from which the representatives units can be chosen are called *sampling units*. For example, in a study on the consumption behaviour of the middle class households, a family is the sampling unit. In order to draw a sample, one must define clearly what we mean by a family, how we distinguish it and how one can observe the units for the purpose of sampling. The sampling units need not necessarily be non-overlapping. However, units should be specified so that each and every elementary unit in the population under study has a probability of being included in the sample. Needless to say, all the sampling units taken together constitute a population.

Another important concept associated with sampling is the concept of a *sample frame*. For using sampling methods, it is essential to have a frame of all the sampling units with proper identification particulars. This may be a list of units with their identification particulars or a map showing the boundaries of the sampling units. The frame must contain all the units of the population and it must exclude the units of other populations. One cannot draw a proper sample unless one has a proper sample frame.

A sample is a collection of sampling units. A sample will be random (probability sample) if its method of selection is governed by certain laws of chance. The sampling units selected in the sample which are termed sample units, are also known as sample observations. The sampling units selected in a sample constitute the *sample size* and a clear specification of all possible samples of a given type with their corresponding probabilities is said to constitute a *sample design*.

9.5 METHODS OF SAMPLING

There are two basic ways of selecting a sample—random and purposive. In this section we shall discuss the method of random sampling. The concept of random numbers – with the help of which random sampling is usually done – will also be discussed in this section.

Sampling theory, as we discussed earlier, is concerned with the ways of estimating and inferring the reliability of the information about the population that we can get from a sample. The basic point that one must remember is that a statistically valid estimate or a statistically valid inference on the reliability of the information cannot be obtained unless the sample is random. This is so because any exercise on statistical validity is based on the theory of probability and the theory of probability cannot be applied unless the observed units are random.

But what is randomness? The term randomness does not mean haphazardness. Randomness is associated with the concept of probability. The essence of random sampling is that each of the individuals included in the population has a given probability of being selected. Sampling on the basis of given probability of being selected is called probability sampling. Random sampling is probability sampling. If every unit in a population has equal probability of being included in a sample, the sample is known as a simple random sample. A sample of a given size is said to be random if every possible sample of this size in the population has a definite probability of being chosen when the population is finite.

A sample selected by a non-random method is termed as a *non-random sample.* A non-random sample, which is drawn using a certain amount of subjective judgement with a view to getting a representative sample, is called a *judgement sample* or a *purposive sample.*

The random and the non-random methods of sampling constitute two broad divisions in the sample. There could be further sub-divisions as described in Table 9.1.

Table 9.1 Alternative designs of sampling

Random sampling	Purposive sampling
Simple random sample, systemic sampling	Block or cluster sampling (area sampling)
Stratified random sampling	Quota sampling
Multi-stage sampling	Convenience sampling
Sequential sampling	Snowball sampling

9.5.1 Simple Random Sample

Simple random sampling refers to a situation in which each member of the population has equal probability of being included in the set of sampled units (sample set). In a population comprising N distinct units, if the researcher plans to draw a sample of n units by the simple random sampling method, the researcher must ensure that each member of N population set has equal probability (chance) of being included in the set of n units drawn from the population. In this particular case, the probability of each member of the population to get entry in the sampled units should be $1/N$. The process of random sampling consists in basing the selection on a chance event such as a draw of lots, throwing of dice and so on. The outcome of a particular draw is determined by the chance or probability assigned to the event. For example, we cannot predict that a particular face of a dice is going to appear in a particular throw. But the chance of a particular face of a dice as an outcome of a particular throw can be assured. Thus, the chance of a particular face appearing as the outcome of a throw is 1/6, because each one of the six faces of the dice is equally likely to occur as the outcome of a particular throw.

9.5.1.1 Simple Random Sampling with Replacement (SRSWR) and without Replacement (SRSWOR)

As already pointed out, in simple random sampling, each member of the population has an equal probability of being included in the set of sampled units. However, the sampling may take place under two different circumstances. From the population set, one may draw an unit randomly and return it to the population before the second draw is undertaken. This procedure is called *simple random sampling with replacement* (SRSWR). When the drawn unit is not returned to the population before the next draw, the sampling is called *simple random sampling without replacement* (SRSWOR). There are several differences between the two procedures. In SRSWR a population unit can be selected more than once; in SRSWOR, a population unit can be selected only once. What does it imply statistically? In SRSWR, since each unit is returned to population before the next draw, the size of the population always remains the same. In a population of size N, the probability of each unit being included in the sample is $1/N$ in each draw. In SRSWOR, on the other hand, since a particular unit selected in one draw is not returned to the population, the size of the population goes on decreasing in the subsequent draws and the probability of selection of the remaining units goes on increasing. Thus, if we have to select n units from a population of size N by SRSWOR, the probability of selection of each of the remaining units in the population is $1/N$ in the first draw, $1/(N - 1)$ in the second and ultimately $1/[N - (n - 1)]$ in the nth draw. Obviously, $1/N > 1/(N - 1) > 1/[N - (n - 1)]$.

In random sampling, each of n sample units is selected independently of another. This implies that probability of selection of any unit in any draw is not influenced by the selection made in any other draw. In SRSWR, this is fully honoured which is why the probability of being included in the sample always remains $1/N$ for each population unit. In SRSWOR, this condition of random sampling is honoured in a truncated way. Here the probability of selection of any unit is not influenced by the selection made in another draw, *provided it has not been selected in any of the earlier draws.* Practically, this means that what we got as the first one in the sampled units affects what we can get for the second one. Mathematically, this means that the covariance between the two isn't zero. Again, in SRSWOR when a population element can be selected only once in a sample, the standard deviation of the sample would be smaller than it is for sampling with replacement. However, note that for a small sample from a large population, sampling without replacement is approximately the same as sampling with replacement, since the odds of choosing the same individual twice is low. When a researcher plans to draw a sample of very small size from a fairly large population it does not matter whether the procedure is SRSWR or SRSWOR.

9.5.1.2 Random Number Table

A *random number table* is a list of numbers, composed of the digits 0, 1, 2, 3, 4, 5, 6, 7, 8 and 9. Numbers in the list are arranged so that each digit has no predictable relationship to the digits that precede it or to the digits that follow it. In other words, the digits are arranged randomly. This is why the numbers in a random number table are called *random numbers.* How do we ascertain which particular unit of the population should enter into the set of sampled units? For this, we need to consult the random number table. Random selection is most conveniently done with the help of the *table of random numbers.* If we have a set of 990 units constituting the population (such as the dealers of a particular consumer durable or the households in a particular locality selected for field survey), the selection of a sample of 10 units can be done by consulting the random number table. How this is actually done will be discussed presently. Before this, we should learn how the random number table is generated. Coming back to the issue of throwing a dice, as we have already observed, the throw of a dice gives one of 6 possible results which are equally likely. If we consider trials of two throws, we understand that this can give $6 \times 6 = 6^2 = 36$ different results which are equally likely. Similarly, a trial of 4 throws will give $6^4 = 1296$ equally likely different results. The results might be recorded as numbers (for example, a result noting the outcome 4, 3, 2, 1 as the faces of the dice has a serial number in the possible set of outcomes in the experiment of four successive trials with a dice). Each outcome thus gets a number (the possible combinations are transformed into numbers). We have thus a set of 1296 numbers *which are equally likely to occur*. Now consider the problem of drawing a sample of 10 units out of the set of 990 units that constitute your population. These 990 units can be assigned to 990 out of 1296 numbers (ordering is not important). These are then random numbers out of which the draw of 10 units is being done. This draw gives a sample which is random in nature. The concept here is one of assigning numbers to 990 units and then drawing 10 units out of the lot of 990 units, after mixing the number plates properly. In practice, this can be done by taking the help of random number tables where the generated set of random numbers is provided.

Consulting a random number table follows a particular rule. The tables usually consist of 1 2, 3 or 4 digit numbers randomly drawn and tested for their randomness. To use these tables one must know which column (digit) he is to use. If the total number in a population does not exceed three digits, we will need to consult the 3-digit or higher order random number table. Again, one may start anywhere in the table and move up, down or diagonally and choose the population units as they occur. One point to note is, the starting point may be arbitrarily chosen, the direction of the movement may also be arbitrarily fixed; but once the direction is set one shall have to follow this direction till all the units are selected. Thus if we want to draw a sample of 10 units out of 990 units, we would consult at least a 3-digit random number table and draw the units starting from anywhere and moving upwards, downwards or diagonally *until* we get 10 such numbers.

Let us explain the procedure. The above mentioned 990 units are numbered from 1 to 990. In this case, we need to use at least a three digit random number table. (A two digit random number table will exclude all the units after 99). In order to draw a sample of 10 units out of this population of 990 units, we may start from anywhere. Suppose we consider column 1 row 8 as the starting point and move downwards, the 10 units to be chosen will be the numbers 058, 452, 757, 149, 639, 648, 573, 879, 676, 235.. We could also start from the top of column 1 and move downwards, in the same column or move diagonally south or north for the numbers. The random number tables are given in Appendices 1, 2 and 3.

9.5.2 Systematic Sampling

In simple random sampling, each possible sample with *n* sampling units has a known and equal probability of being the sample actually selected. This is not so in case of systematic sampling. The permissible samples of size *n* (from a population say, *N*) have a known and equal probability of being selected, the researcher exercises the option of omitting a given number of units systematically until the quota is fulfilled. In other words, we assign a probability of 0 to the candidates who are being omitted. The researcher has a list of elements in the universe of populations from which a probability sample is to be selected. Suppose, in one case the total number of doctors is 600 and the researcher wants to select 60 doctors (as a sample) for canvassing a questionnaire. The chosen procedure is to follow a random number table but in this case the researcher has decided to select the units with a sampling interval of 10. Technically, the procedure is not simple random sampling. Since some units have been dropped systematically, the procedure followed in this case will be termed as *systematic sampling*. The systematic sample may contain the possibility of maintaining circularity, in which case the procedure will be noted as *circular systematic sampling*.

To explain the procedure of systematic sampling, we come back to the problem of selecting 60 doctors out of a panel of 600 doctors. We start from anywhere in the three digit random number table. We move downwards, in the same column or move diagonally south or north till we get a number in the range 1 to 600. This number is the starting point in systematic sampling. Suppose the selected random number is 019.We then calculate the gap which is 600/60 = 10. The next sampled unit will be the 29th unit in the list of 600 doctors that we are working with. The subsequent units will be the 39th, 49th and so on. If the quota of *n* units is not fulfilled even when we reach the end of the list, we select some other point as the next starting point, again by consulting the random number table and follow the same procedure as outlined above until the required number of sample units is obtained. The procedure belongs to the generic group of random sampling because the initial point in the selection process is chosen randomly.

A systematic sample is often drawn without consulting the random number table *per se*. It is assumed that the arrangement of the sample units is random in itself to the characteristics being studied. (Usually the researcher orders the units alphabetically or considering certain characteristics which are not correlated to the issue under study.) The sampling interval is then calculated. In case of selecting 60 doctors out of 600 it is 10 (N/n). For selecting the sample units, one may start with any random number between 1 to 10 (that is, the number given by N/n; if the number involves a fraction, take the nearest whole number). Suppose in this case, the random number is 6, the sample set will consider all the units starting from 6 with an interval of 10 (given by N/n when population is N and the sample size is n). In this case the sample set will be 6, 16, 26 and so on. For this particular example of doctors, we thus have a choice of 10 different possible sample sets.

When the random number table is not consulted, the possible sample set written in each card could then be mixed; thus each set of the samples has a chance of 1 out of 10, of being included as a sample. The universe of 600 doctors is rearranged as 10 clusters of 60 doctors each. A single random number determines all the 60 sampling units to be considered.

The advantages of systematic sampling are:

(a) It is a simple technique, it only has to be a random number in between the interval and then every n^{th} item thereafter will form part of the sample. The nth item will be the interval.
(b) The sample mean of a systematic sample is an unbiased estimate of the universe mean. In the example given above we find that each of the 10 sampling sets have an equal chance of being chosen and hence the repeated trial is expected to give a result that would approximate the mean of the population (average of the sample mean is equal to the universe mean).
(c) It is usually found that in a set of data collected from a field survey without following the method of random sampling, adjacent units in the universe are similar whereas the units that are dissimilar are set apart. This will obviously mean that the stratification is necessary. A systematic sampling can meet the need of stratification when the researcher is not sure what the yardstick for stratification should be.

One major disadvantage of this type of sampling is that it does not strictly adhere to the method of random sampling because the random numbers are chosen at a given interval, the selection of the interval being purposive. However, the method is widely used because stratification of the population is not done a priori, particularly in market research.

9.5.3 Stratified Random Sampling

The technique of the probability method of sampling involves the following stages:

(a) The universe that needs to be sampled is divided into sub-universes which are mutually exclusive and include all items of the universe.
(b) The strata parameters help the universe to be broken up into sub-universes/strata.
(c) The weight of each stratum is decided by the relative number of units of the parent population included in each stratum. The weight is depicted in terms of ratio or percentage.
(d) The proposed (supposed) sample size to be taken from the entire universe is then allotted to each stratum on the basis of the ratio or percentage applicable to it.
(e) The researcher has to draw the sample units randomly within each stratum.

Dividing the universe into sub-universes or strata is based on one or more characteristics of the parent population, such as size of the family, family income, units bought by the family or size of the business.

Let us explain the procedure with the help of an example. Let us suppose we want to study the attitude of individuals towards 'small savings'. A sample of 1000 income earners has to be surveyed. The researcher has the starting premise that the income earners are not homogeneous with regard to their attitude towards small savings; the basis of the premise is the common wisdom that the people in the low income group is more risk averse and therefore they have a positive attitude towards small savings. The parent population which consists of 1,00,000 income earners in a city where a wide variation in income exists should be stratified. The parameter that has to be taken for this stratification should be the level of income that a person earns. The universe based on such a stratification could be as shown in Table 9.2 .

Table 9.2 Relative weights of the strata

Annual income (Rs)	Number of individuals in the population	Relative weights
60,000–1,20,000	30,000	0.30
1,20,000–1,80,000	25,000	0.25
1,80,000–2,60,000	25,000	0.25
2,60,000 onwards	20,000	0.20
Total	1,00,000	1.00

We find that there are four strata from which the sample of 1000 income earners has to be selected. Under stratified random sampling, this sample of 1000 units would be drawn from the four strata. The number of units that is to be selected from each stratum will be decided by the relative weight of the stratum in the population. For the present case, the distribution of weights would be according to the values assigned at the third column of Table 9.2. The number of sample units to be drawn from each stratum is given below (Table 9.3). Thus, for stratum 1, the number of sample units to be drawn is $30{,}000/1{,}00{,}000 \times 1000 = 300$. Allocation of units for the other strata can be done accordingly. The selection of sample units would however be done by consulting the random number table.

Though we have constructed Table 9.3 based on a proportional stratum to the universe, at times it is true that instead of proportionate stratified sampling one can move to disproportionate stratified sampling. In disproportionate stratified sampling, as the name suggests, the size of the sampling units against the stratum is not proportionate to the proportion of the stratum in the universe.

Table 9.3 Allocation of sample units

Stratum	Income group (Rs)	Relative weight (in percentage)	Number of sample units assigned
1	60,000–1,20,000	30	300
2	1,20,000–1,80,000	25	250
3	1,80,000–2,60,000	25	250
4	2,60,000 onwards	20	200
Total		100	1000

A disproportionate stratified sampling is required when we find that the variability among observations within the stratum is high. Under the stated circumstance it becomes imperative that the stratum having higher variability among observations will have more sampling units that proportionate sampling warrants.

Stratified random sampling over simple sampling depends more on how different the statistic (in most cases, the mean) is among the strata. In case the variance is high and within a stratum it is low, stratified random sampling is more important. We can state that in the event of within stratum homogeneity and the among strata heterogeneity, the more suitable method will be stratified random sampling.

9.5.4 Multistage Sampling

Multistage sampling is done in stages, with the ultimate units of selection in mind. The sampling is carried out in various stages – initial, intermediate and final – from where the ultimate units are selected for sample survey. The selection is random at each stage.

Suppose we plan to conduct a sample survey on the expenditure pattern of Indian households, the ultimate sample units are the households. A researcher, in order to get the best representation from India as a whole, would start from the states and select the districts according to certain criteria (such as the distribution of state population over districts). After a proper selection of districts, one will select blocks, towns and villages from where the ultimate units, that is, the households would be selected. Multistage sampling is random sampling because at every stage the procedure of random selection is honoured. The random sample may however be stratified or simple. The size of the sample at each stage will have to be decided by the researcher.

9.5.5 Sequential Sampling

Sequential sampling is widely used in statistical quality control. It requires testing a relatively small sample on the basis of which some decision is made. However, it may so happen that one is not able to arrive at a definite decision on the basis of the results of the first sample. Then, more units are randomly chosen and added to the existing sample until a decision is made on the basis of the enlargement of the sample. Now-a-days, market survey organisations often take up such a procedure in order to arrive at a conclusion with respect to some issues under study. The sample is enlarged and a new survey is taken up with the consequence of higher costs if the concerned issue is considered to be crucial.

9.5.6 Block or Cluster Sampling (Area Sampling)

In probability sampling, the sampling units are independently chosen from the universe. This choice of sampling units sometimes may not be practically feasible, the reason being that the units are physically dispersed. To avoid this problem, one could have selected the units from certain clusters which represent the universe. The universe is first divided into a finite number of clusters. Each cluster should have the same properties that the universe has. The researcher would then select a cluster randomly (sometimes more than one cluster is selected), the sample is drawn from the cluster(s) and not from the universe as a whole.

An example of cluster sampling will bring out its differences from simple random sampling. Let us consider a universe of 20 items arranged arbitrarily into 4 groups (Table 9.4). The researcher knows that each group has the same characteristics as the whole set. One may select one or two clusters and draw the required number of sample units from these clusters and avoid involving the other clusters in drawing the sample. The clusters must be selected randomly.

Table 9.4 Design of clusters

Groups	Elements
1	$X_{11}\ X_{12}\ X_{13}\ X_{14}\ldots\ X_{1n}$
2	$X_{21}\ X_{22}\ X_{23}\ X_{24}\ldots\ X_{2n}$
3	$X_{31}\ X_{32}\ X_{33}\ X_{34}\ldots\ X_{3n}$
4	$X_{41}\ X_{42}\ X_{43}\ X_{44}\ldots\ X_{4n}$

9.5.7 Quota Sampling

The most commonly used technique in market research is *quota sampling*. Basically, quota sampling is stratified non-random sampling. The researcher first defines some strata from which the sample units are to be selected. The actual selection of the sample units does not follow the rules of random sampling. Any member of the stratum can be selected. The target of the field staff would be to meet the required number of units that constitute the quota assigned to the said stratum.

From the operational point of view, quota sampling needs a proper stratification procedure. The researcher defines certain characteristics of the sample and the units are so chosen that these characteristics are honoured in every sample unit. One would realise that this is what a representative sample implies. But under quota sampling, the researcher does not have a complete listing of the members of the universe, which is the starting point of random sampling method for finding the representative sample. Under quota sampling, the researcher has an idea about the population but the complete listing of the members of the population is not available.

Even if the complete listing is available, under quota sampling, the researcher is not bothered with maintaining the representative-nature of the sample by observing the procedure of random sampling. The reason could be that the researcher wants to reduce costs by not waiting for the specific unit that has been selected after consulting the random number table.

The population is sometimes taken care of for fixing the quota of a stratum. Let us suppose the researcher wants to canvas a questionnaire among the residents of a particular area. The research issue is the perception of the residents regarding a shopping mall that has been commissioned recently in the said locality. The crucial factor here is the age and gender of the respondent. Suppose the size of the sample is hundred units, in order to get a better insight into the perception of the people on the incoming shopping mall, the researcher defines strata according to the age and sex composition of the population there. The researcher might opt for complete listing of the population by age and gender and fix the quota for the stratum according to its weight in the population.

1. Selection of the *control characteristics* which are important as parameters of the universe. This means stratification of the universe based on the control characteristics which could be one or more. The resultant classification or stratification that is known as the basis of stratification is referred to as '*controls*'. The basis of stratification is:
   (a) They are supposed to have a correlation with the universe's characteristics that need to be studied.
   (b) Information regarding the existence of the 'control variable' is available with the researcher. Supposing we study the sales of packaged rice, the two control variables are family size and type of store. The table that we form is shown below (Table 9.5).

Table 9.5 Proportion of stratum

Family size	Type of store		
	Retail	**Departmental stores**	**Total**
Less than 5	32%	21%	53%
More than 5	23%	24%	47%
Total	55%	45%	100%

2. Allocation of the sample with reference to the strata. It is necessary to put the percentage against each cell/stratum so that the total sample of 300 (suppose) could be proportionally or non-proportionally shown (Table 9.6).

Table 9.6 Sample size according to proportion of stratum

Description of the customer	Percentage	Number of samples
Less than 5 in family size buying from retail	32%	96
Less than 5 in family size buying from departmental stores	21%	63
More than 5 in family size buying from retail	23%	69
More than 5 in family size buying from departmental stores	24%	72
Total	100%	300

3. The third stage is to allocate the said quota against the cell to researchers, who according to their convenience select the sample units. There is a lot of similarity between stratified random sampling and quota sampling. Till the formation of strata, there is no difference between them. But, after strata formation, the difference is that the units are chosen randomly in stratified random sampling whereas in the case of quota sampling, convenience, choice and time stand in the way of using random numbers to choose the units from a cell or strata.

There are two ways of implementing quota sampling. Suppose the list in the stratum is available, the researcher uses the random number table and is able to locate only 50% of the quota as selection of random numbers has indicated. This could be because the rest of the respondents were not available, the researcher meets those whom he finds convenient to elicit his information, thus the survey has used a quota method of sampling which has become non-probabilistic sampling. In other cases the researcher ab initio goes for convenience in choosing the sampling units.

Quota sampling is a much accepted method but while calculating the mean, one will find that the stratified random sampling is safer as the error will be less. In case the cells are too apart, the mean variance will be high. Quota sampling has a major drawback since at times, it may be difficult to identify the control variable as the expected relationship or correlation between the control and the characteristics to be studied may not be explicit.

9.5.8 Convenience Sampling

The term '*convenience sampling*' refers to a less costly method that is adopted while choosing the sampling units. The researcher chooses the sampling units on the basis of 'convenience' or 'accessibility'. Convenience sampling becomes a must for some market researchers when '*snap studies*' are to be undertaken.

A snap study is often done for framing some working hypotheses with respect to a market research of a bigger scale, particularly when the product is a new one and no a priori knowledge about the behaviour of the consumers exists. Under such a scenario, one may opt for visiting some retail and departmental stores that are accessible and meet a set of consumers chosen according to convenience and develop the perspective for framing the hypotheses for the bigger survey. The study which forms the basis for the working hypotheses is called a snap study.

Of course, even for a regular research, convenience sampling (that is, selecting respondents according to convenience) is often carried out in order to save time and money. In market research, '*intercept interviews*' are often organised at central shopping centres. Essentially, the sampled units here are drawn according to convenience. Intercept interviews may sometimes be based on random sampling. In that case, the researcher shall have to meet every entrant in the shopping centre, without exception, in a given time span. Since the arrival is random, the population should follow a Poisson distribution which ultimately tends to a normal distribution. Usually various surveys, not necessarily those only in market research, follow the method of convenience sampling in order to save time and cost.

It is true that in convenience sampling, sampling bias will be present and sampling error will be on the higher side in comparison to any other probability sampling techniques. Sometimes a trade-off between accuracy and validity on one side and easy accessibility of sampling units and the cost involved in probability sampling on the other, works as a very important consideration. Convenience sampling is opted for when the trade-off favours a non probabilistic sampling.

9.5.9 Snowball Sampling

Snowball sampling is a method in which there is a reference point from which the survey begins. The successive respondents are not drawn from a given list of members in the population. In fact such a list is not available when snowball sampling is undertaken. Additional sample units would be obtained by taking references or information from the initial respondent(s). The major purpose of snowball sampling is to select such units that maintain the determinant characteristics of the population which are rare. Let us suppose among users of automatic washing machines, one may need to interview those units that prefer hot washing of clothes. The initial respondent will act as referral (the salesmen as referrals, the service personnel as referrals). Ultimately it turns out a sample consisting of referrals from referrals thereby justifying the term *snowballing*.

The sampling of rare characteristics is often achieved through a technique known as '*screening interviews*'. A market researcher may use the telephone directory and select numbers randomly without prior knowledge of whether the required attributes of the population are satisfied by the telephone holders. However, by calling these sampled units and ascertaining whether each such unit on its own possesses the characteristics or could refer some other respondent who could be helpful in answering to the queries allows one to find the required sample.

The major disadvantage is that it may overshoot the budget of field survey as time and larger sample (that is, large sample disproportionately high in the population) may need to be considered. The vibrant advantage of this sampling technique is that it substantially increases the probability of finding the desired characteristics in the population with lower mean sample variance.

SUMMARY

- A sample survey is usually undertaken to make inferences about an aggregate, which is known as the population.
- The method involves the logic of induction, to infer from the *part* about the *whole*.
- A sample is a collection of *sampling units* (sample observations). Sampling units in a sample constitute the *sample size*; a clear specification of all possible samples of a given type with their corresponding probabilities is called a *sample design*.
- Units in a sample can be drawn randomly or purposively. Random sampling is probability sampling in which each unit (*random sample*) has an equal probability of being included in the sample. A *purposive*, *judgement* or *non-random sample* is one that is drawn using a certain amount of subjective judgement with a view to getting a representative sample.

ASSIGNMENTS

Q1 Choose the right answers

1. A pen factory produces 300 pens per day, all pens have been observed so:
   (a) It is a sample of the day
   (b) It is a population of the day
   (c) It is partially a sample and partially a census
   (d) None of the above
2. In the case of a census, which of the following is true:
   (a) No error occurs
   (b) Non-sampling error and sampling error are both less
   (c) Sampling errors are less and non-sampling errors are more
   (d) None of the above

3. There are two methods of sampling:
   (a) Random and convenience
   (b) Random and purposive
   (c) Random and quota
   (d) None of the above
4. Quota sampling could initially be:
   (a) Convenience sampling
   (b) Stratified non-random sampling
   (c) Snowball sampling
   (d) None of the above
5. 'Cost effectiveness' in sampling means:
   (a) Cost should be the lowest
   (b) Where benefits equal the cost
   (c) Benefits are maximised
   (d) None of the above
6. 'Convenience sampling' is
   (a) Random in nature
   (b) Non-probablistic sampling
   (c) Systematic sampling
   (d) None of the above
7. Snowballing sampling is
   (a) Multistage sampling
   (b) Convenience sampling
   (c) A variation of cluster sampling
   (d) None of the above
8. The use of 'weights' in stratification is characteristic of:
   (a) Systematic sampling
   (b) Multistage sampling
   (c) Random stratified sampling
   (d) None of the above
9. The concept of a fixed number to be sampled in each category is:
   (a) A concept of quota
   (b) A concept of snowballing
   (c) A concept of multistage sampling
   (d) None of the above
10. In sequential sampling we mean:
   (a) The possibility of the sample size getting enlarged
   (b) The sample size remains constant

(c) The purposive sampling rule operates
(d) None of the above

Answers

1. (b), 2. (d), 3. (b), 4. (b), 5. (b), 6. (b), 7. (d), 8. (c), 9. (a), 10. (a)

Q2 Answer the questions

1. A survey needs to be conducted among the people to find out the attitudes of AIDS victims on sexual psychology. What is the method of sampling you will recommend and why?
2. The difference in earnings of different income categories is responsible for different buying and usage habits of washing powder. You have been asked to conduct a survey and choose a sample. What kind of sampling will you avail? Reason out your answer.

CHAPTER 10

TOOLS OF PROCESSING AND ANALYSIS OF DATA

LEARNING OBJECTIVES

After going through this chapter you will understand

- Quantitative and qualitative data
- Interpolation of data
- Measure of central tendency
- Measure of dispersion
- Coefficient of correlation
- Regression analysis
- Time series analysis
- Econometric modelling
- Analysis of variance (ANOVA)

Key words Quantitative data, qualitative data, population, interpolation, mean, median, mode, standard deviation, coefficient of variation, coefficient of correlation, econometrics, analysis of variance

10.1 INTRODUCTION

Scales are necessary for measuring information available in the form of data. With a given scale, one gets the data either in quantitative or qualitative form. Condensed information in the form of data has to be analysed to reveal the truth which is hidden in the data. The science of statistics has developed certain basic tools in order to unfold what is hidden in the data. In this chapter, we shall discuss these tools in brief. For supplementary reading, the reader is advised to consult any standard textbook on elementary statistics. There is a vast amount of literature on statistical tools. This discussion on statistical tools is intended to provide the reader with the bare outline of the tools and the techniques, and of using the tools for empirical analysis.

The science of statistics considers data with reference to either the population or the sample. Population refers to the universe and the data set is generated by the method of complete enumeration. A sample, on the other hand, refers to a part of the population. If a part of the population is representative in nature, the truth contained in a data set could be generalised.

With respect to both complete enumeration and a sample based study, the truth contained in the data set is captured in terms of a summary. The tools that we refer to have been developed in order to summarise the information available in the form of data.

10.2 QUANTITATIVE AND QUALITATIVE DATA

The science of statistics deals with numerical observations which are known as data. It is sometimes true that the data we collect sometimes comes in the form of quantitative data and sometimes in the form of qualitative data. In the case of qualitative data, the individuals comprising the set are distinguished by the quality or attribute. In case of quantitative data the individuals are distinguished by a measurement of count.

For example, the executives of a company are distinguished among themselves by the ranks that they hold in a company—CEO (Chief Executive Officer), Vice President, General Manager, Area Manager and so on. Placing them in a proper order we get a description which is qualitative in character. The colours of flowers, gender of a person, academic qualifications of a scholar, are some examples of qualitative variables.

The qualitative characters as we have pointed out distinguish the individuals by their attributes. The height of an individual or the turnover of a company are quantitative measures. In quantitative characters, the variation may be continuous or discrete; in qualitative characters, the continuity of a variable can never be conceived—it is always discrete but the discrete numbers will not follow a regular distance as conceived in the ratio scale or the interval scale unless we assign such regularity in order to apply the tools of quantitative techniques to this data (see Chapter 8).

An attribute whose value varies from one individual to another is called a *variable* in mathematical analysis. A variable with an assigned probability is called a *variate* in statistical analysis. While discussing the tools for statistical analysis, one will often find the use of such an expression with respect to the data.

The set of individual values in the entire set or universe is called a *population.* In statistics we often describe a population of working women or a population of sales personnel or even a population of playing cards. The connotation of population is a set of individuals—animate or inanimate. If the researcher selects a part of the population out of the entire set of individual values for his study, the selected set of individual values would be called a *sample.* The individual values that we get either in the form of a population or in the form of a sample are often called the *raw data* in the parlance of statistical analysis. The raw data is the basis of statistical analysis. In order to maintain the quality of statistical analysis, it is imperative for a researcher to carry out a proper scrutiny of the data before storing it for further analysis.

The researcher often stores the data in a computer file for which he must know whether the data is in a qualitative or quantitative form. The qualitative data are stored in a computer in the form of characters and the quantitative data are stored in the form of numerics. The researcher should also know whether there is any outlier in the data set (see 7.2.4 of Chapter 7). All these are constituent elements of the data cleaning process.

After cleaning the data, the researcher might observe that there are missing points in the data set which is why further study on the nature of the variables cannot be done. Instead of rejecting the data set lock, stock and barrel, the researcher might find it prudent to insert some data points based on the mathematical behaviour of the data set. This method is called the method of interpolation. Statistical literature available on this subject is quite rich. We shall develop an outline of this literature in the next section.

10.3 INTERPOLATION OF DATA

Interpolation is the technique of finding the missing value in a set of data. Because of several reasons which are not under the control of the researcher, it so happens that some of the data points are missing. Sometimes the researcher suspects reporting error concerning some particular quantitive information, and in order to rectify the error he may find it necessary to replace the reported information with more reliable data. This can be done by generating a value based on the general trend or pattern of the data. This is done with the help of the tool of interpolation. The technique, which we will discuss now, may also be used for extrapolating the data.

10.3.1 Methods of Interpolation

1. *Method of Linear Approximation*: The most widely used technique for identifying a missing number between two given numbers is to follow the method of linear approximation. In this method, it is assumed that there is no sudden jump in the series

and the missing number belongs to a point that can be approximated by drawing a straight line by involving two known points between which the missing point is located. The underlying assumption is that the rate of growth or decay between two known points remains unchanged at the missing point. Obviously such a method of interpolation ignores the impact of other given values of the variate while interpolating the missing number.

Example 10.1

x	2	3	5
y	5	?	8

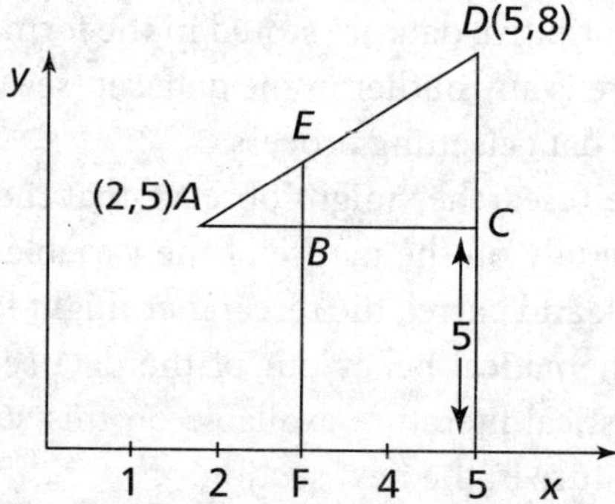

Fig. 10.1 Interpolation by linear approximation

To get the missing number we apply the following relation.

$$\frac{DC}{AC} = \frac{BE}{BA}$$

or
$$\frac{8-5}{5-2} = \frac{BE}{3-2}$$

or,
$$BE = 1$$

Hence, for the missing point $EF = BF + BE = 5 + 1 = 6$

The method is quite handy. However, this can be applied if we have two related series, x and y and it is known that $y = f(x)$. The researcher is advised not to follow this technique unless there is a compulsion because the impact of the other numbers in the series is ignored.

2. *Binomial Approximation*: A suggested alternative is to generate the missing number by following the binomial expression $(y-1)^n = 0$, with y containing the missing number. The expression covers all the data points and fixes the missing number by expanding the series.

Expanding, $(y - 1)^n = 0$

or $$^nC_o(-1)^0 y^n + {}^nC_1(-1)^1 y^{n-1} + {}^nC_2(-1)^2 y^{n-2} + \ldots\ldots + {}^nC_n(-1)^n y^0 = 0$$

The series can be utilised for finding the missing number in the following way. We first ascertain the number of terms (that is, the number of data points, including the missing number) and thus ascertain the the number of terms (value of n). Applying the above formula we find the value of the missing term by equating the sum of all the terms in the series with 0. This may be explained with the help of the following example.

y	180	145	?	131	163	160

There are six terms in the series. The value of n is therefore 6 (from $n = 0$ to $n = 5$). Expanding $(y - 1)^5 = 0$, we get

$$y^5 - 5y^4 + 10y^3 - 10y^2 + 5y^1 - y^0 = 0 \qquad (10.1)$$

In order to apply the formula we write

$$y^5 = y_5 = 160$$

$$y^4 = y_4 = 163$$

$$y^3 = y_3 = 131$$

$$y^2 = \text{missing term} = y_2$$

$$y^1 = y_1 = 145$$

$$y^0 = y_0 = 183$$

Putting these values in Eq. 10.1 we get

$$160 - 5(163) + 10(131) - 10y_2 + 5(145) - 183 = 0$$

Solving, we get $y_2 = \text{missing term} = 119.7$

As a ready reckoner, the following results can be used:

No. of terms	Equation for determining the unknown values
2 or Δ^2	$y_2 - 2y_1 + y_0 = 0$
3 or Δ^3	$y_3 - 3y_2 + 3y_1 - y_0 = 0$
4 or Δ^4	$y_4 - 4y_3 + 6y_2 - 4y_1 + y_0 = 0$
5 or Δ^5	$y_5 - 5y_4 + 10y_3 - 10y_2 + 5y_1 - y_0 = 0$
6 or Δ^6	$y_6 - 6y_5 + 15y_4 - 20y_3 + 15y_2 - 6y_1 + y_0 = 0$
7 or Δ^7	$y_7 - 7y_6 + 21y_5 - 35y_4 + 35y_3 - 21y_2 + 7y_1 - y_0 = 0$
8 or Δ^8	$y_8 - 8y_7 + 28y_6 - 56y_5 + 70y_4 - 56y_3 + 28y_2 - 8y_1 + y_0 = 0$
9 or Δ^9	$y_9 - 9y_8 + 36y_7 - 84y_6 + 126y_5 - 126y_4 + 84y_3 - 56y_2 + 9y_1 - y_0 = 0$

3. *Newton's Formula*: The problem of missing numbers often appears in a bivariate distribution. If all the values in the independent variable are known, a missing number in the data set depicting the values of the dependent variable can be estimated by applying a formula which is due to Newton, the celebrated mathematician and physicist. If x denotes the independent variable with y as the dependent variable, with the values of x given in a ratio scale, we can find the missing value of y by applying Newton's formula. This formula has two different forms. Depending on the position of the missing value we apply one of these formulae. Let us suppose the set of values in ascending or descending order ends at $x = x_n$. If the missing value is nearer to $x = x_0$ we apply *Newton's forward method of interpolation.* On the other hand, if the value is nearer to $x = x_n$ we apply *Newton's backward method of interpolation.* For a value of missing y which is located in the middle of the series, we may apply either of these formulae.

Newton's forward interpolation formula: It is used when the x against which y is being estimated is in between the values of x (which follows a constant interval, of say 5). Let the series be given as:

x	x_0	x_1	x_2	x_3	.	.	.	x_r	.	.	.	.	.	.	.	.	x_n
y	y_0	y_1	y_2	x_3	.	.	.	y_r^*	.	.	.	.	.	.	.	.	y_n

↓
Missing

In order to find the value of y_r^* which is assumed to be nearer to x_0, we apply the following interpolation formula.

$$y = y_0 + u\Delta y_0 + \frac{u(u-1)\Delta^2 y_0}{1\times 2} + \frac{u(u-1)(u-2)\Delta^3 y_0}{1\times 2\times 3}\ldots$$
$$+\frac{u(u-1)(u-2)\ldots(u-n+1)\Delta^n y_0}{1\times 2\times 3\times\ldots\times n}$$

where $u = \dfrac{x - x_0}{h}$, $h =$ the interval or the difference in values of x

Example 10.2

We take a series in which x values maintain a constant difference of 5. This is being considered for the sake of simplicity. The following is the set of given values.

x	=	20	25	30	35	40
y	=	30.5	40.5	45	55	58

We consider the problem of finding the value of y corresponding to the given value of $x = 24$. Applying the formula as given above we generate the following table.

Table 10.1 Difference table

x	y	Δy	Δ²y	Δ³y	Δ⁴y
20	30.5				
		10			
25	40.5		−5.45		
		4.55		0	
30	45		5.45		12.45
		10		−12.45	
35	55		−7		
		3			
40	58				

Here $u = \dfrac{24-20}{5} = 0.8$

$$y = 30.5 + 0.8(10) + \frac{(0.8)(0.8-1)(-5.45)}{2} + (0.8)(0.8-1)(0.8-2)(0)$$
$$+ (0.8)(0.8-1)(0.8-3)$$
$$= 30.5 + 0.8 + 0.436 - 0.219 = 38.717$$

The value of the missing y is derived as 38.717.

The formula can be used for finding any missing value with the set of data that the researcher is handling when we have a set of two variables.

Newton's backward interpolation formula: For a value of missing y which is nearer to x^n we apply the following formula.

$$y = y_n + \Delta y_{n\cdot 1} v + \frac{v(v+1)}{1\times 2}\Delta^2 y_{n-2} + \frac{v(v+1)(v+2)}{1\times 2\times 3}\Delta^3 y_{n-3}$$
$$+ \frac{v(v+1)(v+2)\ldots(v+n-1)}{1\times 2\times 3\times\ldots X_n}\Delta^n y_0$$

When $v = \dfrac{x - x_n}{n}$

Example 10.3

From the following table, estimate y when $x = 0.35$

x	0	0.1	0.2	0.3	0.4
y	0.58	2.48	4.08	5.15	6.12

For simplicity we shall ignore the decimal points while computing the difference.

Table 10.2 Difference table

x	y	Δy	$\Delta^2 y$	$\Delta^3 y$	$\Delta^4 y$
0	0.58				
		190			
0.1	2.48		−30		
		160		−23	
0.2	4.08		−53		66
		107		+43	
0.3	5.15		−10		
		97			
0.4	6.12				

Here $v = (x - x_o)/h = (0.35 - 0.4)/0.1 = 0.5$ [as $h = (x_n - x_{n-1}) = 0.1$]

$$y = 612 + (-0.5)97 + \frac{(-0.5)(-0.5+1)}{2}(-10) + \frac{(-0.5)(-0.5+1)(-0.5+2)}{6}(43)$$

$$+ \frac{(-0.5)(-0.5+1)(-0.5+2)(-0.5+3)}{24}(66)$$

$$y = 612 - 48.5 + 1.25 - 2.69 - 2.58$$

$$y = 559.48$$

Adjusting decimal points we get $y = 5.5948$

10.4 TOOLS OF DATA ANALYSIS

The researcher first gets a description of the data in the form of a frequency distribution. A frequency distribution is often useful for sensing the spread of data and the regions of its concentration. Often the frequency distribution is further arranged in the form of a distribution according to class. Also, it is often helpful to get a graphical representation of the data. Graphical description that we use often comes in the form of a *frequency polygon* or a *histogram*. These are widely used to understand the nature of the data set on which further statistical exercises are to be carried out. Now-a-days, there are several statistical packages (including Microsoft Excel, SPSS) that the researcher can utilise for elementary operations to generate such curves to get the initial exposure (feel) of the data set.

Frequency distribution with its graphical representation may help the researcher in developing an initial understanding regarding the nature of distribution of the data. But we need concise numerical description of the basic features of the distribution for further analysis of the data. The first of such measures is the measure of *central tendency* that gives a representative value of the set of data. The departure from the central value is termed as skewness and the excess or deficiency of frequencies in the centre and the two extremes compared with the flanks is termed *kurtosis*. These are the other two numerical measures that we use to understand the distinctive features of the frequency distribution so that a set of data can be distinguished from the others. We shall not discuss the methods of forming a frequency distribution out of the raw data or the techniques of drawing a histogram or frequency polygon in this book. The reader is advised to consult any elementary book on statistics to learn these techniques.

The second numerical measure attempts to capture another basic feature of the distribution of the data set by considering the spread of the data around the central value (dispersion). However, we shall first discuss the tools for measuring the central tendency of the data set.

10.4.1 Measure of Central Tendency

There are three well known methods of measuring central tendency—*mean (arithmetic mean, geometric mean* and *harmonic mean), median* and *mode.* We discuss them very briefly in this section.

1. Arithmetic Mean

The most widely used measure of central tendency is the *arithmetic mean.* In fact, the statisticians often use the term *arithmetic mean* and *mean* interchangeably. The technique of finding arithmetic mean in a data set is rather simple. If data were grouped into various classes and the number of members in each class (frequency) is recorded, we get a distribution of the data set among various classes (frequency distribution of the variate, that is, the variable under study). For measuring the central tendency of this distribution by arithmetic mean (AM), we identify the mid-value of a class and assume that this value represents all the individual members of the class. The actual calculation of AM is rather easy. The mid-point of each category is multiplied by the number of observations (members) in that category. The general formula is:

$$\overline{X} = \frac{\sum_{i=1}^{n} f_i X_{mi}}{\sum_{i=1}^{n} f_i}$$

$\overline{X}$ = arithmetic mean

X_{mi} = midpoint of the ith class

f_i = frequency in the ith class

Σ = sum of the values, with n denoting the number of classes over which the frequencies are spread.

It is obvious that in case there is no frequency distribution, that is, the data set contains only individual values of the variate, the arithmetic mean is derived by summing the individual values over the entire set and dividing the sum by the number of individual values of the variate in the data set.

The important characteristics of the mean are:

(a) Its value is affected by the value of every observation; therefore a change in the value of any observation will change the value of the mean.

(b) If we have highly skewed distributions, the mean value gets influenced by the direction of the skew.

(c) The sum of the differences between the observed values and the mean is zero.
(d) The formula assumes that all the observations in any class are represented by the middle of the class interval.

We use the arithmetic mean when:

(a) the greatest reliability is required,
(b) the distribution is reasonably symmetrical, and
(c) subsequent statistical calculations are to be made.

2. Mode

The *mode* is the value that occurs most often in the distribution. In other words, the *modal value* of a distribution is the value of the variate that has the maximum frequency. We use the mode when:

(a) the quickest estimate of central tendency is required, and
(b) the most typical value is required.

In order to give a brief idea of the method of calculating mode, let us consider Table 10.5A, which shows the income range and the number of people in the range (in terms of frequency).

Table 10.3 Frequency distribution of income (in Rs)

Income	Frequency	Cumulative *f*
Under 20,000	200	300
20,001–40,000	240	540
40,001–60,000	400	940
60,001–80,000	500	1440
80,001–1,000,000	200	1640
1,00,001–1, 20,000	300	1940
1,20,001–1,40,000	260	2100
Over 1,40,000	400	2500

The following formula demonstrates how the mode may be approximated in mathematical terms for grouped data.

$$M_0 = L_{M_0} + \frac{d_1}{d_1 + d_2} x i$$

where, M_0 = mode

L_{M_0} = lower limit of the modal class

d_1 = difference between the frequency of the modal class and the frequency of the class immediately preceding the modal class

d_2 = difference between the frequency of the modal class and the frequency of the class immediately following the modal class

i = the difference between the lowest value and the highest value in the modal class

Here the modal class is (60001 – 80000) where we have the highest frequency.

Hence $$M_o = 60{,}001 + \frac{100}{100+300} \times 20{,}000 = ₹\,65{,}001$$

The mode is ₹ 65,001.

It is not necessarily true that the frequency distribution of a variate need necessarily have only one peak that might represent the mode. A distribution might be bi-modal or multi-modal. The reader would benefit by reading further on mode as a measure of central tendency.

3. Median

The *median* is the value which is located in the middle of the series when the observations are arranged in an ascending or descending order of magnitude. The idea is that it divides the series into two halves, half the number of observations lying above the median and half below it.

When there are an odd number of observations, the determination of the median is simple. For example, if we have 25 observations ranked in order of magnitude, the 13th observation will be the value of median. In the case of an even number of observations, we may take the average of the two central values. For example, if we have 50 observations then the median will be the value of the average of the 25th and 26th observations, the observations being arranged in the ascending or descending order of magnitude.

With respect to the grouped data, the formula for computing the median M_d is:

$$M_d = L_{M_d} + \frac{(N/2) - C.F}{f_{M_d}} \times i$$

where M_d = median

N = total number of frequencies in the distribution

L_{M_d} = lower limit of the median class

CF = Cumulative frequency of the class immediately below the class containing the median

f_{M_d} = frequency of the median class

i = the difference between the lowest value and the highest value in the median class.

The median of the distribution described in Table 10.3 is calculated below. We can proceed to locate the median class (that is the class in our example which contains the midpoint in the total sample 2500, that is, the 1250th and 1251st respondents).

$$= 60{,}001 + \frac{\frac{2500}{2} - 940}{500} \times 20{,}000$$

$$= 60{,}001 + 0.62\ (20{,}000)$$

$$= 60{,}000 + 12{,}400 = ₹\ 72{,}400$$

If the distribution is highly skewed then a median is a better choice than the mean or mode. When the class intervals are of unequal size, the median is a better measure of central tendency. Thus, the median is used when:

(a) distributions are badly skewed,
(b) the mid-position of the variate is required specifically to address a research issue, and
(c) the distribution is such that extreme values would affect the arithmetic mean disproportionately.

These three measures of central tendency would produce the same value when the distribution is bell shaped. This is so because the highest frequency would be at the peak of the distribution where the arithmetic mean is situated. The frequencies arranged in ascending or descending order will have the mid-value realised at the point where the peak of the distribution is located.

There are two other measures of central tendency—geometric mean and harmonic mean. The methods of calculating these are given below.

Geometric Mean: The geometric mean (GM) of two numbers is found by multiplying both of them and then taking a square root of the product. The GM of 8 and 2 can be calculated thus:

$$\sqrt{8 \times 2} = \sqrt{16} = 4$$

Similarly the GM of three numbers is found by multiplying them together and then calculating the cube root of the product. The GM of the three numbers 1, 3 and 9 is can be calculated thus:

$$\sqrt[3]{1 \times 3 \times 9} = \sqrt[3]{27} = 3$$

The GM of a number is found by multiplying them together and finding the nth root of the product. The form is represented below:

$$GM = \sqrt[n]{X_1 \times X_2 \times X_3 \times ...... \times X_n}$$

For computational advantage, we often utilise the logarithmic values of the original numbers. As we know,

$$\text{if} \quad GM = \sqrt{8 \times 2} = \sqrt{16}$$

$$\log GM = ½[\log 8 + \log 2]$$

$$= (\log 8 + \log 2)/2$$

Antilog of the value would be the GM, which is 4.

The computation can be expressed in symbols for a finite number of values as follows.

$$\log GM = \sum(\log X)/n$$

The antilog is computed; this gives the value of the required GM.

Harmonic Mean: The harmonic mean (x_h) of a variable x_i ($i = 1, 2, ..., n$), is defined as

$$x_h = \frac{n}{\sum_i \frac{1}{x_i}} \quad \text{or} \quad \frac{1}{x_h} = \frac{1}{n}\sum_i \frac{1}{x_i}$$

The second derivation shows that the reciprocal of the harmonic mean of a variable is the arithmetic mean of its reciprocal.

Sometimes the variable may be in the form of '*x* per unit of *m*', for example, rupees per kilogram, kilometers per hour and so on. In such cases, the harmonic mean would be the proper average if equal units of *x* were considered, while the arithmetic mean would be appropriate if equal units of *m* are considered. This may be illustrated with the following example.

Suppose an aircraft moves *n* equal distances, each of *m* units, say, with a speed of *l* miles per hour. The average speed is of course the total distance covered by the total time taken, thus, the average speed is:

$$\frac{nm}{\frac{m}{l_1} + \frac{m}{l_2} + \frac{m}{l_3} + ... + \frac{m}{l_n}} = \frac{n}{\frac{1}{l_1} + \frac{1}{l_2} + \frac{1}{l_3} + ... + \frac{1}{l_n}}$$

this will be the harmonic mean of the given speed.

If, now we consider that the aircraft moves for n equal time intervals, each of length t hours, with the above stated speeds, the average speed will be:

$$\frac{l_1 t + l_2 t + \ldots l_n t}{nt} = \frac{l_1 + l_2 + \cdots l_n}{n}$$

This will be the arithmetic mean of the given speed.

Effectively, we now have five measures of central tendency. The most widely used measure of central tendency is however, the arithmetic mean. This is so because it has certain mathematical properties that can help a statistician in developing theoretical distributions.

There are various dos and don'ts with measures of central tendency. For example, GM becomes useless as a measure of central tendency when there exists a 0 in the series. For further reading, the reader is advised to consult a standard textbook on descriptive statistics, if (s)he does not have exposure to this subject.

10.4.2 Measure of Dispersion

There is a second numerical measure that attempts to capture another basic feature of the distribution of the data. This measure tries to describe the spread of the data around the central value. Technically, this is called the dispersion of the data set.

Why do we measure the spread of the data? This is considered necessary in order to know how the individual observations differ from one another. The central tendency gives an idea about the central value or the typical value of the variate, but it does not tell us anything about the difference among various values of the data set. However, one cannot ignore the extent of difference among the individual values that describes the spread of the data set. This is so because, for the same value of a typical measure of central tendency, one might face a situation where the spread is different and therefore the statistical properties are also different. Consider the following three series:

Series	Data	Arithmetic mean
1	5,5,5,5,5	5
2	4,3,10,5,3	5
3	0,4,4,4,13	5

As one observes, the three series have the same arithmetic mean, namely 5. The difference among the individual values that constitute the series is not the same as examination of the individual series indicates. In statistical analysis of the data, it often matters how the individual values of the set behave which is why we try to comprehend it through a statistical measure. The statistical measure is the measure of dispersion.

There are three measures of dispersion. The most handy and quick to calculate is *range*. The range of a distribution is the difference between the largest and the smallest of observation. Some idea about the dispersion can be gathered from the measure of range, that is, the difference between the two extremes indicates something regarding the spread of the data.

Another measure of dispersion is *mean deviation*. It is calculated by considering the deviation of individual observations from a measure of central tendency. The sign of the deviation is ignored, that is, we take the modulus values. The value of the mean deviation is obtained by dividing the sum of the modulus values of the differences by the number of observations. Mean deviation is the least when it is taken from the median. One would therefore suggest that mean deviation should be taken from median.

The most widely used measure of dispersion is *standard deviation*. Statisticians usually recommend standard deviation as a measure of dispersion because it has some mathematical properties, which are very useful for statistical reasoning. This is why the statisticians usually utilise the tool of standard deviation or variance (which is the square of standard deviation) while examining the spread of the data.

The measure of standard deviation is defined as the 'root mean square deviation' taken from the mean. The idea is that we would first take the deviation of individual values from the mean and then we would take the squared values of these individual deviations in order to ignore the effect of negative values. The mean of these squared deviation values is defined as the variance of the data. The square root this value is defined as the standard deviation of a population represented as σ (σ^2 is the variance).

The measure of dispersion is expressed in the same units of measurement in which the observations themselves are measured. Symbolically the formula for standard deviation is given as:

$$\sigma = \sqrt{\frac{\sum_{i=1}^{n} (X_i - \bar{X})^2}{n}}$$

where, σ = standard deviation

X_i = values of the ith observation

$\bar{X}$ = mean of the observation

n = total number of observations

We use the standard deviation:

(a) because this measure associates itself with a logically sound procedure with the referral point—AM,

(b) it takes care of the extreme values by assigning proportionally higher weightage while measuring the dispersion of the data set, and

(c) it has wide mathematical properties that might be used for further statistical analysis of the data set.

EXAMPLE 10.4

Let us consider a situation where ten respondents have responded to a questionnaire with different scores. The researcher may be interested in the scoring pattern of the respondents. The data is presented in Table10.4.

Table10.4 Calculation of standard deviation of income of the respondents

Respondents	₹ (x)	$x - \overline{X}$	$(x - \overline{X})^2$
1	335	−5	25
2	330	−10	100
3	345	5	25
4	320	−20	400
5	325	−15	225
6	355	15	225
7	360	20	400
8	350	10	100
9	345	5	25
10	330	−5	25
	3400	0	1550

$$\overline{X} = \frac{\sum x}{n} \qquad \sigma = \sqrt{\frac{(x - \overline{X})^2}{n}}$$

$$= \frac{3400}{10} \qquad = \sqrt{\frac{1550}{10}}$$

$$= 340 \qquad = \text{Rs. } 12.44$$

The important characteristics of the standard deviation are:

(a) change in observed values affects the standard deviation,

(b) Skewness of the distribution will affect the standard deviation, and

(c) the standard deviation cannot be computed from open-ended distribution.

In the case of a sample, the symbol of standard deviation is usually denoted by *s*.

Coefficient of variation: Dispersion is an absolute measure expressed in the same unit in which the data are recorded. In order to compare the dispersion of two different distributions measured in different units, it is necessary that we make them unit free. This is done by introducing a new measure which is known as the coefficient of variation. Given the population mean $\overline{X}$, the coefficient of variation (*cv*) is defined as $\sigma/\overline{X}$. Often we use percentage as a measure of *cv*. The *cv* is then defined as $\sigma/\overline{X} \times 100$. In the example given in the Table 10.4, the *cv* is computed as follows.

$$cv = \frac{12.44}{340} \times 100 = 3.65$$

The coefficient of variation remains unaltered when we change the scale but it is affected by the change of origin which affects the mean.

10.4.3 Measurement of Simultaneous Variation

Variation in the values of one variable is measured by dispersion. Simultaneous variation in the values of two or more variables is a problem that we often confront. Dispersion is not the tool with which we can assess the extent of such a variation. In statistics, we have a separate set of tools to analyse the simultaneous variation in two or more variables. These are the tools of correlation and regression analysis.

When the variation in the value of one variable is associated with the variation in the value of another variable, one understands that a variable is related to another variable. When we do not consider which variable is the cause of change, and only observe the extent of association between two variables (variate), the tool that we use is *correlation between the two variables.* For example, when we consider the simultaneous variation in the values of height and weight of a set of individuals, we use the statistical tool of correlation between the height and weight of the individuals. Similarly we may measure the correlation between the price of a commodity and the business turnover with respect to the same commodity. When we measure this correlation, we do not consider whether a variation in price causes a variation in business turnover or whether the variation in business turnover causes a variation in price. What we try to assess is the *degree or extent of association* between price and business turnover.

The correlation could be positive or negative. If an increase in one variable is accompanied by an increase in the other, the variables are said to be positively correlated. If, on the other hand, an increase in one variable is accompanied by a decrease in the related variable, the variables are stated to be negatively correlated. If a change in one variable is not associated with a change in the other variable, the variables are said to be uncorrelated.

As stated earlier, while measuring correlation, we considered the simultaneous variation in the values of two variables without discussing the cause and effect relationship between the variables under consideration. Let us probe the issue further. If two variables change their values simultaneously, there must be a factor that causes this change. At the very outset, one should find out the possibility that the two variables under consideration might change their values as a result of change of a third variable that affects both the variables under consideration. While taking up a numerical exercise on a two variable *cause and effect* related relationship, one should understand first whether such a relation can at all exist between the variables under consideration. Theory would be the best guide in this regard. The relation captured by the numerical exercise in quantitative terms might be spurious, if there is no theory or no rationale to justify the relation.

Consider the other possibility, namely, the possibility that the cause of change is endogenous; among two variables under consideration, one is causing the change in the other. Business turnover changes because of the change in price. An iron bar expands (captured by length in millimetre) because of an increase in temperature (captured by centigrade).These are sensible hypotheses backed by theory. One may therefore study the nature of the relationship (correlation) without risking the possibility of finding a spurious correlation.

The correlation between temperature (in centigrade) and length (in millimetre) can further be specified with temperature as the cause variable and length of the iron rod as the effect variable. Mathematically this is noted as a functional relation in which the temperature (T) is the independent variable and length of the iron rod (L) is the dependant variable. This can be represented as $L = f(T)$. More specifically the relation may be written as $L=\alpha+\beta T$ or $L=\alpha+\beta T^2$ and so on, depending on the mathematical specification of the relation.

In statistical theory, we discussed the cause and effect relation in terms of a regression analysis. In regression analysis, we specify the functional form among the variables and try to measure the change in a dependant variable as a result of a change in an independent variable. In the above mentioned example, $L=\alpha+\beta T$, $\frac{dl}{dt}=\beta$ is the measure of change in L when temperature changes by a very small amount. The measure of this change is called the regression coefficient, the independent variable is called the *regressor* and the dependant variable the *regressand*. In statistics, we have the tools to estimate α and β so that, for a given value of T we can estimate L (the estimated value is written as $\hat{L}$).

The literature that has developed to consider the relation between two sets of variables is based on the basic idea, as developed by Karl Pearson, which states that the measure of correlation is the covariance of a bivariate distribution, placed as the ratio of the product of the standard deviations of individual variates. The measure is therefore unit free also. The idea was developed further which gave rise to a vast literature of regression analysis that served as the basis of the present day econometric analysis. We shall now describe these measures in terms of a few simple formulae which might be useful for beginners. Now-a-days software packages are available in user friendly modes that might take care of the numerical exercises associated with this literature.

10.4.4 Coefficient of Correlation

Given two variables X and Y, the degree of association between them is measured by *product moment correlation coefficient* due to Karl Pearson. In case the entire universe of the variates is considered, the correlation is indicated by ρ. If we define correlation with respect to a sample of observations it is indicated by r. The product moment correlation coefficient is defined as:

$$\rho_{xy} = \frac{Cov(X,Y)}{\sqrt{v(X)}\sqrt{v(Y)}}$$

In brief

$$\rho_{xy} = \frac{\sum(Y_i - \bar{Y})(X_i - \bar{X})}{\sqrt{(\sum Y_i - \bar{Y})^2}\sqrt{(\sum X_i - \bar{X})^2}} \tag{10.1}$$

For grouped data with frequency, the formula boils down to :

$$\rho_{xy} = \frac{\sum_{i=1}^{n} f_i(X_i - \bar{X})(Y_i - \bar{Y})}{\sqrt{\sum f_i(X_i - \bar{X})^2}\sqrt{\sum f_i(Y_i - \bar{Y})^2}}$$

$$= \frac{(\sum f_i X_i Y_i) - (1/N)(\sum f_i X_i)(\sum f_i Y_i)}{\sqrt{\sum f_i X_i^2 - (1/N)(\sum f_i X_i)^2}\sqrt{\sum f_i Y_i^2 - (1/N)(\sum f_i Y_i)^2}}$$

Example 10.5

The following are the data in reference to consumption of rice and the income of each respondent.

Respondents	Yearly consumption of rice (kgs), (*Y*)	Yearly income of respondents (₹), (*X*)
1	200	10,000
2	400	15,000
3	700	25,000
4	800	30,000
5	900	35,000
6	1000	40,000

We want to know the extent of correlation that might exist between yearly consumption of rice (Y) and yearly income (X) of the respondents. For this we shall apply the formula Eq. 10.1. To facilitate the calculation, the Table 10.5 is constructed.

Table 10.5 The computation of correlation

X ('000)	Y ('00)	$X-\bar{X}$	$(X-\bar{X})^2$	$(Y-\bar{Y})$	$(Y-\bar{Y})^2$	$(X-\bar{X})(Y-\bar{Y})$
10	2	−15.8	249.64	−4.7	22.09	74.26
15	4	−10.8	116.64	−2.7	7.29	29.16
25	7	0.8	0.64	0.3	0.09	0.24
30	8	4.2	17.64	1.3	1.69	5.43
35	9	9.2	84.64	2.3	5.29	21.16
40	10	14.2	201.64	3.3	10.89	46.86
155	40		670.84		47.34	177.11

$\bar{X}=25.8,\ \bar{Y}=6.7$

The sample correlation coefficient is noted as r_{xy} or r (note that r_{xy} is the same as ρ_{xy}). If the relationship between variables is positive, the value of r will be 0 $0<r\leq+1$ and for a negative correlation the value or r will be $-1\leq r<0$. At $r=0$ we have a situation where there exists no relationship. If r has a value of 0.5, we infer a favourable relation. When the r value is above 0.8, we say the relation is still stronger. The formula of r as in case of ρ_{xy},

$$r=\frac{\sum(Y_i-\bar{Y})(X_i-\bar{X})}{\sqrt{(Y_i-\bar{Y})^2(X_i-\bar{X})^2}}$$

$$r=\frac{177.11}{178.20}=0.99$$

The relationship between variables X and Y is 0.99, which indicates that there exists almost a perfect correlation between income and the consumption of cereal. We infer from the results that there is a high positive relationship between income and consumption of rice, according to the given data set.

10.5 REGRESSION ANALYSIS

As we have already discussed, a correlation analysis does not consider the causal relationship that might exist between the variables. What is stated here is the existence of relationship in terms of positive or negative correlation.

When the degree of association is measured in terms of a causal relationship among the variables, the discussion is done in terms of a regression analysis. If the relation is drawn in terms of two variables, the regression is a two variable regression or a simple regression in which the *cause* variable is noted as the independent variable and the *effect* variable is stated to be the dependent variable. In case we have more than one independent variable the regression is known as multiple regression. Usually we assume a linear relationship among the variables (nonlinear cases are often translated into linear models by considering log-linear forms).

We come back to the data contained in Table 10.5 to discuss the method of regression analysis. It is assumed that the yearly consumption of rice in kilograms depends on the yearly income of the respondents. In other words it is assumed that yearly consumption of rice = *f*(yearly income). More specifically,

$$Y = f(X)$$

where X = yearly income and Y = yearly consumption of rice.

We assume a linear relation $\quad Y = a + bX$

where a is the intercept and b is the slope of the curve.

The hypothetical line showing the relation is shown in Fig. 10.2. It is understood that the regression will estimate the intercept a and the slope b of the hypothetical line.

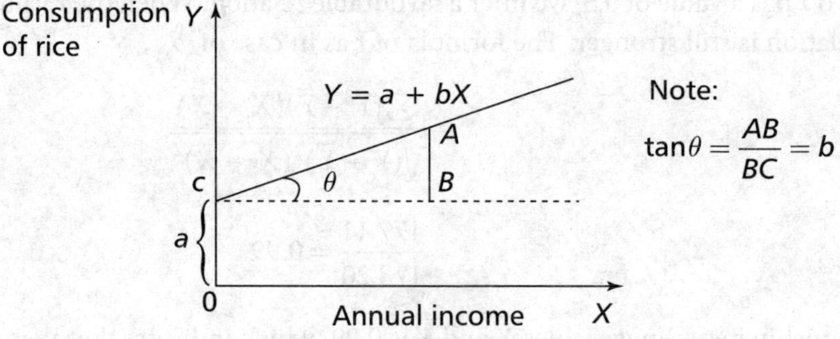

Fig. 10.2 The linear regression

The estimated values of a and b known as $\hat{a}$ and $\hat{b}$ will be given by the following formula.

$$\hat{b} = \frac{N\sum XY - (\sum X)(\sum Y)}{N\sum X^2 - (\sum X)^2}$$

$$\hat{a} = \frac{\sum Y - \hat{b}\sum X}{N}$$

(The summation is to involve all the values of the variable.)

Using the above formula, in the previous example of consumption of rice (annually) and the annual income, we get the data arrangement as shown in Table 10.6.

Table 10.6 The computaton of regression

X ('000)	*Y*('00)	*XY*	X^2	Y^2
10	2	20	100	4
15	4	60	225	16
25	7	175	625	49
30	8	240	900	64
35	9	315	1225	81
40	10	400	1600	100
155	40	1210	4675	314

$$\hat{b} = \frac{6(1210)-(155)(40)}{6(4675)-(155)^2} = \frac{7260-6200}{28050-24025}$$

$$= \frac{1060}{4025} = 0.26$$

$$\hat{a} = \frac{40-0.26(155)}{6} = \frac{40-40.3}{6}$$

$$= \frac{-0.3}{6} = -0.05$$

The estimating equation turns out to be:

$$\hat{Y} = -0.05 + 0.26X$$

where $\hat{Y}$ is the estimated value of Y.

With the estimated equation, we can now predict the consumption of rice among people of different levels of annual income. Supposing the annual income is ₹ 50,000, the consumption of rice should be:

$$\hat{Y} = -0.05 + 0.26(50)$$
$$= 12.95 \times 100 = 1{,}295 \text{ kg}$$

The coefficient a tells us the estimated value of Y when X is equal to zero. The more important coefficient $\hat{b}$ indicates the amount of change in $\hat{Y}$ due to 1 unit change in the variable X.

Robustness of the regression

Whenever regression is performed, it is necessary to know how well it captures the relation which is hidden in the data. If it captures the truth to the fullest, the estimated value is supposed to be the most robust. But how do we assess the extent to which the estimated regression has succeeded? The statistician would suggest the measurement of the *coefficient of determination*, which is identified as R^2 for testing the robustness of the regression. The coefficient has a value of +1.00 as the maximum limit and 0 as the minimum; that is, it varies between 0 and +1. An R^2 value of 1.00 indicates that the variance of the data around mean is the same as the variance of the data around the estimated value of Y. The implication is that the estimated regression line explains 100% of the variance in the dependent variable about its mean. In other words it indicates that the estimated regression gives us the line of best fit. An R^2 value of 0, on the other hand, indicates that the estimated regression equation cannot capture the truth in the data to any extent.
The formula for R^2 is:

$$R^2 = \frac{\text{(Total variance in the dependent variable)} - \text{(Variance 'unexplained' by regression equation)}}{\text{Total variance in the dependent variable}}$$

The unexplained variance occurs when the regression line fails to explain the variance and residuals are noticed in the scatter diagram. When it is a best fit line and no residual is present, the R^2 is computed as under.

$$R^2 = \frac{\left(\text{Total variance in dependent variable}\right) - 0}{\text{Total variance in the dependent variable}} = 1$$

The exact formula of R^2 is:

$$R^2 = \frac{\Sigma Y_i - \bar{Y})^2 - \Sigma(Y_i - \hat{Y})^2}{\Sigma(Y_i - \bar{Y})^2}$$

$\hat{Y}$ is the estimated value through the regression equation.

where Y_i = i^{th} value of the dependent variable (i = 1, 2, 3 .... n)

$\overline{Y}$ = mean of the dependent variable, that is, observed values

$\widehat{Y}_i$ = estimated value of Y_i in the regression equation.

With respect to the example that we have considered, R^2 is calculated in the following way.

Table 10.7 Calculation of R^2

Y ('00)	$\widehat{Y}$	$Y_i - \overline{Y}$	$Y_i - \widehat{Y}$
2	2.55	−4.67	−0.55
4	3.85	−2.67	0.15
7	5.45	0.33	0.55
8	7.75	1.33	0.25
9	9.05	2.33	−0.05
10	10.35	3.33	−0.35
40		**0.02**	**0**

$$\overline{Y} = 6.67$$

$$\widehat{Y} = -0.05 + 0.26(X)$$

So the values of $\widehat{Y}$ for values of X = 10, 15, 25, 30, 35, 40 are −0.55, 0.15, 0.55, 0.25, −0.05, −0.35.

Hence we get,

$$R^2 = \frac{(-0.02)^2 - 0}{(-0.02)^2} = 1$$

The estimated regression line can be considered to explain 100% of the variance of the data. Usually a regression line keeps an unexplained part, that is, R^2 is not equal to 1.

Multiple regression: When the independent variables to be considered is more than one, the regression is known as multiple regression. Here we consider the possibility that the change in the dependent variable is due to more than one independent variable. Supposing the variables take the form shown:

$$Y = f(X_1, X_2, \ldots\ldots X_n)$$

The linear equation is,

$$Y = a + b\,X_1 + c\,X_2 \ldots\ldots\ldots$$

where, a = intercept in Y, b = regression coefficient of variable X_1, c = regression coefficient of variable X_2.

Now instead of X_1, X_2, X_3 we could work it by:

$$y = Y - \bar{Y}$$

$$x_1 = X_1 - \bar{X}_1$$

$$x_2 = X_2 - \bar{X}_2$$

The transformed figures are then used to calculate the five columns of data

$$(yx_1, yx_2, x_1x_2, x_1^2 \text{ and } x_2^2)$$

Therefore for an equation: $y = a + b X_1 + c X_2$, the estimated value of b, c and a will be

$$\hat{b} = \frac{(\sum yx_1)(\sum x_2^2) - (\sum yx_2)(\sum x_1x_2)}{(\sum x_1^2)(\sum x_2^2) - (\sum x_1x_2)^2}$$

$$\hat{c} = \frac{(\sum yx_2)(\sum x_1^2) - (\sum yx_1)(\sum x_1x_2)}{(\sum x_1^2)(\sum x_2^2) - (\sum x_1x_2)^2}$$

The coefficient $\hat{a}$ will be calculated after the $\hat{b}$ and $\hat{c}$ values have been worked out. For this we use the following:

$$Y = a + bX_1 + bX_2$$

Hence $$\bar{Y} = a + b\bar{X}_i + c\bar{X}_2$$

Hence $$\bar{Y} = \hat{a} + \hat{b}\bar{X}_i + \hat{c}\hat{X}_2$$

Or, $$\hat{a} = \bar{Y} - \hat{b}\bar{X}_1 - \hat{c}\bar{X}_2$$

10.6 USE OF THE TOOLS OF REGRESSION IN TIME SERIES ANALYSIS

Forecasting or predicting is an important tool in the decision making process. Time series is used to detect patterns of change in statistical information over regular time intervals. We project these patterns to arrive at an estimate for the future. We normally have two sets of data, the time or year set of data and the observations or values against each time or year. A scatter diagram shows the two variables, that is, the time as the independent variable and observations or values of the variable for which the forecast has to be made as the dependant variable. From the scatter, we try to anticipate whether the pattern of the relation is linear or curvilinear.

Accordingly, we draw a hypothetical relation. When we anticipate a linear trend, the trend equation would be written as

$$Y = a + bx$$

Y is the dependant variable, X is the independent variable (time), a is the Y-intercept, b is the slope of the trend line.

The estimated value of:

$$b = \frac{\sum XY - n\overline{XY}}{\sum X^2 - n\overline{X}^2} \quad \text{(summed over } n \text{ values)} \qquad (10.2)$$

$$a = \overline{Y} - \mathrm{b}\overline{X} \qquad (10.3)$$

These are derived by applying the least square method (not discussed here) on the observed values of Y and the associated value of time (X). $\overline{Y}$ is the mean value of the dependent variable, $\overline{X}$ is the mean value of the independent variable, n is the number of data points in the time series, a is the Y-intercept, b is the slope. The relation between Y and X is assumed to be linear.

Table 10.8 Coding of time series

Case 1: Odd number of sample elements			**Case 2: Even number of sample elements**			
X	$X = \overline{X}$	**Code time(x)**	X	$X = \overline{X}$	$X = \overline{X} \times 2$	**Code time(x)**
1994	1994–96	−2	1994	$1994–1996\frac{1}{2}$	$-2\frac{1}{2} \times 2$	−5
1995	1995–96	−1	1995	$1995–1996\frac{1}{2}$	$-1\frac{1}{2} \times 2$	−3
1996	1996–96	0	1996	$1996–1996\frac{1}{2}$	$-\frac{1}{2} \times 2$	−1
1997	1997–96	1	1997	$1997–1996\frac{1}{2}$	$\frac{1}{2} \times 2$	1
1998	1998–96	2	1998	1998–1996	$1\frac{1}{2} \times 2$	3
			1999	$1999–1996\frac{1}{2}$	$2\frac{1}{2} \times 2$	5
9980			**11,979**			

The set of x values that were taken for the calculation were derived by shifting the origin from 0, that is, the beginning of the Christian calendar year to the year 1996. For the given series, 1996 is the mid-point. Hence we generated the $X - \overline{X}$ series with origin at 1996. In the case of an even number of years, the mid-point is a mid-year point. The transform scale would therefore assign a fraction to each figure, which can be eliminated by multiplying the derived values by 2. The procedure is given below in detail.

Mean time or mean year for Case 1 is 1996, which can be derived by summing the numerical values of the years and dividing by the number of years. Thus, for Case 1,

$$\overline{X} = \frac{9980}{5} = 1996$$

For Case 2,

$$\overline{X} = \frac{11979}{6} = 1996\frac{1}{2}$$

The coded times are then derived as in Table 10.8. Coding has been done in order to simplify the calculations.

Now we return to our calculation of slope and the Y intercept to determine the line of best fit. Since we are using the coded variable x, we replace X and $\overline{X}$ by x and $\overline{x}$ in the above equation. Again the mean of our coded time variable $\overline{x}$ is 0, we can substitute 0 for $\overline{x}$ in Eqs 10.2 and 10.3.

$$b = \frac{\sum XY - n\overline{X}\overline{Y}}{\sum X^2 - n\overline{X}^2}$$

$$= \frac{\sum xY - n\overline{x}\overline{Y}}{\sum x^2 - n\overline{x}^2}$$

[$\overline{x}$ (the coded variable) substituted for $\overline{X}$ and x for X]

$$= \frac{\sum xY}{\sum x^2}, \text{ as } \overline{x} = 0$$

In Eq. 10.3 the substitution of $\overline{x}$ will help in reformulating a.

$$a = \overline{Y} - b\overline{X}$$

$$= \overline{Y} - b\overline{x} \text{ (substitution of } \overline{x} \text{ for } \overline{X})$$

$$= \overline{Y} - \text{b0 (value of } \overline{x} = 0)$$

$$= \overline{Y}, \text{ as } \overline{x} = 0$$

Example 10.6

Let us now consider two sets of data, the time and the cattle population. The researcher is required to predict the future growth of the cattle population.

Table 10.10 Calculation for trends of cattle population

X	*Y* ('000)	Code (*X*)	*xy*	x^2
1990	28	−5	−140	25
1991	35	−4	−140	16
1992	42	−3	−126	9
1993	55	−2	−110	4
1994	65	−1	−65	1
1995	70	0	0	0
1996	85	1	85	1
1997	70	2	140	4
1998	85	3	255	9
1999	90	4	360	16
2000	80	5	400	25
21945	**705**	**0**	**659**	**110**

$$\overline{X} = \frac{21945}{11} = 1995,\ \overline{Y} = \frac{705}{11} = 64.09,\ b = \frac{\sum xy}{\sum x^2} = \frac{659}{110} = 5.99$$

$$a = \overline{Y} = 64.09$$

The general linear equation for forecasting is

$$Y = 64.09 + 5.99x$$

Let us suppose the data is being projected for the year 2002, the coded time is (2002 − 1995 = 7). Thus fitting it in the estimator equation we get,

$$\widehat{Y} = 64.09 + 5.99(7) = 106.02 \times 100 = 10{,}602$$

The estimated cattle population in 2002 is 10,602.

We assume a linear relation while considering the above mentioned data set. There are cases in which the line of best fit should not be derived from a linear relation between X and Y. The researcher would then be advised to try some other relation, which is non-linear in nature. For example, the suggested relation between Y and X for $Y = f(X)$ may be described as:

(a) $Y = a + bX + cX^2$
(b) $Y = a + bX + cX^2 + dX^3$
(c) $Y = a + bX + cX^2 + dX^3 + eX^4$

From mathematics we know that these are polynomial equations and they can be used as and when necessary to determine the line of best fit. The technique is the same as in the case of linear equations. We follow the method of least squares to find the necessary normal equations and on solving those equations we get the values of the coefficients (a, b, c,...). For n number of observations, the method can be described with respect to the following hypothetical relations:

$$Y = a + bx + cx^2$$

The three normal equations that can be derived following the least square method (not discussed here) are:

$$\sum_{i=1}^{n} Y_i = \sum_{i=1}^{n} a + \sum_{i=1}^{n} bx_i + \sum_{i=1}^{n} cx_i^2$$

$$= na + b\sum_{i=1}^{n} x_i + c\sum_{i=1}^{n} x_i^2 \tag{10.4}$$

Multiplying each side of Eq. 10.4 with x_i and summing over n number of places we get the normal equation.

$$\sum x_i Y_i = a\sum_{i=1} x_i + b\sum_{i=1} x_i^2 + c\sum_{i=1} x_i^3 \tag{10.5}$$

Similarly the normal equation, Eq. 10.6 is derived by multiplying each side of Eq. 10.4 by x^2 to get:

$$\sum x_i^2 Y_i = a\sum_{i=1} x_i^2 + b\sum_{i=1} x_i^3 + c\sum_{i=1} x_i^4 \tag{10.6}$$

Solving Eqs 10.4, 10.5 and 10.6 we get the values of three unknowns—a, b and c. Given the observed values of Y for n number of years, in a time series we can find the estimated values of a, b and c, namely $\hat{a}, \hat{b}$ and $\hat{c}$ by solving the above mentioned equations.

Example 10.7

Let us suppose a company has sold the following amount of cement (in tonnes) over five years, and by using the scatter diagram we find that the parabolic curve is visible.

Table 10.11 Annual sales of cement

Year (*X*)	1991	1992	1993	1994	1995
Quantity in million bags (*Y*)	15	30	75	120	180

In the scatter diagram considering *X* and *Y* axis we get a parabolic curve. In **Table 10.12** we perform the intermediate calculation for computing the trend.

Table 10.12 Calculation of trend

Y	X	$X-\overline{X}=x$	x^2	x^4	xY	x^2Y
15	1991	−2	4	16	−30	60
30	1992	−1	1	1	−30	30
75	1993	0	0	0	0	0
120	1994	1	1	1	120	120
180	1995	2	4	16	360	720
420	**9965**	**0**	**10**	**34**	**420**	**930**

In the above mentioned equations, year 1993 has been considered as the mid-point; thus, shifting the origin to 1993, we get:

$$\sum(X_i - X_0) = \sum_{i=1}^{5} x_i = 0 \quad (i=1\ldots5)$$

Similarly
$$\sum_{i=1}^{5} x_i^3 = 0$$

Hence the normal equations in context of this example are reduced to

$$\sum Y_i = na + c\sum x_i^2$$

$$\sum x_i Y_i = b = \sum x_i^2$$

$$\sum x_i^2 Y_i = a\sum x_i^2 + c\sum x_i^4$$

With respect to the above example, we have thus formed three equations. We can form three other equations:

$$420 = a(5) + c(10) \tag{10.7}$$

$$420 = b\,(10) \tag{10.8}$$

$$930 = a\,(10) + c(34) \tag{10.9}$$

From Eq. 10.8 we get,

$$b = \frac{420}{10}$$

Solving Eqs 10.7 and 10.9 we get:

$$\begin{aligned} 840 &= \quad 10a + 20c \\ -930 &= -10a \pm 34c \\ \hline -90 &= -14c \end{aligned}$$

$$\therefore \qquad c = 6.42$$

Substituting the value of c in Eq. 10.7 we get the value of a

$$420 = 5a + 6.42\,(10)$$

$$a = 71.16$$

Hence the estimated trend line.

$$\begin{aligned} \hat{Y} &= \hat{a} + \hat{b}x + \hat{c}x^2 \\ &= 71.16 + 42x + 6.42x^2 \end{aligned}$$

If we want to predict the number of bags in 1996 the x is (1996 − 1993 = 3) = 7 1.16 + 42(3) + 6.42 (9) = 255 million bags (approximately).

10.7 AN OUTLINE OF ECONOMETRIC MODELLING

A researcher while handling quantitative data finds the statistical tool of regression analysis, as outlined above, very useful in pursuing his analysis. To the extent the research design is in the nature of casual studies (see Chapter 2), the researcher finds that the independent variables or the set of independent variables as introduced in the regression analysis are 'the causal factors' and the dependant variable is the 'effect variable'. Assuming that the truth is revealed in cause and effect relation, such a structure has the amazing quality of pursuing the quantitative analysis or even analysis with qualitative variables to its every possible end. While outlining the statistical technique of correlation and regression analysis, we discussed only the bare outline based on the basic concept developed by Karl Pearson. The potential of such an analytical study was explored later by developing a new branch of applied statistics. Since the tools with respect to such analysis had been developed basically to perform the quantitative analysis of the economic variables, this branch of knowledge was eventually termed as *Econometrics*.

Econometrics is now a branch of knowledge which is immensely useful in causal study. Initially the study was confined to the analysis of quantitative data. Econometrics can now incorporate the analysis of qualitative data as well. The researchers had realised the potential of the subject further in recent years with the development of computer-based techniques of regression analysis. There are now software packages which are very user friendly, anyone with some basic knowledge of statistics can apply such tools to understand almost every aspect of the interrelation among the variables and the variables may be described in quantitative as well as in qualitative terms. Software packages like SPSS (statistical package for social sciences) or SAS (statistical analysis system) contain manuals that may help one understand even the basic rules, without going for a course on the econometric theories (we do not suggest that the researcher should not go for a course work on the econometric theory. It may often be dangerous to apply a software package without knowing the underlying theory properly).

In order to apply the tools of econometric analysis a researcher should take up the following route

- Step 1: Scrutinise the data; edit the data; check the nomenclature with respect to each data set and assign the abbreviation.
- Step 2: Go to theory and specify the causal structure; hence identify the dependent and independent variables.
- Step 3: Qualitative data may exist in the original data set. This must be identified. The econometric model introduces the qualitative variables as categorical variables. The categorical variables may enter the model as independent or dependent variables. For categorical variables as dependent variables, the appropriate model is logistic regression. Qualitative or categorical variables as independent variables can be tackled by introducing the concept of dummy variables.
- Step 4: Suggest the regression model specifying the alternative models and identify the simulation process.
- Step 5: Run the regression.
- Step 6: Check multi-collinearity, check heteroscadasticity, check auto-correlation for the time series data, try co-integration.

Step 7: Revise the regressions accordingly.
Step 8: Analyse the results.
Step 9: Write the report.

Most of these steps would seem to be obvious to the students who have had an exposure to the econometric theory. The best way to learn the process is to start with an empirical problem and try to solve the emerging difficulties by going back to the theory and also the manual of the software package (the manual may mislead you, if you do not have an exposure to the basic theory). A researcher must depend on his own analytical faculty while performing the exercise with the help of the machine. He must not put the machine above his reasoning capacity. One must know that no empirical exercise can produce a spectacular result out of the software. The quality of the research depends heavily on the quality of the basic data and the quality of the theory that the empirical findings try to analyse.

This section is concluded with a note on how to write a report on the results of an econometric analysis. If the researcher plans to write the report after receiving the results from the machine, he is often placed under the pressure of time particularly when there is a deadline for submitting the report. It is advisable to prepare a topic report while conceiving the work. The topic report may contain:

(a) the research question,
(b) a list of possible relevant variables,
(c) the hypotheses to be tested, and
(d) whatever the researcher knows about the data source.

After organising the data, the researcher gets the first set of results from the computer. The researcher should prepare a preliminary report that describes the results and contains some sort of a SWOT analysis of the results. Finally the researcher should improve upon the topic report under preliminary report and write the final report in the following format.

1. *Introduction*

Research question and a brief outline of what is coming.

2. *The econometric model*

(i) Conceptual variables
(ii) Relationship among conceptual variables
(iii) Transformation and other adjustments of the variables
(iv) Working hypothesis (expected signs of the regression co-effluents)
(v) The functional form of equations

3. *Data*
   (i) Specific variables used, meaning of the variables
   (ii) Sources of data
   (iii) Strength and weakness of the data
4. *Analysis of the regression results*
   (i) The results
   (ii) Interpretation of the results in the framework of a theory
5. *Summary of the findings*

10.8 USE OF ANALYSIS OF VARIANCE (ANOVA) IN QUANTITATIVE RESEARCH

In quantitative research we often face a situation where the information with respect to a particular query needs to be analysed further in order to ascertain if the quantitative data contain a statistical pattern that could not be captured by the ordinary tools of descriptive statistics, such as mean or variance. For example, suppose a departmental stores chain maintains six stores at six different locations of the city and the marketing department wants to know the differences between the various stores or the nature of variation in sales in 24 months. One might start with a quantitative description in terms of means (among stores and among months). But this hardly helps one to understand whether the difference is serious enough for making a policy intervention. In technical terms, the observed differences between the places or months might be due to random fluctuations in the data (in which case no policy intervention is possible) or it might have followed a pattern which is not due to sampling fluctuation (indicating that the business scenario might be different in different places). How should the researcher address the problem?

The intuitive answer to this query might be as follows. Had the observed differences between the places and months been entirely due to random fluctuations, we would have expected that the various mean squares would be of the same order. This gives us a clue to the way by which the problem has to be tackled. A researcher would start with a hypothesis that the differences are indeed due to statistical randomness contained in the data set. He would therefore consider the mean square due to any cause (location or month as in the case of this example), and the error mean square. *A comparison of mean square due to any cause and the error mean square provides a test of significance arising from that particular cause.* The comparison is done by finding the ratio of the mean square concerned (mean square due to location or due to month) to the error mean square. This ratio is known as the *variance ratio*. In a theoretical distribution, such a ratio is denoted by *F*. The theoretical values of F at various degrees of freedom can be constructed for various levels of significance (see Appendix 9.5 for F table at 1% and 5% level of significance). With the help of these theoretical values, one may test whether there is strong evidence in favour of the contention that the difference in means (squared) due to sampling error is at a tolerable level.

The F test has the powerful property of identifying whether the variations among the various data sets is entirely due to sampling error. *In fact, the F test actually has wider applications because it also provides an overall test of several differences.* It is more powerful than the t test because the t test provides a test of a single difference. In the example that we started with, the application of the t test will be confined to each of the two places with monthly data; the test would be run on the basis of the hypothesis that the sales (Rs) data at two places can be regarded as independent samples with no associations on account of the months being the same for the corresponding values. One would follow the non-paired t test in this case. We would however, point out that even in such a situation, one can carry out the test of variation following the F test.

This being so, in quantitative research, one needs to know the technique of analysis in the variation of the variable under study. This is done under *analysis of variance.* The example given above is in fact a typical case where the analysis of variance would be the proper tool for studying the nature of significance of differences in locations and also the months. The idea is that total variation in the present case is due to (i) the variation between locations and (ii) the variations within locations due to seasonality. This in fact leads to a technique of analysis which is described below.

The technique is really simple. Given a data set involving more than two variables, we may derive the arithmetic means of the data set. We want to know whether the means are significantly different. To apply the technique of analysis of variance, the variance of means *between* the different groups and the variance of mean within the different groups are considered. We thus find the total variance, distributed over between groups and within a group. The spirit is that one cannot take a rational decision regarding whether the means are significantly different by considering only the pairwise comparison (typical t test). The suggested test of significance of the total variance, both between and within group, is the F test. The F distribution to be followed for this purpose is generated by the ratio of these two variances in the population. The specific form of F to be utilised for this purpose is as follows:

$$F = \frac{\text{Estimate of population variance based on between sample variance}}{\text{Estimate of population variance based on within sample variance}}$$

In order to explain how this ratio is derived, we shall have to consider first what we are trying to test. Any observation, that is, the observed value of a variable can be broken into three parts, which are additive. An observed value = overall mean + deviation of group mean from overall mean + deviation of the observed value from the group mean. Let us explain this with a simple numerical example. We consider the responses in terms of number of consumers in reference to three promotional tools across four places (Table 10. 13).

Table 10.13 Promotional tools

Places	Toothpaste (T_1)	Toothbrush (T_2)	Drinking mugs (T_3)
1 (W_1)	15 (T_1W_1)	13	15
2 (W_2)	20	17	25
3 (W_3)	25	15	30
4 (W_4)	20	15	30
$\overline{X}$	$\overline{X}_1 = 20$	$\overline{X}_2 = 15$	$\overline{X}_3 = 25$
Grand mean = 20			

Let us consider the cell value (T_1W_1) = 15. Using the formula stated above, this value can be split as shown below.

$$15 = 20 + (20 - 20) + (15 - 20) = 15$$

This is true with respect to the values in the other cells as well.

The deviation of a group mean from the overall mean represents the effect on each observation belonging to that particular group. Deviation of an observation from its group mean represents the effect of all variables other than the variable under observation, on that observation. One takes a clue from this, and tries to assess the variation in terms of the deviation of the observation from the average of the group as well as the deviation existing among the groups. One thus gets a concept of inter-group variation and intra-group variation.

When we encounter a set of grouped data, the statistical issue to address is whether there is heterogeneity in the data. The distribution that the sample follows becomes important in this context. We first consider the variation existing within the group and then check variation between groups. The tool used to measure variation is *statistical variance*. A theoretical distribution is then conceived and a hypothesis is formed. This will help in testing whether the data set is from the same universe. If sufficient evidence is not found in favour of the hypothesis, the researcher concludes that homogeneity might not exist in the data set.

In the numerical example above, a marketing agency took up a promotional exercise on a particular product—a 500 grams packet of detergent. Three promotional tools of roughly the same price were offered – a tube of toothpaste, a tooth brush or a drinking mug – free with the purchase of the product. A buyer could choose any one of these three.

The weekly sales over places vary. The variation might be due to variation in effectiveness of the tools; it might be also due to variation in brand preference across places (the particular brand of the detergent with which the promotional tools are tagged might fail to get preference over a competitive brand among the buyers visiting the shop during each week). There are thus two sources of variation. How can we test which variation is more powerful?

Variation across promotional tools is inter-group variation. Variation across places with reference to a specific promotional tool is intra-group variation. There are thus three intra-group variations. In the above example, if there is more variation in inter-group than intra-group, one would understand that variation in the outcome of the treatment variable. When there is only one aspect of study, it is called *one way ANOVA*. When we study two aspects simultaneously drawn from two different populations we have the *two way ANOVA*.

10.8.1 One Way ANOVA

One way ANOVA refers to only one population and two way ANOVA refers to two independent populations. Let us suppose, we have a set of data on the endurance of electric bulbs produced by different companies. Thus, we have data on the lifetimes of bulbs selected from different companies. The population refers to the lifetimes of bulbs under experiment. The difference in endurance over various companies will be captured by one way ANOVA. Now suppose we consider the performance of different sales persons in different territories, we have a data set that refers to two populations—population of sales persons and the population of territories. ANOVA in this case shall refer to both the populations. It will therefore be called two way ANOVA. The numerical example that we started with – the effect of different promotional tools in different places – is a typical example of two way ANOVA.

Which statistical technique will suit our purpose? We have a grand mean of 20 in the above example. How is the grand mean derived? We have three group means from which a grand mean is calculated. Now consider the deviations of the individual cell values from the grand mean. For example, for T_1W_1 the deviation from grand mean is $20 - 15 = 5$. We need to explain this deviation in terms of factors within groups and factors between groups. Taking care of the fact that individual variations from the grand mean might be positive or negative, the summation of these numbers might not help us to understand the total variation. So, we calculate the squares of the deviations and add them to get total sum of the squares of deviations (SS) from the grand mean $\overline{\overline{X}}$. This is typically what is done for calculating variance.

Mathematically, it looks like $\left(X_{ij} - \overline{\overline{X}}\right)^2$, where i indicates the ith row and j indicates the jth column. Summed over all cells it appears as $\sum_{i=1}^{4}\sum_{j=1}^{3}\left(X_{ij} - \overline{\overline{X}}\right)^2$ in the example above. Calculating, we get the Total Sum of Squares (TSS). In the above example,

$$\text{TSS} = [(15-20)^2 + (20-20)^2 + (25-20)^2 + (20-20)^2 + (13-20)^2 + (17-20)^2 + (15-20)^2 + (15-20)^2 + (15-20)^2 + (25-20)^2 + (30-20)^2 + (30-20)^2]$$
$$= 408$$

Variance is not just the total sum of squared deviations but its mean. We obtain in this case as well, as mean square (MS) of the deviations. This is rather easy. It is obtained by dividing the TSS by the respective degrees of freedom. *Degree of freedom* is the number of independent observations—in the example above, we have 12 observations over 3 treatment variables (promotional tools). If we want to get deviations we shall have to keep one promotional tool fixed. The denominator therefore is $12 - 1 = 11$; in other words, the degree of freedom (df) in this case will be $12 - 1 = 11$. In this particular example, the MS will be

$$\text{MS} = \frac{408}{11} = 37.09$$

The idea is that we can look upon the total variation represented by the mean square as arising from two causes—variation due to treatment variables and variation due to places. We shall discuss presently how variations can be captured in statistical terms. Before we do this, a caveat has to be put in. Variations would be calculated (as in the case of total variation in considering the respective sum of squares as suggested above), will not add up to the total sum of squares of the deviations of the observations from the grand mean. This is because the treatment variable does interact with the variable representing places. This has an impact on the total variation which is represented by the total sum of squares. It can be proved that TSS = SS between + SS within + interaction SS.

We shall now discuss how the individual SSs (Sum of Squares) are calculated. We shall consider SS between first. This is the deviation of the *sample mean* from the *grand mean* squared and multiplied by the number of observations in the sample. This is shown below.

$$= n_1\left(\overline{X}_1 - \overline{\overline{X}}\right)^2 + n_2\left(\overline{X}_2 - \overline{\overline{X}}\right)^2 + \ldots\ldots N_n\left(\overline{X}_n - \overline{\overline{X}}\right)^2$$

n = number of observation in the specific sample. In the above case it is stated as under:

$$= [4(20-20)^2 + 4(15-20)^2 + 4(25-20)^2] = 200$$

We calculate the mean square between (MS between) the groups, this is done by dividing SS between by the degrees of freedom. The degree of freedom is one less than the number of groups. Here k refers to number of treatment variables. If the number of groups is k, the degree of freedom is $k - 1$. Since we have three groups, the degree of freedom is $3 - 1 = 2$. The MS between in this case is:

$$\text{MS between} = \frac{200}{3-1} = 100$$

In a similar way we can calculate other Sum of Square deviations within (SS within) the group which will be needed for ANOVA. This is the deviation of the cell value from the sample mean squared. The formula is:

$$= \sum_{i=1}^{4} \sum_{j=1}^{3} \left(X_{ij} - \bar{X}_j\right)^2$$

For the above example, it can be computed as:

$$\begin{aligned} &= [(15-20)^2 + (20-20)^2 + (25-20)^2 + (20-20)^2] + \\ &\quad [(13-15)^2 + (17-15)^2 + (15-15)^2 + (15-15)^2] + \\ &\quad [(15-25)^2 + (25-25)^2 + (30-25)^2 + (30-25)^2] \\ &= 208 \end{aligned}$$

One has to calculate the mean square within (MS within) the group. This is done by dividing the 'SS within' by the degrees of freedom. The degrees of freedom in case of within groups consist of the total number of observations minus the number of groups, that is, $n - k$.

$$= \frac{208}{12-3} = 23.11$$

The TSS should be split into 'between' and 'within' sum of squares of the deviation. If there is no interaction between variables represented in columns and the variables represented in rows, there will not be any interaction between these two variables. There is no necessity to calculate the interaction SS in such cases. This typically happens in the case of one way ANOVA. TSS in such cases will be equal to SS between + SS within. If we assume that there is interaction between the two attributes under study (places and promotional tools in the given example, for instance) the TSS will not be equal to SS between + SS within, since interaction SS which represents the Sum of Squares due to interaction will have to be calculated.

We shall consider this possibility presently. The given numerical example has been designed for this. Let us consider a scenario in which the promotional tools are expected to be place neutral. The assumption is that the variation in sales is *solely due to the variation in the effect of having the promotional tools or not.* In other words, we are considering the heterogeneity in one attribute and homogeneity in the other attributes. (The consumers in the given example are homogeneous across places.) Typically, this is now a problem of one way ANOVA. In many textbook examples, it is found that the same type of problem is sometimes considered under one way ANOVA and sometimes under two way ANOVA—the reason is the difference in perception of the problem by the researcher. If the researcher concentrates on the effect of one attribute, the problem boils down to one way ANOVA. The other attribute does not interact with the variable under consideration. The total variation will therefore be equal to SS between + SS within. The interaction SS will be equal to 0.

In order to continue with the given numerical example in the context of one way ANOVA, we shall at this stage concentrate on the findings of SS between and SS within. We shall check whether the promotional tools have any impact at all on the sales of the product. In the numerical example, there were observable differences in the cell values. The question is whether the differences are entirely due to sampling fluctuations. If we find that there are statistically valid evidences in favour of the hypothesis that the differences are due to sampling fluctuations, one may conclude that there is a sound basis to reject the hypothesis that the promotional tools affect the sales of the product. If the hypothesis is rejected, the statistical basis for understanding that the promotional tools do matter, get strengthened.

But how would we perform such a test? Recall that the F test has the powerful property of identifying whether the variations among various data sets is entirely due to the sampling error or not. We perform F test after defining the proper test statistic. The test statistic F is the ratio of the 'MS between' and 'MS within' at the appropriate degrees of freedom. In the above case, degrees of freedom would be 2 ($3 - 1 = 2$ with respect to the promotional tools) and 9 ($12 - 3 = 9$ with respect to the cell frequencies). The calculated F is:

$$F = \frac{100}{23.11} = 4.33 \text{ at (2,9) degrees of freedom}$$

We choose a level of significance, say 5%, in this case. The table value of F at 5% level of significance and (2,9) degrees of freedom is 4.26 which is lower than the computed value. Since the computed value is larger than the table value, the hypothesis of no effect (of promotional tools on sales) stands rejected. The implication is that the promotion should have its impact on the sales of the product.

The summary of the findings (of the above example) is given in Table 10.14.

Table 10.14 Summary of results

Source of variation	SS	df	MS	F ratio	F value at 5% level of significance and (2,9) degrees of freedom
Between groups	200	3 – 1 = 2	100	4.33	4.26
Within groups	208	12 – 3 = 9	23.11		
Total	408	12 – 1			

We now consider another example where steps involved in one way ANOVA have been elucidated. Consider the following numerical example.

A firm gives gifts as treatment variables in the retail stores of the same territory ensuring that the extraneous factors that affect all the retail outlets are relatively equal in effect. The question was of sales of 500 grams packets of washing powder in the stores with such variations in the gifts. The experiment was conducted for 6 weeks repetitively across the three stores. The outcome was recorded in terms of the number of detergents packets sold. The researcher is interested to find whether the gifts have impacted the sales. There are 18 observations (Table 10.15).

Table 10.15 Sales of 500 g (size) packet with gifts

Weeks	Gifts			Total (packets)
	Teddy bear (packets)	Buckets (packets)	Eating plates (packets)	
1	15	24	21	60
2	25	26	28	79
3	30	34	35	99
4	30	40	46	116
5	40	40	45	125
6	40	40	41	121
Total	180	204	216	600
$\bar{\bar{X}}$	30	34	36	

The issue is to assess whether the types of gifts had any impact on the number of packets sold. We shall consider first the column wise mean. This will capture average sale per week with respect to each of the treatment variables.

Step 1: Column wise average (sample means)

$$\bar{X}_1 = \frac{180}{6} = 30, \ \bar{X}_2 = \frac{204}{6} = 34, \ \bar{X}_3 = \frac{216}{6} = 36$$

Step 2: The means of the sample means would be

$$\bar{\bar{X}} = \frac{30 + 34 + 36}{3} = 33.33$$

Step 3: Deviation of the column-wise means from the grand mean are then calculated. We need the total sum of square (SS) of these deviations from the grand mean. This is SS between the groups. The numerical value is as follows

$$\text{SS between} = n_1\left(\bar{X}_1 - \bar{\bar{X}}\right)^2 + n_2\left(\bar{X}_2 - \bar{\bar{X}}\right)^2 + n_3\left(\bar{X}_3 - \bar{\bar{X}}\right)^2$$

$$\text{SS between} = 6(30-33.33)^2 + 6(34-33.33)^2 + 6(36-33.33)^2$$
$$= 112.02$$

Step 4: To calculate the mean square (MS) between which would be obtained by dividing the 'SS between' with the total number of columns minus one. This is the degree of freedom pertaining to one way ANOVA.

$$\text{MS between} = \frac{\text{SS between}}{(k-1)}$$

$$\text{MS between} = \frac{112.02}{3-1} = 56.01$$

k = number of columns

Step 5: We next consider the sum of square (SS) of the deviation of the individual values from the group mean. Symbolically this comes as 'SS within'.

$$\text{SS within} = \sum\left(X_{1i}-\bar{X}_1\right)^2 + \sum\left(X_{2i}-\bar{X}_2\right)^2 + \sum\left(X_{3i}-\bar{X}_3\right)^2$$

$$\begin{aligned}\text{SS within} = {} & [(15-30)^2 + (25-30)^2 + (30-30)^2 + (30-30)^2 \\ & + (40-30)^2 + (40-30)^2] + [(24-34)^2 + (26-34)^2 + \\ & (34-34)^2 + (40-34)^2 + (40-34)^2 + (40-34)^2 + \\ & (40-34)^2] + [(21-36)^2 + (28-36)^2 + (35-36)^2 + \\ & (46-36)^2 + (45-36)^2 + (41-36)^2] \\ = {} & 1218\end{aligned}$$

Step 6: We then calculate the mean square (MS) within, which is

$$\text{MS within} = \frac{\text{SS within}}{n-k}$$

$$\text{MS within} = \frac{1218}{n-k} = \frac{1218}{18-3} = 81.20$$

N = number of observations

Step 7: We then get SS for total variance as given below:

$$\text{SS for total variance} = \sum\left(\bar{X}_{ki} - \bar{\bar{X}}\right)^2$$

$$\text{SS of total variance} = [(15-33.33)^2 + (25-33.33)^2 + (30-33.33)^2 + (30-33.33)^2 + (40-33.33)^2 + (40-33.33)^2] + [(24-33.33)^2 + (26-33.33)^2 + (34-33.33)^2 + (40-33.33)^2 + (40-33.33)^2 + (40-33.33)^2] + [(21-33.33)^2 + (28-33.33)^2 + (35-33.33)^2 + (46-33.33)^2 + (45-33.33)^2 + (41-33.33)^2]$$

$$\text{SS of total variance} = 1330.02$$

Thus we calculate all the variances and prepare the set of information for performing the statistical test, in this case the F test. The F ratios are calculated as below.

Step 8: Finally, the F ratio is worked out as shown below.

$$\text{F ratio} = \frac{\text{MS between}}{\text{MS within}}$$

$$\text{F ratio} = \frac{56.01}{81.20} = 0.689$$

Since we are interested in one way ANOVA, we shall consider only the between sample variation and perform the F test. The information in summary form is given in Table 10.16.

The computed value of the F ratio 0.689, at degrees of freedom (2,15), is less than the Table value of F (3,68) at 5% significance level with degree of freedom (2,15). Therefore the gift element did not impact the sample. The difference is insignificant.

Table 10.16 Summary of results

Source of variation	SS	df	MS	F ratio	F value at 5% level of significance and (2,15) degrees of freedom
Between groups	112.02	(3 – 1) = 2	56.01	$\frac{56.01}{81.20} = 0.689$	3.68
Within groups	1218.00	(18 – 3) = 15	81.20		
Total	1330.02	(18 – 1) = 17			

10.8.2 Two Way ANOVA

Let us suppose the researcher is placed in a situation where there exist reasonable grounds to hold that the effectiveness of promotional tools among the buyers does not depend only on the type of the promotional tool (toothpaste, toothbrush and drinking mug) but also on the place to which the buyer belongs. Technically speaking, this implies that promotion is an attribute that interacts with another attribute, the location of the sales outlet. The cell values now represent the resultant of interaction between these two attributes as well. In fact, this is the essence of a situation that needs the application of two way ANOVA.

The two way ANOVA takes into consideration two factors. The data are classified on the basis of two factors, for example, type of promotional tool and the type of place where the sales outlet is situated. Many more such cross tabulations based on two factors or variables are conceivable. Such tabulations could accommodate data with repeated measurement and non-repeated measurement as well. In this discussion we will consider only cases with non-repeated measurement.

Unlike in the case of one way ANOVA, interaction between factors is also accommodated in two way ANOVA. For the measure of variance, therefore, the TSS would also be different from what was in case of one way ANOVA.

$$\text{TSS} = \text{SS between} + \text{SS within} + \text{interaction SS}$$
$$\text{Interaction SS} = \text{TSS} - (\text{SS between} + \text{SS within})$$

which is often stated as residual SS. We shall describe in a tabulated form how these elements can be calculated in a simple way (Table 10.17).

Table 10.17 Outline of computational steps

Source of variation	Sum of squares (SS)	Degrees of Freedom (d.f.)	Mean Square (MS)	F ratio
Between column treatment	$\sum\frac{(T_j)^2}{n_j} - \frac{(T)^2}{n}$	$(c - 1)$	$\frac{\text{SS between column}}{(c-1)}$	$\frac{\text{MS between column}}{\text{MS residual}}$
Between rows treatment	$\sum\frac{(T_i)^2}{n_i} - \frac{(T)^2}{n}$	$(r - 1)$	$\frac{\text{SS between rows}}{(r-1)}$	$\frac{\text{MS between rows}}{\text{MS residual}}$
Residual or error	Total SS − (SS between columns + SS between rows)	$(c - 1)(r - 1)$	$\frac{\text{SS residual}}{(c-1)(r-1)}$	
Total	$\sum X_{ij}^2 - \frac{(T)^2}{n}$	$(c.r - 1)$		

where, T_j = total of jth column, n_j = number of items in j^{th} column, T_i = total of ith column, n = total number of items, T = grand total, c = number of columns, r = number of rows.

Thus MS residual variance serves as the basis of the significance test. Between columns and rows, the residual variance or MS residual ratio is worked out to tabulate the F ratio between column and rows. These are compared with the table values of F pertaining to degrees of freedom and chosen level of significance. In case the computed value of F is more than the table value, the variable related to the concerned attribute is considered to significantly affect the cell values. In case the tabulated value of F is less than the table value, the difference is considered to be significant and the cause is likely to be due to sampling fluctuation.

We shall now explain the working of two way ANOVA with respect to the previous example, with reference to the effect of promotional tools and the location of the sales outlet on cell values of sales of detergent packs (Table 10.18).

Table 10.18 Promotional tools

Places	Toothpaste (T_1) (packets)	Toothbrush (T_2) (packets)	Drinking mug (T_3) (packets)	Total (packets)
1 (W_1)*	15	13	15	43
2 (W_1)*	20	17	25	62
3 (W_1)*	25	15	30	70
4 (W_1)*	20	15	30	65
Total	80	60	100	240

W_1 = week one

Let us are compute the results of above example.

$$\frac{(T)^2}{n} = \frac{(240 \times 240)}{12} = 4800$$

T (grand total) = 240, n (number of observations) = 12

$$\text{Total SS} = \sum X_{ij}^{\ 2} - \frac{(T)^2}{n} \text{ or } \frac{(240 \times 240)}{12}$$

$$= (225 + 400 + 625 + 400 + 169 + 289 + 225 + 225 + 225 + 625 + 900 + 900) - \frac{(240 \times 240)}{12}$$

$$= 408$$

$$\text{SS between columns} = \sum \frac{(T_j)^2}{n_j} - \frac{(T)^2}{n}$$

$$= \left[\frac{80\times 80}{4}+\frac{60\times 60}{4}+\frac{100\times 100}{4}\right]-\left[\frac{(240\times 240)}{12}\right]$$

$$= 200$$

$$\text{SS between rows} = \sum\frac{(T_i)^2}{n_i}-\frac{(T)^2}{n}$$

$$= \left[\frac{43\times 43}{3}+\frac{62\times 62}{3}+\frac{70\times 70}{3}+\frac{65\times 65}{3}\right]-\left[\frac{(240\times 240)}{12}\right]$$

$$= 139.32$$

$$\text{SS residual error} = \text{Total SS} - (\text{SS between column} + \text{SS between rows})$$

$$= 408 - (200 + 139.32) = 68.68$$

$$\text{MS between column} = \frac{\text{SS between columns}}{(c-1)}$$

$$= \frac{200}{(3-1)} = 100$$

$$\text{MS between row} = \frac{\text{SS between rows}}{(r-1)}$$

$$= \frac{139.32}{(4-1)} = 46.44$$

$$\text{MS residual or error} = \frac{\text{SS residual or error}}{(c-1)(r-1)}$$

$$= \frac{68.68}{(3-1)(4-1)} = 11.45$$

$$\text{F ratio between columns} = \frac{\text{MS between columns}}{\text{MS residual}}$$

$$= \frac{100}{11.45} = 8.73$$

$$\text{F ratio between rows} = \frac{\text{MS between rows}}{\text{MS residual}}$$

$$= \frac{46.44}{11.45} = 4.06$$

Table 10.19 Summary of findings

Source of variation	SS	Degrees of freedom (df)	MS	F ratio	Table value of F at 5% level of significance
Between columns	200	3 – 1 = 2	100	8.73	F(2,6) = 5.14
Between rows	139.32	4 – 1 = 3	46.44	4.06	F(3,6) = 4.76
Residual or error	68.68	(3 – 1)(4 –) = 6	11.45		
Total	408	4 × 3 – 1 = 11			

We choose a level of significance, say 5% in this case. The table value of F between columns at 5% level of significance and (2,6) degrees of freedom is 5.14 which is lower than the computed value. Since the computed value is larger than the table value, the hypothesis of no effect (of promotional tools on sales) stands rejected. The implication is that the promotion should have its impact on the sales of the product.

Consider now the second attribute. We choose a level of significance, say 5% in this case also. The table value of the F between rows at 5% level of significance and (3,6) degrees of freedom is 4.76 which is higher than the computed value. Since the computed value is less than the table value, the hypothesis of no effect (of places on sales) stands accepted. The implication is that the places should have no impact on the sales of the product.

Let us consider another example showing the steps involved in the calculation of two way ANOVA.

Table 10.20 shows the monthly sales (in thousand rupees) of a certain firm in three different states with reference to four different salesmen.

Table 10.20 Monthly Sales (000 Rupees) in three different states

States	Salesman				Total (sales)
	A (sales)	*B* (sales)	*C* (sales)	*D* (sales)	
X	4	6	4	7	21
Y	6	7	4	8	25
Z	5	7	7	10	29
Total	15	20	15	25	75

Step 1:

$$\frac{(T)^2}{n} = \frac{75 \times 75}{12} = 468.75$$

T (grand total) = 75, n (number of observation) = 12

Step 2:

$$\text{Total SS} = \sum X_{ij}^{\;2} - \frac{(T)^2}{n}$$

$$= (16 + 36 + 25 + 36 + 49 + 49 + 16 + 16 + 49 + 49 + 64 + 100) - \left[\frac{75\times 75}{12}\right]$$

$$= 36.25$$

Step 3:

$$\text{SSb between columns} = \sum \frac{(T_j)^2}{n_j} - \frac{(T)^2}{n}$$

$$= \left[\frac{15\times 15}{3} + \frac{20\times 20}{3} + \frac{15\times 15}{3} + \frac{25\times 25}{3}\right] - \left[\frac{75\times 75}{12}\right]$$

$$= 22.91$$

Step 4:

$$\text{SS between rows} = \sum \frac{(T_i)^2}{n_i} - \frac{(T)^2}{n}$$

$$= \left[\frac{21\times 21}{4} + \frac{25\times 25}{4} + \frac{29\times 29}{4}\right] - \left[\frac{75\times 75}{12}\right] = 8$$

Step 5:

$$\text{SS residual error} = \text{Total SS} - (\text{SS between columns} + \text{SS between rows})$$

$$= 36.25 - (22.91 + 8.00) = 5.34$$

Step 6:

$$\text{MS between columns} = \frac{\text{SS between columns}}{(c-1)}$$

$$= \frac{22.91}{(4-1)} = 7.64$$

Step 7:

$$\text{MS between rows} = \frac{\text{SS between rows}}{(r-1)}$$

$$= \frac{8.00}{(3-1)} = 4.00$$

Step 8:

$$\text{MS residual or error} = \frac{\text{SS residual or error}}{(c-1)(r-1)}$$

$$= \frac{5.34}{(4-1)(3-1)} = 0.89$$

Step 9:

$$\text{F ratio between columns} = \frac{\text{MS between columns}}{\text{MS residual}}$$

$$= \frac{7.64}{0.89} = 8.58$$

Step 10:

$$\text{F ratio between rows} = \frac{\text{MS between rows}}{\text{MS residual}}$$

$$= \frac{4.00}{0.89} = 4.49$$

Table 10.21 Summary of findings

Source of variation	SS	Degrees of freedom (df)	MS	F ratio	Table value of F at 5% level of significance
Between columns	22.91	4 – 1 = 3	7.64	8.58	F(3,6) = 4.76
Between rows	08.00	3 – 1 = 2	4.00	4.49	F(2,6) = 5.14
Residual or error	05.34	(4 – 1)(3 – 1) = 6	0.89		
Total	36.25	4 × 3 – 1 = 11			

Since the tabulated F value of 8.58 between columns is more than the Table value (4.76) at 5% level of significance for (3,6) degrees of freedom, it most probably implies that salesmen have impacted sales. This is to state that the differences in the mean are not due to sampling.

Since the tabulated F value of 4.49 between rows is less than the Table value (5.14) at 5% level of significance for (2,6) degrees of freedom, it implies that the differences in mean are owing to sampling fluctuation and not because of the variable 'different states'.

SUMMARY

- Numerical observations are known as data. The data that we collect sometimes comes in the form of quantitative data and is sometimes qualitative in nature.
- Interpolation of data is a technique used for finding the missing value in a set of data through linear approximation, binomial approximation and by Newton's formula.

- Techniques of data analysis involve measurement of central tendency, measure of dispersion, measurement of simultaneous variation and coefficient of correlation.
- Existence of relationship between the variables is carried out by correlation analysis and the result is expressed in terms of positive and negative correlation.
- Regression analysis and multiple regression analysis are carried out to determine the changes in the dependent variable due to one (or more than one) independent variable(s) respectively.
- Time series analysis is carried out to detect the pattern of change in the variables over regular time intervals.
- Econometric analysis involves determining the cause–effect relationship between the variables. Now-a-days, software packages such as SPSS or SAS are extensively used for such analysis.
- Analysis of variance (ANOVA) is frequently used in research data analysis to ascertain a statistical pattern of change of variables that could not be captured by other simpler means. ANOVA can be one way or two way depending upon the nature of relationships which are studied among the variables.

ASSIGNMENTS

Q1 Choose the right answers

1. The well known methods of measuring central tendency are:
   (a) Mean and standard deviation
   (b) Mean and mode
   (c) Mean, median and mode
   (d) None of the above
2. Arithmetic mean could be used when:
   (a) Only a typical value is required
   (b) The distribution is reasonably symmetrical
   (c) Extreme measures would affect the mean disproportionately
   (d) None of the above
3. The median is used when:
   (a) The greatest reliability is required
   (b) Subsequent statistical calculations are to be made
   (c) Distribution is badly skewed
   (d) None of the above
4. The mode is used when:
   (a) The most typical value is required
   (b) Extreme measures would affect the mean disproportionately
   (c) Subsequent statistical claculations are to be made
   (d) None of the above

5. A low value of standard deviation implies:
   (a) The data set is dense
   (b) The data set is widely dispersed
   (c) Arithmetic mean of the data set is low
   (d) None of the above
6. Newton's Backward Interpolation is required:
   (a) When the missing value is nearer to $x = x^0$
   (b) When the missing value is nearer to $x = x^n$
   (c) When the missing value is only in univariate distribution
   (d) None of the above
7. Regression analysis is required when:
   (a) Only degree of association is required
   (b) Degree of association and causal relationship is required
   (c) No degree of association exists
   (d) None of the above
8. The set of data can be distinguished from other set by means of:
   (a) Central value and dispersion
   (b) Central value, dispersion and skewness
   (c) Central value, dispersion, skewness and kurtosis
   (d) None of the above
9. The variation in one variable is measured by dispersion:
   (a) True
   (b) False
   (c) Sometimes true and sometimes false
   (d) None of the above
10. The binomial method of interpolation is:
   (a) A graphical method
   (b) Algebraic method
   (c) A graphical method and algebraic method
   (d) None of the above

Answers

1. (c), 2. (b), 3. (c), 4. (a), 5. (a), 6. (b), 7. (b), 8. (c), 9. (a), 10. (b)

Q2 Answer the questions

1. The following are the sales in units for a specific month of a group of salesmen (Table B_1). Another group of 10 salesmen different from the first group have also recorded sales in units (Table B_2).

Table B_1 Data from the first group of salesmen

Salesmen	1	2	3	4	5	6	7	8	9	10
Sales (units)	250	300	325	280	400	350	280	288	300	350

Table B_2 Data from the second group of salesmen

Salesmen	1	2	3	4	5	6	7	8	9	10
Sales (units)	300	320	400	286	280	350	400	320	330	250

You have been asked to find out which group is more consistent in their sales performance. [Hint: Find out the standard deviation of each group in reference to sales (units), the one with lesser standard deviation is more consistent.]

2. The following are the sales of washing powder in different years. Forecast the sales for the year 1996 and 1997.

Year	Units in million (bags)
1990	230
1991	285
1992	315
1993	350
1994	375
1995	400

3. The following are the figures for different years against which the sales of cement is stated except for the year 1993. You have been asked to find out the missing sales figure.

Year	1991	1992	1993	1994	1995	1996
Sales of cement (tons)	400	350	?	435	450	375

4. The agriculture department introduced three types of seeds in 6 different blocks and the adaptation of the farmers are as follows:

Blocks	Seeds		
	A_1	A_2	A_3
1	22	30	24
2	34	42	38
3	20	28	30
4	34	52	40
5	20	28	24
6	28	40	24
Total	158	228	180

The extension agronomist is interested to find out whether the type of seeds has had an impact on adoption by the farmers and whether the adoption has varied over the blocks. The decision has to be arrived at through ANOVA.

Solving: The F ratio between columns at (2,10) degrees of freedom is 12.58, the table value of F ratio at 5% level of significance with (2,10) degrees of freedom is 4.10. Thus the tabulated value is more than the table value which implies that the type of seeds has had an impact on the adoption by the farmers.

The F ratio between the rows at (5,10) degrees of freedom is 12.616, the table value of F ratio at 5% level of significance with (5,10) degrees of freedom is 3.33. Thus, the tabulated value is more than the value which implies that there has been an impact on the adoption by the farmers of different blocks where the seeds were introduced.

5. Three types of organic fertilisers were administered on 6 block of a district. The topography of the blocks are same or homogeneous. The agricultural firm is interested to verify whether organic fertilisers of three different types have really impacted the production level of potatoes. The table below cross tabulates the production of potatoes in tonnes vis-à-vis the blocks.

The production of potatoes in tonnes

Blocks	Organic fertilisers		
	O_1	O_2	O_3
1	5	6	4
2	5	7	4
3	4	5	5
4	7	8	7

Blocks	Organic fertilisers		
	O_1	O_2	O_3
5	8	8	7
6	7	8	6
Total	36	42	33

(This is one-way ANOVA)

Solution: The computed value of the F ratio 1.78, at degrees of freedom (2,15), is less than the table value of F (3,68) at 5% significance level with degree of freedom (2,15). Therefore the three varieties of organic fertiliser did not impact the sample. The difference is insignificant.

6. Discuss the reason for using analysis of variance. When should one use 'one way ANOVA' and when should one use 'two way ANOVA'? Discuss.
7. The features of the car, from a marketing point of view, are colour, shape, engine power, seating capacity, brand image. Respondents have been asked to rank them using an ordinal scale. The analyst has been told that the tool flexibility is restricted to descriptive statistics for final ranking. What descriptive statistic will one use and why?

CHAPTER 11

Sampling, Sampling Errors and Testing of Hypotheses

LEARNING OBJECTIVES

After going through this chapter you will understand

- Distinction between population and sample
- Population distribution and sampling distribution
- Confidence limits of estimates
- Reliability of estimated mean
- Reliability of estimated standard deviation
- Statistical significance of difference between two means
- Testing of hypotheses
- Null hypothesis and alternate hypothesis
- Selecting a level of significance
- Application and usage of two-tailed test
- Chi square as a non-parametric test

Key words Sampling, normal distribution, sampling distribution, standard error, critical ratio, hypothesis testing, null hypothesis, chi-square test

11.1 INTRODUCTION

Statistical theory was developed primarily for helping a researcher to unveil the reality which is hidden in a data set. In the previous chapter we saw how calculating the central tendency of the data or the dispersion of the data can reveal some truths contained in the data set. While it is true that such uses of statistical tools are important, particularly for getting summary results from the data set, statistical theory has more powerful tools in its arsenal that a researcher can use. For example, consider the following problem. Let us suppose the total number of households in the given locality is known to be 4000. A researcher visits only 100 households and collects the data on monthly consumption expenditures of these households. By analysing the data, he finds that the average level of consumption expenditures of these households is Rs 5740 per family. The researcher, for some reason, is unable to collect data on the monthly consumption expenditure from all the households of the locality. However, he wants to know whether it would be wise for him to accept Rs 5740 as a reasonable approximation of the average monthly consumption expenditures per family of the 4000 households in the locality. Ordinarily, it seems that such an inference cannot be drawn on the basis of the information about the consumption expenditures of 100 households out of 4000 households in that locality. Usually, one would advise the researcher to visit each of the 4000 households, collect the required information and then calculate the average to get the right answer to the problem. Statistical theory however suggests that one can reduce the cost and time involved in visiting all the 4000 households by estimating the average consumption expenditures of the 4000 households on the basis of the information collected from only 100 representative households. Some error will exist, but the statistician would be able to help the researcher to estimate even the extent of error in this estimated value. He may also help the researcher to know the probability that the average consumption expenditure per family of the 4000 households in the locality would indeed be Rs 5740. Statistical theory has this power.

To put issues in order, we will point out that in the previous chapter, various statistical tools for summarising the information contained in the data set, as well as the techniques for finding the relation between or among the data set were outlined. These are indeed very useful in social research. We shall now discuss another set of statistical tools which may help the researcher in his effort to draw inferences regarding the behaviour of a larger set of data on the basis of the information collected from a smaller set. In fact, this is the most powerful contribution of statistical tools and techniques in various areas of social science. A researcher in applied areas of the subjects in social science should be equipped in such a way that he can draw statistically valid inferences about the universe of his study on the basis of the limited information that he is exposed to. In this chapter we give a brief outline of how this can be done. There is a vast amount of literature in this branch of knowledge. For further reading, a textbook on statistical theory should be consulted.

11.2 POPULATION AND SAMPLE

It is important to learn some technical terms. In statistical theory, two terms - population and sample - are widely used. The term population has a special meaning in statistical theory. It means the sum total of the objects or events—not necessarily human beings. For example, in statistics we very often talk about the population of a particular plant (number of mango trees in a mixed orchard), the population of an industrial product (number of cars in a city) or the number of events in a sports programme in a club. All these would be termed as a 'population'.

As one understands, the examination of the entire population for studying a certain feature is often either impossible or impractical. For example, studying the quality of mangoes in an orchard is never done by plucking every mango in the orchard and sending it to the laboratory. Again, a market research team will never visit every customer for studying the consumer psyche with respect to a particular brand. The usual practice is to examine a limited number of individual cases which are a part of the whole set (population). Such a set of a limited number of individual cases is known as a sample. We can study the statistical properties of a sample precisely. For example, if we take a sample of 100 mangoes from the orchard and measure their weights we can precisely find out the average weight of the mangoes in the sample. Again, we can record the brands of a set of 500 cars plying in a city road at a particular period in a particular day of a particular year and record the percentage of cars of a particular brand in the set of 500 cars. Getting the information on the percentage of a particular brand of cars plying in a city road on an average in a typical day is rather difficult if not impossible (even if we go by the records of car registration in a city, we may not be able to find the precise percentage of a particular brand of cars in a city because a car registered in a city need not necessarily ply in the same city).

The theory of statistical inference can help us to estimate how many cars might be plying in a city in a typical day, provided we take a properly selected sample of cars. Similarly one may infer the average weight of a mango in a particular orchard without plucking every mango if only a representative sample of mangoes is plucked (thus not destroying the orchard). The technique of choosing a representative sample and utilising it for inference with the help of sampling theory is therefore important. The issue of selecting a proper sample, that is, a random sample, is discussed in **Chapter 9** of this book where the advantages of a sample survey vis-à-vis that of a complete enumeration are considered. For making statistically valid inferences from a sample, the necessary prerequisite is that a sample must be unbiased. In other words, a sample must be drawn from the population in a statistically random manner.

11.3 POPULATION DISTRIBUTION AND SAMPLING DISTRIBUTION

Population distribution: In Chapter 10, we started with the concept of frequency distribution. To recapitulate, a *variate* can assume different values. For example, monthly expenditure per household in a select set of localities is a variate in statistical analysis. The frequency count for the number of times a particular value of a variate occurs is noted. The description is usually given in numerics in the ratio scale. It can also be given in terms of a histogram, a bar diagram or a frequency curve. Now consider a sample drawn from a population. We now have a sample of observations which can be considered as the frequency distribution of the concerned variate. For a continuous variate we will get a continuous frequency distribution which can be described as a frequency curve. This curve may take any shape depending on the nature of the sample. Suppose the sample is taken repeatedly, the nature of the frequency distribution will also change. Consider now a situation where the trial, that is, the drawing of the sample is done repeatedly. What would be the shape of the frequency distribution? The problem was tackled by considering a hypothetical situation of trial with a coin and noting the outcomes (head or tail). It was observed that the distribution was a bell-shaped curve. Theoretically also, it has been proved that if the number of trials increases infinitely, the frequency distribution would be bell-shaped. The highest frequency would be on the central value or mean of the distribution.

In the bell-shaped curve, the variate is assumed to be continuous so that the frequency distribution is also a continuous curve. The frequencies are evenly spread around the central value of the variate, which is known as the mean of the distribution. The dispersion of the frequencies is such that 68% of all the cases will lie around mean $\pm$ standard deviation (Std Dev or σ). The values of the variate, that lie within mean $\pm 2\sigma$ will cover 95% of the frequencies and 99.7% of the cases will be covered by a value of the variate that lies within mean $\pm 3\sigma$. This distribution, which is to take place with respect to any population in which the continuous variate can move from $+\alpha$ to $-\alpha$, was conceived by the mathematician Karl Friedrich Gauss (1777–1855) and therefore the distribution is known as *Gaussian distribution.* The statisticians considered this as the norm with the theoretical distribution and therefore this is called *normal distribution*.

How do we conceive this distribution? Suppose the variate under consideration is *x*. The probability of *x*, denoted as *P*(*x*) under Gaussian distribution which is a continuous distribution, is given by:

$$f(x,\mu,\sigma)=\frac{1}{\sigma\sqrt{2\pi}}e^{-\frac{(x-\mu)^2}{2\sigma^2}} \tag{11.1}$$

where μ is the population mean and σ is the standard deviation, $\pi = 3.14159$ and $e = 2.71828$.

The mean, median, and mode are equal for this family of distributions. The area under the curve over a range represents the probability for that range. The total area under the curve from $+\alpha$ to $-\alpha$ is unity. But the highest probability is concentrated near the mean value (Fig. 11.1).

If we assume that the sample is drawn from a normal population, the properties of the normal curve can be utilised for testing a hypothesis (the rules for testing the hypothesis are

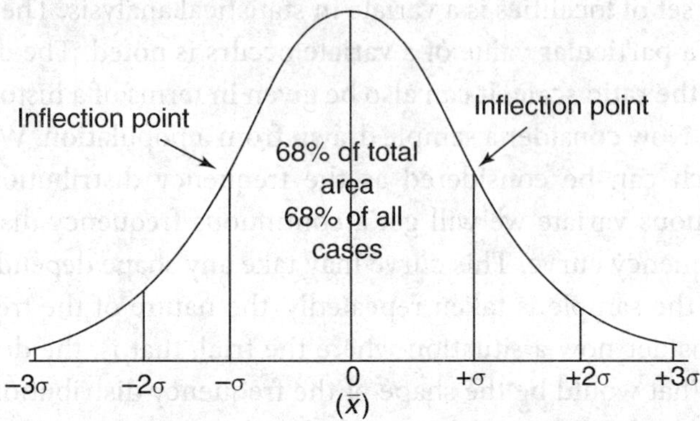

Fig. 11.1 Relationship between the area under the curve for a normal probability distribution and distance from the mean measured in standard deviation

discussed in another section of the chapter). There could be other theoretical distributions such as *Binomial* and *Poisson*. For an infinite trial, both these distributions would tend towards normal distribution. For some statistical tests, the population is assumed to follow a binomial or a Poisson distribution.

Sampling distribution: When we take a sample, its distribution cannot approximate the normal distribution unless the size of the sample is very large. But we can make inferences about the properties of the population (what should be the mean, what should be the standard deviation) from a representative sample even when the sample size is small. In order to understand how to do this, we shall have to start with the concept of a sampling distribution.

Consider any measure that characterises a population. For example, consider the mean of a population. Suppose a number of samples of the same size are taken from a population. If we measure the mean of each sample, we will observe that the individual values are not the same; they differ from each other. If now we consider the frequency distribution of such measures of mean we get a distribution which is known as a sampling distribution of mean. What could be the nature of the distribution of the sample mean? If the trial is repeated infinitely, it would also approach the normal distribution. Suppose we now take a specific sample in a statistically regular way (units are drawn randomly). The specific value of the mean is derived from the given sample. Call it $\bar{x}$. Let us suppose we now want to know how reliable it is to take $\bar{x}$ as the mean of the population. If one can take $\bar{x}$ as a fair approximation of the true mean of the population, then it would be absolutely unnecessary to consider each unit of the population and find the true mean through a lengthy, time consuming and costly process. The sampling theory addresses this issue.

The issue is addressed in the following way. Suppose the population mean is μ. The issue under consideration is whether $\bar{x}$ can be considered as the same as μ, that is, whether $\bar{x} - \mu = 0$. Common sense would tell one that $\bar{x}$ will most likely not be same as μ, that is, $\bar{x} \neq \mu$. The statistician however, would put the issue differently and would ask how reliable it will be to take $\overline{x}$ as a true approximation of μ. In other words, how much error could there be if we take $\overline{x}$ as a measure of μ?

Let us consider a situation in which the samples are taken from a bell-shaped parent population and assume that the samples are not small, then the sample distribution is closer to the normal distribution. For all practical purposes, when samples contain not less than 50 cases (or not less than 30 cases) this property of a representative sample will remain valid.

The implications are quite interesting. If we consider the mean of a representative sample and repeat the process (that is, draw another representative sample from the population and find its mean) an infinite number of times, it is quite likely that the central tendency of these means would be towards the mean of the population and about 68% of all the means will lie around the mean of the sample means ± 1 standard deviation of the distribution of sample means. The values of the sample means that lie within mean of sample means ± 2 standard deviation of the distribution of sample means will cover about 95% of the frequencies and about 99.7% of the cases will be covered by a value of the sample means that lies within mean of sample means ± 3 standard deviation of the distribution.

The standard deviation of the sample means about the true population mean is known as the standard error of the mean. The standard error or the mean is thus the standard deviation of a sampling distribution of the means. If in any particular sample, the mean is found to be lying outside these regions (which of these regions is not decided by any statistical theory; one shall have to apply one's own judgement about the tolerance limit of the estimate), one would infer that the sample mean is most unlikely to be a proper estimate of the population mean.

11.4 CONFIDENCE LIMITS OF ESTIMATES

Let us consider the issue from the point of view of the user of the technique. What is the crux of the issue? The user applies the theory of statistics, draws the representative sample and calculates the mean as the summary description of the behaviour of the data set. Now he wants to know whether it would be logical to infer that the calculated mean can be taken as a good approximation of the population mean. In other words, the user desires to estimate the population mean from the mean of the representative sample that he has drawn. To estimate the mean of a population we take a sample from the population and calculate its mean. We then try to infer whether this mean can be considered as the mean of the population. In other words, we *estimate* the true population mean from the mean of a sample. For example, let us suppose a researcher plans to find out the % of a family's budget spent on cereals with respect to 1000 families residing in a locality. Instead of meeting 1000 households, the researcher takes a sample of 100 households to minimise the cost of the survey. The sample has been drawn scientifically, that is, by the method of random sampling. From the information collected from 100 households, the researcher finds that the average expenditure on cereals per household is Rs $\overline{x}$. The question that the researcher faces is whether *it can be regarded as an estimate of the mean expenditure on cereals by 1000 households in the locality.*

From a statistical point of view, the answer is yes because the sample is drawn scientifically, that is, the sample is a representative of the population. The next question that the researcher faces is: would $\bar{x}$ be the exact figure for average expenditure on cereals by the 1000 households of the locality? The answer from the statistical point of view is that the researcher is not sure whether it is true; in fact this is why $\bar{x}$ is an *estimated* value and not claimed to be the exact value. The logical next question therefore is how good such an estimate is. To what extent is the researcher confident that the estimated value can represent the true value of the population mean?

Statistical theory can answer this question. If the sample is large, then the mean computed for the representative sample will most probably not lie farther than three times the standard errors below and above the true mean. (99% of the cases will lie in this range, only 1% is outside this range.)

To proceed further, let us go back to Eq. 11.1. Assume $\mu = 0$ and $\sigma = 1$. The normal distribution is then transformed to standard normal distribution ±1.96 area around mean (which is zero) which will include 95% of the population. Taking a clue from this, we could state that, in a large sample, only 5% of the sample mean will be outside the area $\pm 1.96\sigma_M$ of the true mean. If the true mean in smaller than the $1.96\sigma_M$ then the true mean lies on the extreme left of the bell-shaped curve. The probability of the mean being that much below is 1/2 of 0.05, that is, 0.025.

If the mean is larger than the estimated one and lies $1.96\sigma_M$ or more above it, than the estimated mean will lie somewhere in the extreme right portion of the mean. The probability that the true mean will be within $1.96\sigma_M$ of the estimated mean, it will be 1 – (0.025 + 0.025) = 0.95. Such a range describes the confidence limits of an estimated value of a variate (Fig. 11.2).

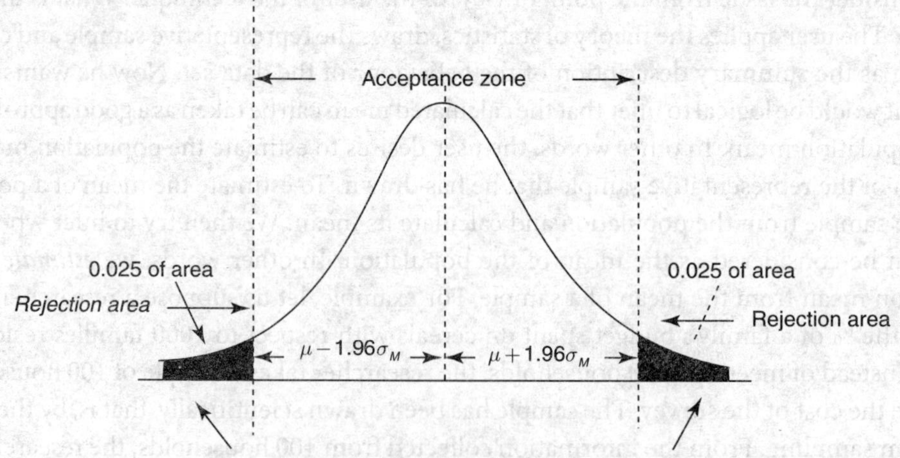

Fig. 11.2 5% level of significance

The reliability of the statistic is stated in terms of the probability of the true value being within a certain distance of the estimated one.

11.5 RELIABILITY OF AN ESTIMATED MEAN

Accepting that there is a given agreed risk of being wrong, we can express the reliability of an estimated population mean by stating the confidence limits above and below it. The precision of the estimate or the reliability of the statistic, is stated in terms of the probability of the true value being within a certain distance from the estimated one.

The distance here is conceived in terms of confidence limits and confidence limits are expressed in terms of standard error of the sample mean. The standard error has a relation with the standard deviation of the population.

If we consider σ as standard deviation of the population, and n the number of units in the sample, the standard error of the mean will be:

$$\sigma_{\bar{x}} = \frac{\sigma}{\sqrt{n}}$$

We shall not discuss how this relation has been derived. Instead, we will explain what it implies. Even a casual look at the formula will explain that larger the σ (population standard deviation) the more scattered will be the means of the sample. Further, more the units that exist in the samples, the less scattered will be the sample mean. The smaller the number of units in the sample, the more scattered will be the sample means; in fact, the standard error of the mean is inversely proportional to the square root of the units in the sample. Usually, we expect that n should be 30 units or more, in which case we expect to get a good approximation of the parameters.

We normally assume that with respect to a representative sample, the estimated population mean is simply the sample mean (reliability in estimation should be taken care of by attaching the upper and lower limits within which the true value will lie). We will now add that a good estimate of the standard deviation of population is given by the standard deviation of the sample which is standard error.

Having calculated the $\bar{x}$ and the standard error of the sample, the population mean can be estimated with reliability. We will explain how this can be done.

Example 11.1

Let us suppose that the mean of expenditure (per month) on toys is Rs 150 in a sample of 120 households. The standard deviation is Rs 25 for the population of households. Work out the reliability of the estimate of the mean of Rs 150.

The standard error of mean stated in the case is:

$$\sigma_{\bar{x}} = \frac{25}{\sqrt{120}} = \text{Rs } 2.28$$

Therefore on basis of probability of 0.01 (level of confidence limit), the upper and lower limits of likely monthly average consumption of the population will be

$$\text{Rs } 150 \pm 2.58 \times 2.28 = \text{Rs } 150 \pm \text{Rs } 5.88$$

The lower limit of monthly expense on toys will be Rs 144 and the upper limit will be Rs 165.

11.6 RELIABILITY OF ESTIMATED STANDARD DEVIATION

We are now in a position to estimate the standard deviation of the population by the same logic. We have the formula for the standard error of the standard deviation. The formula is:

$$\sigma_6 = \frac{\sigma}{\sqrt{2n}}$$

For a higher degree of confidence, that is, at the probability of 0.01, the estimated standard deviation must be in the range of $\sigma \pm 2.58\,\sigma$.

Example 11.2

Consider Example 11.1. The data are n = Rs 125, M = Rs 150, σ = Rs 25. The standard error of the standard deviation is

$$\sigma = \frac{25}{\sqrt{2 \times 150}} = \text{Rs } 1.44$$

Therefore, on the basis of a probability of 0.05 (level of confidence), the upper and lower confidence limits regarding the value of the estimated standard deviation are

Rs 25 ± Rs 1.96 × σ σ = Rs 25 ± Rs 1.96 × 1.44 = Rs 25 ± Rs 2.82. The lower limit of income variation in the population will be Rs 22.18 and the upper limit will be Rs 27.82.

11.7 THE SIGNIFICANCE OF DIFFERENCE BETWEEN TWO MEANS

Suppose we take one sample from a specific population and calculate its mean. Similarly another sample is considered and its mean is likewise calculated. If the mean of the second sample is close enough to the mean of the first sample it could be concluded that the second sample was drawn from the same population. In case it is otherwise, it is most likely that the second sample has not been drawn from the same population. *The problem is referred to the as the problem of significance of the difference between the means.* The difference between two sample means is not due to change or due to fluctuation in the samples. The difference is significant if it is at least 1.96 its standard error at 5% level of significance, or at least 2.58 its standard error at 1% level of significance.

We have already seen that $\sigma_{\bar{x}} = \frac{\sigma_1}{\sqrt{n_1}}$

When n_1 = sample size and σ_1 = sample standard deviation of sample 1 and σ_{M1} = the standard error of mean for sample 1.

Similarly, for the second sample we get,

$$\sigma_{\bar{x}_2} = \frac{\sigma_2}{\sqrt{n_2}}$$

The standard error of the difference between two means may be expressed in terms of

σ_1 = standard deviation of first sample, σ_2 = standard deviation of second sample, n_1 = size of the first sample, n_2 = size of the second sample

$$\frac{(M_1 - M_2)}{\sigma_D} = \sqrt{\left(\frac{\sigma_1^2}{n_1} + \frac{\sigma_2^2}{n_2}\right)}$$

Now if M_1 is the mean of the first sample and M_2 is the mean of the second sample, the difference between these means divided by σ_D is known as the *critical ratio* (CR).

$$\text{CR} = \frac{(M_1 - M_2)}{\sigma_D}$$

If the critical ratio is equal to or greater than 1.96, then the probability that two samples are drawn from the same population is equal to 0.05. At 1% level of significance, if the CR is more than or equal to 2.58, the samples are from the same population.

Example 11.3

Let us suppose the size of the sample in two groups is 120. The mean score is Rs 150 and Rs 145 as expenditure per month on alcohol for group 1 and group 2 respectively. The standard deviation of group 1 and group 2 is Rs 20 and Rs 30 respectively.

The standard error of the difference between the two means is,

$$\sigma_D = \sqrt{\frac{20^2}{120} + \frac{30^2}{120}} = \sqrt{3.33 + 7.5} = 3.29$$

$$\text{The critical ratio: } \sigma - \frac{M_1 - M_2}{\sigma_D} = \frac{150 - 145}{3.29} = 1.52$$

The samples are different in origin if tested at 5% level of significance as it is lesser than 1.96. Thus group 2 has been drawn from a population different from that of group 1.

11.8 TESTING OF HYPOTHESES

The universe from which the sample is drawn is not known in most of the cases of social research. The only thing we know is that, if the original population is distributed normally or even approximately so, the distribution of the means of a random sample is normal. The researcher utilises this theorem to find out the limits within which any given proportion of sample means would lie. From this, one can develop the concept of confidence limits and confidence interval, that is, the range between the two confidence limits.

In applied investigations we are often interested in comparing some characteristics of a group with a specified value, or in comparing two or more groups with regard to their characteristics. For example, we may be interested in comparing the mean incomes of two groups of sales personnel working in two different companies or we may wish to compare the variation in the incomes of two groups of sales persons in two companies. One may even want to know whether having an MBA degree would make any difference to the total emoluments in these two companies.

How should one proceed? Should we rely on mere numerical magnitudes of the index of comparison such as the mean variance or measure of association? Any researcher who is exposed to the discussion on the relation between population and sample would understand that this may not be the right approach. Each group here is represented only by *a sample of observations and if another sample were drawn, the numerical value would change.*

In other words, sampling fluctuations exist which affect the observed differences between groups. One cannot therefore take the difference between the observed values (of mean or dispersion) as the real difference.

With the help of statistical theory, we can develop a procedure to distinguish whether the observed difference is merely due to sampling fluctuations or whether it is due to some real differences among the groups. Such a procedure is called a *test of significance.* We shall discuss this topic briefly.

11.8.1 Null Hypothesis and Alternate Hypothesis

If the difference between two attributes is purely due to sampling fluctuations, we understand that the difference between the two will not be statistically significant. For example, when we test the difference between the mean emoluments of sales personnel of two companies (see above), we shall understand that the two samples could be taken to be drawn from the same population and therefore the difference between their means is associated with the scatter that might have been in a homogeneous population; that is, two companies do not *basically* differ in their pattern of emoluments offered to the sales personnel—we are then considering the *null hypothesis* (H_o). This hypothesis asserts that no true difference exists between two means.

Alternate hypothesis (H_a) states that the difference between two samples is not due to sampling fluctuation but due to the fact that they are drawn from different populations. However, rejecting the H_o does not necessarily mean that the H_a is true. In the H_o, the statement is in the negative form. For example, with respect to the two sample means related to the emolument of the sample personnel, the statement for the H_o would be:

H_o: The difference between the two means is *not* statistically significant.

Selecting a significance level: It is defined as that percentage of certainty with which one has to state the probability of a particular hypothesis being true. There is no single standard for level of significance. In some cases 1% level of significance, in other some 5% level of significance is used. One may even test a hypothesis at 10% level of significance. The percentages only indicate the extent of robustness of the inference.

Figure 11.3 illustrates a hypothesis test at three different significance levels—0.01, 0.10, and 0.50. In part (a) and (b) the range of rejection is small whereas in part (c) it is large.

11.8.2 Decision Rule

Rejecting a null hypothesis when it is true is called Type I error and accepting a null hypothesis when it is false is referred as Type II error. The probabilities of Type I and Type II errors are referred to as α (alpha) and β (beta) respectively. There is a trade off between the two types of errors; the probability of reducing one type of error will lead to the increase in the probability of another type of error. In other words if we want to reduce Type I, this will increase the probability of Type II error. In Fig. 11.3 , when we consider part (c), we are trying to safeguard the occurrence of Type II error, but in the process we have increased α. To deal with this trade off in a professional situation, we decide the appropriate level of significance by examining the penalties attached to the type of error.

For example, rejecting a consignment would mean a lot of work will be undertaken to redo the contract while allowing the consignment may mean that there is a possibility of poisoning the consumer. Increasing Type I error results in reduction of Type II error. From a management perspective, this is the required solution for the situation.

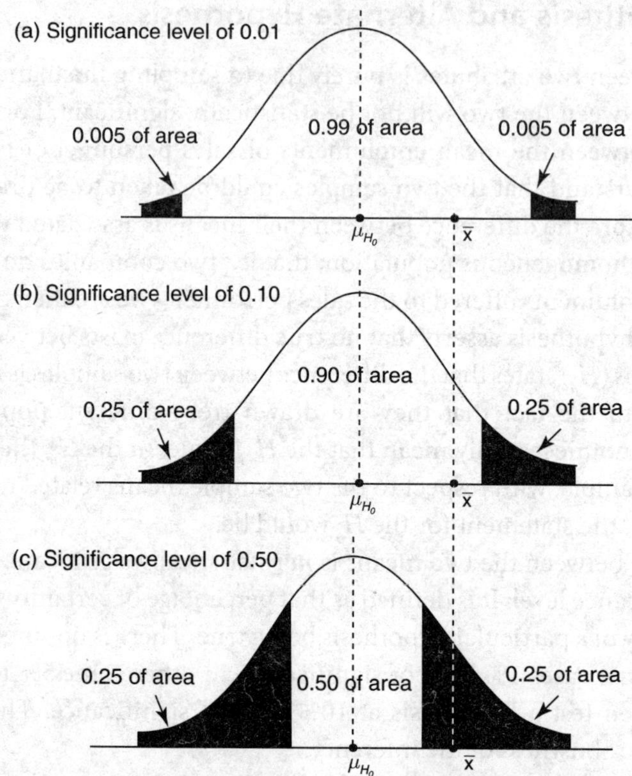

Fig. 11.3 Different levels of significance

11.8.3 Application and Use of Two-tailed Hypothesis Testing

Let us suppose we have a scenario where the product (a transistor) should be such that its temperature must be 1000°C. In case it is less than 1000°C, the other components of the circuit breaker will not get activated. Again, in a situation where the temperature is above 1000°C, the circuit breaker will burn out.

$$\text{Null hypothesis } H_0 = M = 1000°\text{C}$$

$$\text{Alternate hypothesis } H_1 = M \neq 1000°\text{C}$$

This states that the sample which necessarily has a mean of 1000°C will be accepted and the null hypothesis will be rejected.

11.8.4 Application and Use of One-tailed Hypothesis Testing (Left-tailed)

Let us consider a situation when the transistor should preferably have a temperature of 1000°C. If it is more it is acceptable as no extra cost is involved, but under no circumstance should the temperature be less than 1000°C.

$$H_0 = M = 1000°C$$

$$H_1 = M < 1000°C$$

The sample is acceptable if it at least has a mean temperature of $H_0 = M = 1000°C$ and it is also acceptable if $H_1 = M < 1000$. It rejects the H_0 if the sample has a mean life which is below 1000°C (Fig 11.4).

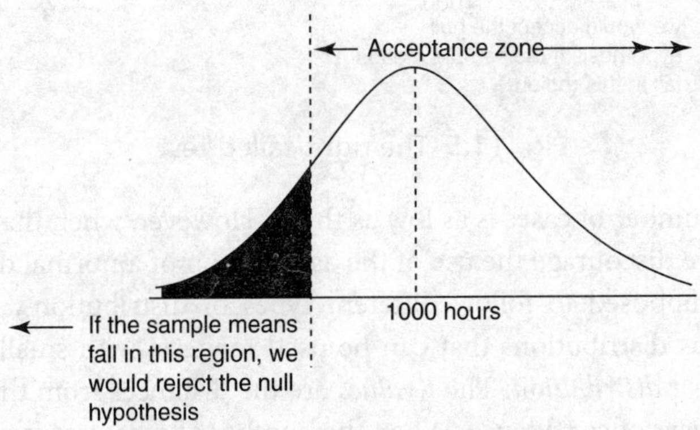

Fig. 11.4 The left-tailed test

This test is referred to as *left-tailed test*. A left-tailed test is used when the following conditions exist. H_0: $M = MH_0$ and H_1: $M < MH_0$.
Use and application of one-tailed test (right-tailed test):
A right-tailed test is applicable when H_0: $M = MH_0$ and H_1: $M > MH_0$.

A sales manager expects that the commission payable to a sales person up to Rs 1000/- is acceptable but an amount above Rs 1000/- is not so. The null hypothesis and alternate hypothesis are the following:

Null hypothesis H_0: $M =$ Rs 1000/-

Acceptance hypothesis H_1: $M > 1000$/-

The null hypothesis is rejected when the salespersons have a mean above Rs 1000/-. Figure 11.5 shows the rejection zone.

11.8.5 Sampling Distribution (Large and Small Samples)

So long, we have assumed that the population distribution is normal. This assumption is true when the population is large. Again in case of a sample, the sampling distribution would be normal only when the sample size is large. This however depends on the number of cases in the sample. Strictly speaking, the theory is true when the number of cases is infinitely large (which in effect is an unattainable condition). For all practical purposes, we maintain the assumption of normality when the number of cases is equal to or greater than fifty. This assumption is also supposed to be

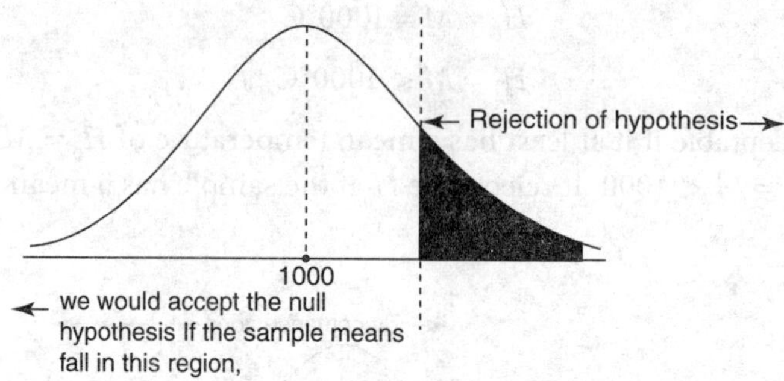

Fig. 11.5 The right-tailed test

valid even when the number of cases is as low as thirty. However, when the number of sampled units is less than 30, we discourage the use of the assumption of a normal distribution. Samples of smaller sizes are supposed to follow different types of distributions. In fact, statisticians have developed various distributions that can be used for tests with small samples. One such distribution is *student's t distribution.* The *t values* are the distances from the mean value which correspond to given levels of confidence. When the number of cases per sample (*n*) is very large, the *t* distribution tends to be normal. The lower the value of *n,* higher the *t* value for the same level of confidence. The *t* distribution curves are symmetrical around the mean and they are bell-shaped curves having higher peaks and longer tails than the normal distribution. For testing, the *t* values are set against the number of degrees of freedom which would be $n-1$.

Other small sample distributions are *Snedecor's F distribution* (used for testing the variance), *Fisher's Z distribution* (used for testing the combined estimates of correlation coefficients) and *chi-square distribution* (used as a test of goodness of fit). Chi-square distribution will be discussed elaborately. It is widely used when the distribution of the parent population does not specify any parameter that can be estimated. One should however be aware of the fact that this distribution provides some powerful tools for testing various statistical hypotheses. A course on sampling theory and the theoretical distribution related to large and small samples would be very useful for the researcher in handling empirical research.

11.9 CHI-SQUARE AS A NON-PARAMETRIC TEST

It is primarily used for testing the agreement of observed frequency with those expected upon a given hypothesis. For instance, comparison of the observed frequency distribution with a theoretical one such as normal distribution. The test is used as—a test of goodness of fit and a test of independence.

A goodness of fit: The chi-square (χ^2) test enables us to see how the observed data matches with the theoretical distribution (such as binomial distribution, Poisson distribution or normal distribution). In case of a perfect fit, the result of the χ^2 will be 0, which rarely happens. The outcome is usually some positive value due to sampling fluctuation.

As a test of independence, this test enables us to explain whether or not, two or more attributes or variables are associated. One could be interested to know whether a promotional tool has an association with any particular stratum of population and similar issues. Under the circumstance, it is imperative that one works out the *expected frequency* relative to the observed frequency first and then works out the χ^2. Symbolically this formula could be written as,

$$\chi^2 = \sum \frac{(O_{ij} - E_{ij})^2}{E_{ij}}$$

where O = observed frequency, E = expected frequency, O_{ij} = observed frequency of the cell in the ith row and j^{th} column, E_{ij} = expected frequency of the cell in the ith row and j^{th} column.

In market research, one uses the chi-square test mostly in relevance to *test of independence.* In other words it is *testing of independence of classifications in what are known as contingency tables.* When a group of individuals can be classified in two or more ways, the result of classification can be stated as in Table 11.1.

Table 11.1 Contingency table

Classes	A_1	A_2	A_3
B_1	N_{11}	N_{21}	N_{31}
B_2	N_{12}	N_{22}	N_{32}
B_3	N_{13}	N_{23}	N_{33}
...			

A or B classes refer to types of classifications. The number N_{11} refers to cross tabulation—cell of A_1 classification with B_1 classification. Thus the cell frequency is tabulated. The cell frequency and the observed frequency have to be absolute numbers (not percentages). In case the cell frequency is less than 5, the cell has to be merged with an adjacent cell. The χ^2 value is tabulated based on two dimensions—degree of freedom and level of significance, that is, 1, 2 or 3 for degree of freedom and 0.01 level of significance or 0.05 level of significance and so on. The contingency table shows the observed frequency in each such cross tabulated cell pertaining to the classifications. For working out the χ^2 the Expected Frequency Table has also to be computed. The tabulated value of χ^2 is matched with the table value in the respect to the degree of freedom and level of significance. In case of the contingency table, the degree of freedom is calculated as $(r - 1)(c - 1)$, where r refers to number of rows and c refers to number of columns.

The expected frequency in each cell is computed as shown below.

$$\text{Expected frequency} = \frac{(\text{Row total of the rows of the cell}) \times (\text{Column total of the columns of that cell})}{\text{Grand total}}$$

The tabulated value of χ^2 being lower than the table value (considering the specific degree of freedom and level of significance) will indicate that the classification variables have no association. In case the tabulated χ^2 is more than the table value (considering the specific degree of freedom and level of significance), it would indicate that there is association among the classification variables. The degree of association cannot be stated by χ^2. An example will help in understanding the concept.

Example 11.4

One wants to test the association of usage volume of detergent powder with the size of the family, the contingency table is given below.

Contingency table showing use of detergent with family size

Family size	**Packet size (Numbers)**		
	500 g (A_1)	**1 kg or more 1–5 (A_2)**	**Total**
1–5 (B_1)	80 (A_1 B_1)	40 (A_2 B_1)	120
More than 5 (B_2)	20 (A_1 B_2)	100(A_2 B_2)	120
Total	100	140	240

Expected frequency table showing use of detergent with family size

Family size	**Packet size (Numbers)**		
	500 g (A_1)	**1 kg or more 1–5 (A_2)**	**Total**
1–5 (B_1)	$\frac{120 \times 100}{240} = 50$ (A_1 B_1)	$\frac{120 \times 140}{240} = 70$($A_2$ B_1)	120
More than 5 (B_2)	$\frac{120 \times 100}{240} = 50$($A_1$ B_2)	$\frac{120 \times 140}{240} = 70$($A_2$ B_2)	120
Total	100	140	240

Table showing the calculation of χ^2

Groups	Observed frequency O_{ij}	Expected frequency E_{ij}	$(O_{ij} - E_{ij})$	$(O_{ij} - E_{ij})^2$	$\frac{(O_{ij} - E_{ij})^2}{E_{ij}}$
(A_1, B_1)	80	50	30	900	18.00
(A_1, B_2)	20	50	–30	900	18.00
(A_2, B_1)	40	70	–30	900	12.85
(A_2, B_2)	100	70	30	900	12.85
				$\sum\frac{(O_{ij} - E_{ij})^2}{E_{ij}}$	61.70

$$\chi^2 = \sum\frac{(O_{ij} - E_{ij})^2}{E_{ij}} = 61.70$$

Degrees of freedom $(r - 1)(c - 1) = (2 - 1)(2 - 1) = 1$

The table values at 0.01 (1%) or 0.05 (5%) level of significance with 1 degree of freedom are $\chi^2 = 3.841$ and 6.635 respectively.

Since the computed value is more than the table value, one concludes that packet size of detergents have association with family size.

11.9.1 Yates' Correction

There could be situations where one may not like to club or merge the cells in order to maintain the classification in the proper perspective. This is to say that the cells may have a cell frequency less than 5. Yates has proposed correction in the χ^2 value calculation in the cases of (2 × 2) tables in cases of cell frequency being less than 5. The correction suggested by Yates is referred to as *Yates' correction*. It refers to the reduction of deviation of observed frequency from the expected frequency which in turn reduces the value of χ^2. The rule of the correction is to reduce the deviation for each cell by 0.5. The formula is:

$$\chi^2 = \sum\frac{[(O_{ij} - E_{ij}) - 0.5]^2}{E_{ij}}$$

One must reiterate that such corrections are only done in cases of contingency table of the 2 × 2 format.

Example 11.5

A sample of 40 was chosen to understand whether the promotion tools are associated more with urban or rural localities. The observed frequency is shown below:

Table showing the cross classification of promotion tools with localities

Localities	Promotion tools		
	Tea spoon (numbers) [A_1]	Face powder (numbers) [A_2]	Total
Urban (numbers) [B_1]	2 [A_1B_1]	8 [A_2B_1]	10
Rural (numbers) [B_2]	12 [A_1B_2]	18 [A_2B_2]	30
Total	14	26	40

Expected frequency table showing the cross classification of promotion tools with localities

Localities	Promotion tools		
	Tea spoon (numbers) [A_1]	Face powder (numbers) [A_2]	Total
Urban (numbers) [B_1]	$\frac{10\times14}{40} = 3.5$ [A_1B_1]	$\frac{10\times26}{40} = 6.5$ [A_2B_1]	10
Rural (numbers) [B_2]	$\frac{30\times14}{40} = 10.5$ [A_1B_2]	$\frac{30\times26}{40} = 19.5$ [A_2B_2]	30
Total	14	26	40

Table showing the calculation of χ^2(using Yates' correction)

Groups	Observed frequency O_{ij}	Expected frequency E_{ij}	$(O_{ij} - E_{ij})$	$[(O_{ij} - E_{ij}) - 0.5]^2$	$\frac{[(O_{ij} - E_{ij}) - 0.5]^2}{E_{ij}}$
A_1B_1	02	3.5	−1.5	1	0.29
A_1B_2	12	10.5	1.5	1	0.10
A_2B_1	08	6.5	1.5	1	0.15
A_2B_2	18	19.5	−1.5	1	0.05
					0.59

$$\chi^2 = \Sigma\frac{[(O_{ij} - E_{ij}) - 0.5]^2}{E_{ij}}$$

The table value of 0.01 (1%) or 0.05 (5%) level of significance with 1 degree of freedom is $\chi^2 = 3.841$ and 6.635. The association does not exist because the tabulated value of χ^2 is 0.59 which is less than the table value at 1% and 5% level of significance.

Further it is worth noting that the Yates' correction decreases the value of χ^2 vis-à-vis such correction not being undertaken. Such an exercise is taken up below.

Table showing the calculation of χ^2

Groups	Observed frequency O_{ij}	Expected frequency E_{ij}	$(O_{ij} - E_{ij})$	$(O_{ij} - E_{ij})^2$	$\frac{(O_{ij} - E_{ij})^2}{E_{ij}}$
$(A_1 B_1)$	02	3.5	–1.5	2.25	0.64
$(A_1 B_2)$	12	10.5	1.5	2.25	0.21
$(A_2 B_1)$	08	6.5	1.5	2.25	0.35
$(A_2 B_2)$	18	19.5	–1.5	2.25	0.16
				$\sum\frac{(O_{ij} - E_{ij})^2}{E_{ij}}$	1.36

Degrees of Freedom $(r - 1)(c - 1) = (2 - 1)(2 -) = 1$

The table value of 0.01 (1%) or 0.05 (5%) level of significance with 1 degree of freedom is $\chi^2 = 3.841$ and 6.635. The association does not exist because the tabulated value of χ^2 is 1.36 which is less than the table value at 1% and 5% level of significance.

Please observe that with Yates' correction, the value of χ^2 is 0.59 and without the correction the value of χ^2 is 1.36.

SUMMARY

- In research study, the word *population* is used to include the sum total of the objects, events or people; it does not mean only human beings.
- A sample drawn randomly from the population is representative of the population.
- Population distribution and its sampling distribution are studied to determine mean value standard deviation and other important information about the population distribution.
- In a hypothesis, testing is done at different levels of significance.
- Specific criteria are used in accepting or rejecting a null hypothesis.
- The chi-square test enables us to examine how the observed data matches with its theoretical distribution.

ASSIGNMENTS

Q1 Choose the right answers

1. A hypothesis by its origin is a :
   (a) Simple statement
   (b) A proposition likely to be true or false
   (c) A statement that is vague
   (d) None of the above
2. An alternative hypothesis is one in which one wishes:
   (a) To prove the untruth
   (b) To prove the truth
   (c) To prove neither the truth nor the untruth
   (d) None of the above
3. A type 1 error is said to occur when:
   (a) H_0 is actually true but the decision rule has made H_0 false
   (b) H_0 is actually false but the decision rule has made H_0 true
   (c) A mistake in the sample has been found
   (d) None of the above
4. A two-tailed test is said to occur when:
   (a) Null hypothesis has many values
   (b) Null hypothesis has a specific value or specified value
   (c) Null hypothesis has mixed values
   (d) None of the above
5. A one-tailed test is said to occur when:
   (a) The population mean has to be less than the hypothesis value
   (b) The population mean and sample mean are the same
   (c) The population mean is greater than the hypothesised value
   (d) None of the above
6. The null hypothesis claim is usually rejected when:
   (a) The computed value is less than the theoretical value of the statistic
   (b) The computed value is more than the theoretical value of the statistic
   (c) The computed value is similar to the table value of the statistic
   (d) None of the above
7. A sampling distribution is one in which:
   (a) The units of the sample are uniformly distributed
   (b) The samples are equally distributed

(c) The distribution of value of measures of a statistic in each sample of the population
(d) None of the above

8. The reliability of estimated means are:
(a) Computed by tallying one mean with another
(b) Computed on the basis of a level of significance
(c) Computed randomly
(d) None of the above

9. The *decision rule* is the rule of:
(a) Deciding which sample to choose
(b) Decision on the type of measurement of the sample distribution
(c) Decision on acceptance or rejection of null hypothesis
(d) None of the above

10. The test statistics are decided on the basis of:
(a) The sample characteristics
(b) The type of distribution and the type of variable
(c) The population characteristic
(d) None of the above

Answers

1. (b), 2. (b), 3. (a), 4. (b), 5. (c), 6. (b), 7. (c), 8. (b), 9. (c), 10. (b)

Q2 Answer the questions

1. You are given a sample of 50 consumers who are classified by two variables—occupational category and consumption expenditure.

Contingency table showing occupational category and consumption expenditure

Occupational category (members)	Consumption expenditure (Number)		
	Upto 20% on grocery (A_1)	More than 20% on grocery (A_2)	Total
Business (B_1)	14 (A_1B_1)	07 (A_2B_1)	21
Non-business (B_2)	13 (A_1B_2)	16 (A_2B_2)	29
Total	27	23	50

Use the χ^2 test to examine their association.

Solving: The tabulated value of χ^2 is 2.338. The table value is 6.635 and 3.841 at degrees of freedom 1, the level of significance is at 1% and 5% respectively. There exist no associations because the tabulated value is less than the table value for both the levels of significance.

2. An agricultural scientist is interested in finding out whether the colour of hibiscus has any association with the leaf shape of the plant. The data at his disposal is present in the contingency table below.

Leaf shape	**Colour of hibiscus**		
	Yellow	**White**	**Total**
Broad	249	717	966
Narrow	80	236	316
Total	329	953	1282

You, as a researcher, have been asked to find out whether there exists any association between the shapeof the leaf and the colour of the flower.

Solving: The tabulated value of χ^2 is 0.026 at (2 – 1)(2 – 1) degrees of freedom. The table value of χ^2 at 1% level of significance with (2 – 1)(2 – 1) degrees of freedom is 6.635. The null hypothesis is accepted. The difference in value is insignificant.

3. A sample of 13 dealers depict the market behaviour in relation to duration of credit and amount of credit (%). The market research analyst is verifying whether the firm has a logical credit based policy relating to the sales of aluminium corrugated sheets. The contingency table is given below.

Credit amount	**Duration of credit**		
	Till 7 days	**Above 7 days**	**Total**
Credit amount 25%	01	00	01
Above 25%	03	09	12
Total	04	09	13

Solving (using Yates' correction): The tabulated χ^2 is 0.188 at (2 – 1)(2 – 1) degree of freedom. The table value of (2 – 1)(2 – 1) degrees of freedom at 5% level of significance is 3.841. Since the tabulated value is less than the table value, we finally observe that the null hypothesis is accepted, that is, the difference in values is not significant. There is not likely to be any association between duration of credit and credit amount. The firm's policy is not logically based.

4. One records the data of sales (Rs) vis-à-vis percentage of commission, in regard to sales of gunny bags in reference to a sample of 16 sales persons.

Commission	Sales (Rs)		
	Till 50,000	Above 50,000	Total
Till 25% commission	03	03	06
Above 25%	01	09	10
Total	04	12	16

Solving (using Yates' correction): The tabulated χ^2 is 1.42 at (2 – 1)(2 – 1) degree of freedom. The table value of (2 – 1)(2 – 1) degrees of freedom at 5% level of significance is 3.841. Since the tabulated value is less than the table value, we finally observe that the null hypothesis is accepted, that is, the difference in values is not significant. There is not likely to be any association between sales and commission of the sales person.

5. An export order has been received and the rejection of the lot is expected when the defects are 80 units per 1,00,000. Less than 80 units will lead to rejection of the lot. More than 80 also will lead to rejection. A sample of 1000 units was obtained where 50 units were rejects. A testing of hypothesis in the case should conceptually be a two-tailed testing or a single-tailed testing. (Hint: It is a two-tailed test)

6. The null hypothesis is that 15% of the passengers travel in business class. There could be a possibility of this being more or less. A random sample of 300 passengers had 60 passengers in business class. Can we reject the null hypothesis at 95% level of confidence or 5% level of significance? (Hint: Two-tailed test of proportion)

$P_{Ho} = 0.15$ – hypothesised value of population proportion of travelling in business class

$Q_{Ho} = 0.85$ – hypothesised value of population proportion who will not travel in business class

$n = 300$

$p = 0.20$ – sample proportion of probables who use business class

$q = 0.80$ – sample proportion of probables who will not use business class

One wants to test the hypothesis that 0.15 employees are business class travellers at the 0.05 significance level.

$H_o: p = 0.15$ (null hypothesis)

$H_a: p \neq 0.15$ (alternate hypothesis)

We calculate the standard error of the proportion, using the hypothesis value of P_{Ho} and Q_{Ho}. The equation is stated below.

$$s_p = \sqrt{\frac{(PH_o)(QH_o)}{n}} = \sqrt{\frac{(0.15)(0.85)}{300}} = \sqrt{0.000425} = 0.021 \text{ (approx)}$$

Next we standardise the sample proportion and the z is to be calculated by the equation.

$$z = \frac{p - PH_o}{\sigma p} = \frac{0.20 - 0.15}{0.021} = 2.38$$

Thus the computed z value is greater than the table value at 0.05 level of significance (95% confidence level), that is, the table value is 1.96 and the computed value is 2.38, which is more than the table value and therefore we accept the alternate hypothesis. This is to state that the proportion of business class travellers is not 0.15.

7. In the market, two different promotions were tested. The first promotional variable evoked a favourable response of 100 in a sample of 400. The second variable evoked a favourable response of 300 in a sample size of 600. The researcher wants to test whether there is a difference between the efficiency of two promotional variables at 5% level of significance. (We are using Appendix 11.1)
Using the above figure in the problem we get:

$$S_{\text{difference}} = \sqrt{\frac{(50)(50)}{600} + \frac{(25)(75)}{400}}$$

$$= \sqrt{4.16 + 4.24} = 2.89$$

H_o: Observed difference is statistically significant
H_a: Observed difference is not statistically significant
We calculate the Z value

$$Z = \frac{50\% - 25\%}{2.89} = 8.65$$

The observation difference is equivalent to 8.85 standard error. Since the computed value is larger than 1.96 the table value at 0.05 level of significance (or 95% confidence level), we reject the null hypothesis. Thus we conclude that the promotion was responsible for bringing about a difference in the favourable response.

APPENDIX 11.1

The calculation of z statistic is:

$$z = \frac{After\% - Before\%}{S_{difference}}$$

The numerator of this relationship is the observed differences between two samples. The denominator is the standard error of two sample means percentage ($S_{\text{differences}}$).

The formula of standard error of a percentage is:

$$S_P = \sqrt{\frac{pq}{n}}$$

p = percentage that has the characteristics, q = percentage that is other than the p, that is, $(100 - p)$, n = sample size.

In reference to the above problem

$$S_{\text{difference}} = \sqrt{s_a^2 + s_b^2}$$

s_a = estimated standard error of the after sample percentage, s_b = estimated standard error of the before sample percentage.

Table value of Z

In the table shown below we find the level of confidence and the corresponding Z values are specified.

Desired confidence level	Critical Z value
90%	1.64
95%	1.96
99%	2.58

CHAPTER 12

Data Analysis and Report Writing

LEARNING OBJECTIVES

After going through this chapter you will understand

- Interim report and final report
- Preparation of final tables containing all useful information
- Analysis of data
- Some common mistakes in organising, storing and analysis of data
- Interpretation of results
- Outline of report
- Research and its limitations

Key words Research report, tabulation, research hypothesis testing, research outcome

12.1 INTRODUCTION

The end product of research is the report or findings of the research. The report can be furnished in the form of a scientific paper usually addressed to fellow researchers. However, a report is often required to be furnished to persons who do not have technical expertise in the subject. For example, research reports are often prepared by consultants who are required to present the findings in the form of a report that can be utilised by a client who is not expected to have technical expertise in the subject. While preparing the report, the researcher should therefore identify the clientele first and then prepare the report so that it becomes user friendly. In other words, a report is client specific. Much depends on the nature of the client. One must know the target so that the report becomes user oriented.

Whosoever be the target, a research report should be written in such a way that it follows a proper format. A researcher who has no training in the methodology of report writing may often fail to communicate the fruits of the research efforts to fellow researchers or the generalist. The focus might be lost. Much of the research that he himself has carried out may remain uncommunicated. We therefore find it prudent to discuss the salient features of a proper research report.

One point, however, should be emphasised at the very outset. Writing a good report banks heavily on the extent of clarity on the part of the researcher in understanding the subject in which he is pursuing the research. A good understanding of the methodology and strict compliance of the dos and don'ts in report writing cannot improve the quality of the research, unless the researcher develops a deep understanding on the subject of his research.

12.2 INTERIM REPORT AND THE FINAL REPORT

A research problem is taken up within a time frame. Often the researcher is required to present an interim report before the final observations are reported. The interim report is basically a progress report in which the researcher is expected to give an account of the extent of progress that has been achieved in the given period. In market research, the client often insists on getting regular feedback so that the findings of the research that has been done so far could be utilised by them immediately. In case the client needs certain information that he wants to utilise immediately, the researcher would carefully provide this information. It is not expected that the analysis based on the information would be carried out elaborately at this stage. In most of the interim reports, some highlights are provided with the necessary backup information. Care should be taken so that the report does not mislead the client. A regular meeting with the client before providing such information may help the researcher shape his understanding regarding the expectations of the client and to what extent his work is proceeding in that direction. The interim report would try to meet this expectation. Since the interim report does not contain much analysis, the researcher should not find any difficulty in submitting such a report within the time schedule, even though the work is still continuing and the researcher is mostly busy in running the research project, that is, monitoring the work that is in progress.

A final report is different from the interim report(s). Here the researcher is expected to wrap up his study and put the findings in the form of a report which should be of lasting value. Such a report can be prepared only after going through every step of research. One should remember that the interim reports provide the necessary foundation for the final report. An authentic final report should not contradict the findings that have been reported previously (unless the scenario has changed in the meantime). A final report should also contain a comprehensive analysis addressing the research issue and describing the research methodology, data sources and the findings of the research, in sequence. Rigour in analysis and precision in reporting the findings are the major qualities of a good research report. Even if the client does not need that amount of rigour that a fellow researcher would have needed, there should be no compromise on the question of maintaining quality by imparting rigour. However, rigorous analysis might be placed in the appendix of the report, if the researcher feels so. The final report of an empirical research must have the following sections—introduction, literature review, discussion on methodological issues, field area, results of the field survey, interpretation and conclusions. The limitations of the report should also be discussed. All these are elaborated upon in Section 12.6.

In empirical research, the main plank of the final report is the set of final tables that describe the empirical content of the research work which the report articulates. It is therefore necessary to discuss how to prepare the final tables from the data. Before we discuss the outline of the final report, we will elaborate upon this issue.

12.3 PREPARING THE FINAL TABLES

In the context of an empirical research, the starting point is data which could be quantitative as well as qualitative. We have discussed, rather elaborately, how the data set is generated[1] and how one can handle the data. We have also discussed how one can identify the type of research that one needs to pursue. The starting point of course is to identify the research question. As soon as one identifies a research question properly one also understands the research issues and the design of the research[2].

A particular research design is not something sacrosanct that one should adhere to during the entire course of the research. One may change the design during the course of the research. In fact, it is often found that a research question comes into sharper focus as the researcher pursues his research. He learns better as he explores the research problem. Consequently one gets a better understanding of the research issue; the research design might be changed or the initial design might be supplemented with another that effectively lays the truth bare. For example, a researcher may start with an explorative design and after getting further exposure to the problem in the course of his research, he might switch over to a causal research that may handle the problem in a better (more rigorous) manner.

The researcher is ultimately responsible for the findings of his research project. In empirical science the findings are often placed in the form of *final tables* which are expected to reveal the features of the phenomenon under study in summarised forms. Such tables are derived

1 Chapter 3
2 Chapter 2

out of the initial tabulation of the raw data following the norms of data entry, as given in computer software packages. The most user-friendly form is Excel which can transfer the data for statistical analysis under various software packages (such as Mathamatica, SPSS, SAS and others).

The initial data set should be scrutinised carefully in order to eliminate the outliers and wrong and incomplete entries. Statistical tools are then used for studying the inner logic of the data set. The tools of descriptive statistics are widely used for this exercise. While sophisticated statistical tools are very useful in preparing the final report, one should remember that the researcher would benefit if the analysis is started with simple diagrams, charts, univariate and bivariate tables, some of which could be utilised in the final report and many of which could be for the researcher's own understanding about the behaviour of the data so that he or she can use more sophisticated computer package based exercises. In other words, such an exercise with descriptive statistics primarily helps the researcher to understand the hidden logic in the behaviour of the variable(s) under study.

While preparing a report, the researcher has to first of all, visualise the necessary final tables. If and when the data set is generated from field surveys, the researcher after comprehending the research issues would identify the areas in which the information must be gathered from the target group of respondents. This is better done in a structured setting where the stimuli are imparted systematically and the responses are expected to come systematically. If the form of communication is written, this method will be called the questionnaire (closed ended) method. It is advisable that the researcher should prepare a set of dummy tables from the blank questionnaire itself and instruct the data entry operator to store the necessary information in such a way that these can be retrieved to meet the requirements of the final tables, the dummies of which have already been prepared. In a research involving field surveys, it is often found that a researcher prepares a questionnaire without having a clear understanding on what final tables will be utilised in the report. This develops out of the researcher's lack of clarity on the research questions and the research issues involved in his empirical research. However the immediate consequence is that the questionnaire often misses some vital questions that are necessary for analysing the research issue. In order to guard against such a possibility – the damage cost of which is pretty high – the researcher often goes for a questionnaire that contains the provision for answers to such questions which ultimately might transpire to be unnecessary for writing a report. The researcher should avoid both of these possibilities and select an optimum set of questions—otherwise the field survey may become inefficient in terms of cost and the quality of data. Needless to say, the researcher can develop an optimum set of questions only when he has a clear comprehension regarding the research question and the related research issues. The final tables are prepared in two or three stages. With the advent of data processing through the computer, researchers have the time to try out various alternatives with the same set of data so that the basis of induction becomes powerful. In order to pursue research in this line, the researcher first develops bivariate tables to get a first approximation of the hidden relation among the variables under study. After checking the consistency, the researcher concentrates on such tables that would bring the features of the phenomenon under study into sharp focus. The inclusion of tables that diffuse the issue must be avoided. The researcher should also not go for tailor-made tables that suits one's purpose—to prove or disprove a research hypothesis.

At the second stage, the researcher studies the association among the variables with the help of other statistical techniques. Often the quantitative truth contained in a single variate is also studied (for example, considering mean, standard deviation, coefficient of variation and other tools for univariate analysis). In order to study the interrelationships among the phenomena, as captured in the data set, it is necessary that the tools of bivariate or multi-variate analysis are utilised. The researcher takes up such experiments with the help of software packages which are user-friendly and quite fast (SPSS and SAS are two efficient packages which are user-friendly). However while applying such techniques, one must know the strengths and weaknesses of the statistical device that the researcher is applying. For this, an exposure to statistical theory is necessary.

12.4 ANALYSING THE DATA

For a large-scale survey, now-a-days computers are used to perform the tabulation of the data, data storage and the necessary analysis of the data. These are done with the help of software packages. In earlier chapters we have briefly mentioned how some computer packages function and what the researcher is expected to get from them during his research endeavour. After preparing the final tables, the researcher would again check his research hypothesis and plan the analysis of the data accordingly. Research is like taking a voyage in an unchartered route in the sense that the researcher does not know whether the empirical finding would corroborate the research hypothesis that has been drawn a priori on the basis of the received knowledge of the subject. In fact, the empirical research may gather evidence that does not go with existing understanding on the issue. However, this is what one expects to get out of a research—it attempts to develop a new frontier, a set of findings that may pave the way for reassessing the worth of an existing theory.

This is why, in empirical research we need a good deal of flexibility in our approach towards unfolding the empirical truth hidden in the data. Before the advent of the present generation computers, it was very difficult to exercise such an option because the labour involved in every statistical operation, particularly with respect to large samples and large surveys, was prohibitive. Labour involves cost. Since a project is supposed to operate under a budget constraint, it has to minimise the cost—particularly that involved in the preparation of final tables and further statistical operations, every change in which, would escalate the cost. Now-a-days, thanks to software packages, such costs have reduced significantly. But, for a better outcome, a good researcher has to pre-plan every step on the basis of what he requires to get out of the final tables and, based on this, what statistical calculations would be necessary to pursue his project. The flexibility that a good research requires has to be considered against the cost involved in pursuing flexibility.

One would, however, remember that with the advent of appropriate software, the researcher can exercise a tremendous amount of flexibility with very little impact on the marginal cost of labour so that the benefit remains well ahead of cost. A researcher can utilise this opportunity to delve deeper into data sets, so that every aspect of the truth hidden in the data gets exposed to him. The researcher needs a clearly defined research issue and the research design. The researcher will have to collect the necessary information, check the quality of the data and store it in a computer (usually with the help of a data entry operator). The primary memory acting on the CPU (central processing unit) can generate the possible outputs from the set of inputs that the researcher has stored in the computer (copied to the hard disk from a compact disc or memory stick). With the help of software packages, the researcher can perform the analysis of the data with a previously unheard of flexibility.

As we know, empirical research now-a-days banks heavily on regression analysis (Chapter 9). There are user-friendly packages that can help the researcher in getting the results of the regression with amazing speed. The researcher can also go for alternatives just by changing the instructions to the computer. The researcher selects the best regression results after analysing the strength or weakness of each regression. This of course requires knowledge of statistical tools and a good amount of understanding of their strengths and weaknesses; the appropriateness of the tool, with respect to the research issue should also be judged properly. And finally, the researcher must know how to interpret the regression results. One may not comprehend the implications of the regression results unless one knows the theoretical implications and mathematical properties of regression analysis. It is easier to comprehend the means of using simple statistical tools following the chartered course of a software package. But getting a command over a statistical tool is not so simple. This is particularly true with respect to regression analysis. For proper utilisation of regression related software packages, one must have a good deal of formal training in regression analysis as a subject, which has made tremendous progress during last 30 years, thanks to the efforts of the econometricians.

All this does not mean that one can comprehend the truth contained in the data set just with the help of statistical techniques. One cannot analyse the empirical findings unless one knows the subject on which the empirical research is being performed. A tool becomes useless and often dangerous if it is utilised by someone who is not properly trained in the subject matter of enquiry.

12.5 SOME COMMON MISTAKES

In organising, storing and analysing the data, the researcher often makes some mistakes that should be checked. A good researcher should maintain a check list so that such mistakes can be avoided. No research can be fool proof, errors and omissions would remain. However, there could be some errors which are very costly. A researcher should avoid such errors by scrupulously checking whether the research contains such mistakes. In this section we highlight some such mistakes—this list, however, is not exhaustive:

(a) *The data*: Any empirical research must have the *necessary* data with the help of which the analysis is carried out. Unless the researcher knows what the necessary variables are, one would fail to address the issue properly. A researcher should maintain a checklist of the variables that are absolutely necessary to perform the analysis. If after a proper search, it is found that some attributes (some variables) are still missing, he or she should go back to the theory and try for a proxy variable that may serve the research purpose with respect to the attribute that has not been captured in the existing results. However, such a roundabout way should be avoided as far as possible. One should try to identify the variables cautiously and solve every problem pertaining to field data before going for a research on the issue.

(b) *Tabulation and compilation*: The quality of an empirical research depends on the quality of data. One may draw a wrong set of conclusions simply because there are fundamental mistakes in the data. The data should be scrutinised at every stage. As a precautionary step, a small sample should be taken up randomly to check the robustness of the data before tabulation and compilation of the data. The implication of the attributes with respect to which the set of information has been collected must also be understood properly so that the data can capture these attributes properly. The common mistake is that a variable is defined in terms of a certain attribute and while getting the empirical mapping, the information is collected in terms of certain measures which do not capture the proper implication of the variable as discussed in the theory.

(c) *Estimation and testing*: Another common mistake is that a researcher with his insufficient training in statistical theory applies all the advanced statistical tools to judge the validity of his research hypothesis without being sure whether such tools could at all be applied to his data. Thus a researcher very often applies the tools of testing a statistical hypothesis on his data set even though the data had not been collected from a sample frame that adheres to the statistical theory of randomness. Often the researcher fails to realise that the robustness of statistical estimation depends on the robustness of sample frame which he might often be unable to comply with. No tool of estimation or testing a statistical hypothesis can be applied unless the basic data pertains to a sample which has been randomly selected from a population.

In fact, empirical research often fails to adhere to the very first step in statistical research. Before someone starts collecting the primary data, one must understand the 'population' from which the 'sample' is drawn. Some research may even be based on complete enumeration of the elements in the universe. If the study is based on complete enumeration there cannot be any sampling error. Consequently, there is no problem of estimating the sampled statistic and finding its error in estimation and setting a 'confidence interval' for a statistic to represent the true value of the parameter. All these are redundant because the entire population is being studied here. Such problems crop up as soon as we try to predict something on the nature and characteristics of the population on the basis of the results that we get by analysing a sample. Assessing something about the whole from the knowledge of the part is similar to making a generalisation from a particular observation. The theory of statistics is a science related to induction. The theory would help one make an induction about the nature and behaviour of the population itself when a proper sample is chosen.

The whole theory maintains its usefulness by developing certain devices to understand whether the sample is truly drawn from the population. Suppose we have taken a sample from the field study without knowing the population, there will be errors in estimation and this will be error due to sampling. If the sample has not been drawn on the basis of random sampling these errors cannot be assessed with the help of statistical tools and the power of induction of the estimated values cannot be assessed properly. However, the errors will exist even if the sample is drawn randomly (by adhering to the statistical principle of drawing a random sample) but by using proper statistical techniques one can contemplate whether the error is well within the approximation. Naturally, the error related to a sample which is non-random cannot be assessed with the help of these techniques. A researcher must know this point very clearly before he applies these tools to his research.

(d) *Misconception about regression analysis:* Now-a-days, empirical research very often utilises the tools of regression. Thanks to the development of sophisticated statistical packages and path-breaking research in regression analysis, such tools are available in almost every area of empirical research. But, this often gives rise to some problems, the consequences of which might even be disastrous in some cases. A researcher may often be tempted to utilise such techniques without knowing the basic limitations of a so-called powerful tool and the field to which the tool should be applied. A researcher must remain aware of two basic facts—no tool can reveal a truth which is not contained in the data set and a tool may lead to a wrong conclusion about the universe unless it is used properly. A high regression value (with low multi-collinearity and so on) does not necessarily mean that the phenomenon has really been explained satisfactorily by the explanatory variable, unless a good and sensible theory can justify the results. Empirical research is useless unless the research is founded on a robust theoretical base. While applying the regression analysis, the researcher must also be aware of some basic facts about the theoretical basis of the tools that he is using. For example, the researcher must know that he should not go for any regression analysis if the degrees of freedom (defined as number of observations – the number of explanatory variables minus one) is not sufficiently high.

The other important point is that the researcher must know the irrelevant variables included in the model and the relevant variables that have been omitted from the model. The inclusion of irrelevant variables decreases the precision of R^2 (R^2 adjusted for degrees of freedom) and results in higher standard errors and lower t scores. The effect of omission of relevant variables creates bias and inconsistency in the estimated coefficients of the included variables. The researcher should immediately go back to the theory behind the empirical analysis and check the robustness of his research hypothesis.

(e) *Interpreting the results*: After going through all the statistical operations the researcher would take up the task of interpreting the results. The elementary mistake that the researcher must not make while interpreting the results is that the interpretations must maintain consistency and aim at unfolding the inner truth of the data, step by step. A researcher must not over stretch the implications of the findings—he must also avoid wrong interpretation by defending the results in a wrong way. A result must not be defended by advocating wrong interpretations. A better course of action would be to rerun the regression with a proper software package that might suggest which variables should be included and which are to be dropped.

Interpreting a regression from the computer results often leads to mistakes that could be avoided by taking proper precautions. Such mistakes often crop up because of insufficient exposure to the theory of econometrics. It is advisable that the researcher should go through a textbook on econometrics and prepare a regression user's checklist and guide for regression users before taking up a regression analysis, so that the researcher can fall back upon the econometric theory if he or she faces problems in interpreting the regression results derived by utilising software packages. Finally, one must remember that the ethical researcher does not revise the findings to suit his purpose—the findings arrived at after adhering to rigour in every step is something that an ethical researcher would never suppress or avoid.

12.6 OUTLINE OF A FINAL REPORT

The end product of a research, from the point of view of a researcher is the final report that contains the description of a research issue, the way the issues have been handled and the results of the research. The researcher would find it rewarding to follow a preconceived format. A tentative structure of a model research report is described below.

OUTLINE FOR THE FINAL REPORT

TITLE OF THE PROJECT

1. **Introduction**
   (a) Identifying the problem and the research question.
   (b) A brief description of methodology adopted.
   (c) Outline of the major findings.
   (d) A brief appraisal of the results with special reference to the existing literature.
   (e) Limitations of the study and the issues for further research.
2. **Literature Review**
   (a) Background.
   (b) Brief description of the major contributions in the research area.
   (c) The research gap.
   (d) The plan of work (a brief outline of what is coming).
3. **The Methodological Issues**
   (a) The research issues and research hypothesis.
   (b) Type of research (exploratory, descriptive, causal or a combination).
   (c) The empirical issues: the data requirement.
   (d) The data: primary and secondary sources.
4. **The Field Area, the Population and the Sample**[3]
   (a) The field area—the relevant socio-economic features (if required).
   (b) The population and the design of the sample survey.
   (c) The questionnaire.
   (d) The logistics of the survey and the possible sources of non-sampling error.
5. **The Findings**
   (a) The theory and hypotheses.
   (b) Working hypotheses.
   (c) The preliminary results.
   (d) Evaluation of results and interpreting the findings.
   (e) Summary and conclusion.
6. **The Causal Study—An Econometric Analysis of the Data**[4]
   (a) Conceptualising the variables.
   (b) Relationships among the variables, as perceived in theory.
   (c) Proxy variables, dummy variables and other adjustments for modelling.

---

3 The section may be omitted if the study does not involve the collection of the primary data.

4 This section may be omitted if economic model building is not included in the study.

(d) Working hypothesis redefined in terms of the regressor and the regressant.
(e) Functional forms for equations: co-integration for understanding causality.
(f) Modelling with a software package: describing the final results.
(g) A brief description of the data (strength and weakness of the data and the results).[5]

7. **The Concluding Remarks**
(a) The research issue again.
(b) The identified research gap.
(c) Focussing on the major findings.
(d) Theoretical implication.
(e) Future research.

While writing a report, the researcher shall have flexibility in the format that he would use. He must communicate the work that he has done without concentrating on the irrelevant facts, in an organised manner. The format outlined above may serve as a ready reckoner to a researcher so that he does not miss the essential issues that a report should address.

Finally, the most important point that a researcher must keep in mind is that the report must be written in a lucid manner with clarity ensured at each step. A researcher should not write a single clumsy sentence because that will serve as a deterrent to whatever he wants to communicate. Writing well is at least as important as the field research and understanding the results of a study. It is difficult to suggest a method that can improve the style of writing, books on good writing are helpful (Strunk W, Jr and White E B, *Elements of Style*, 1979, MacMillan Publishing Co, and Turabian L, *A Manual for Writers of Term Papers, Thesis and Dissertations*, 1973, University of Chicago Press). One develops a good style of writing by observing the styles followed in lucidly written papers and dissertations. The golden rule is to understand a point clearly and to communicate it in simple, non-ornamental language.

12.7 THE RESEARCH AND ITS LIMITATIONS

A research work is based on a particular paradigm of reasoning. The strengths and weaknesses of a research are derived basically from the paradigm to which it belongs. It is not enough to observe that the empirical research does or does not corroborate a particular theory. A theory is a generalisation. The generalisation which forms the basis of a contribution to the theory is based on the logic of induction. The results of the research would therefore be limited by the weakness of induction as a method of reasoning. A good researcher should remain aware of this particular weakness of empirical research while trying to derive a generalised conclusion from his empirical study. Again, placed in a different paradigm, the same set of information

5 This part is taken from Johnson A C, Jr , Johnson M D and Buse R C, *Econometrics Basic and Applied*, 1989, MacMillan Publishing Co., New York, USA.

might be utilised for developing a different theory. In social research, we often face such a situation. A researcher should take this point into consideration while defending his results.

While defending the results, the researcher often fails to realise that his findings might not have been derived in such a way that statistical regularity is honoured. For example, a researcher often fails to draw a sample by following the rule of statistical randomness. In case this is so, no estimation or drawing of inference can be done from the data set. Strictly speaking, the results derived from the sample will not represent the characteristics of the population. A researcher having poor exposure to statistical theory may often miss this point and derive some unwarranted conclusions.

Finally, the researcher should be aware of the fact that even a good piece of research has its limitations. In most cases, it would explain the issue under consideration only partially. This is so because even though an empirical research is framed within the paradigm of inductive logic, it often fails to take all the factors that may provide a robust basis of induction, into consideration. It happens partly because of the limitations of the theory (limitation of the existing knowledge). In many cases, this may also occur because the researcher does not have a sound grasp over the theory, so much so that a limitation might remain in an empirical research work, even though the quality of such work is excellent. One cannot expect an empirical research to be excellent unless one has a good grasp over the theory that forms its basis.

SUMMARY

- The interim report is basically a progress report in which the researcher is expected to give an account of the extent of progress that has been achieved in the given period. A final report is not just a compilation of interim reports and is supposed to contain much more information and analysis.
- In empirical science, the findings are often placed in the form of final tables which are expected to explain the features of the phenomenon under study in summarised forms. Tables and charts should be neatly presented.
- Analysis of data and interpretation of data after statistical analysis is the critical factor that gives an insight into the quality of the research study and the quality of its reporting. A researcher must not over stretch the implications of the findings—the researcher must also avoid wrong interpretation by defending the results in a wrong way.
- The researcher should follow a pre-planned format while writing a report. However, the researcher shall have flexibility in the format that he would use. He must communicate the work that he has done in an organised manner. Care must be taken to avoid any mistake in the research report in terms of the data presented, tabulation and compilation, estimation and testing.
- A reseacher should remember that a research work is based on a particular paradigm of reasoning. The strengths and weaknesses of a research is derived basically from the paradigm to which it belongs. The researcher should remain aware of the fact that even a good piece of research has its limitations. In most cases, it would explain the issue under consideration only partially.

ASSIGNMENTS

Q1 Choose the right answers

1. The end product of a research is :
   (a) Analysis of data
   (b) Report writing
   (c) Defining the scope of study
   (d) None of the above
2. The report should be focused towards:
   (a) Area of knowledge
   (b) Need identified by the client
   (c) The knowledge of the researcher
   (d) None of the above
3. Which of the statements is not true:
   (a) An interim report is of lasting value
   (b) An interim report has been submitted on the requirement of client
   (c) An interim report is also a monitoring of the work in progress
   (d) None of the above
4. Which of the following statements is not true for the final report:
   (a) Such a report is prepared only after going through every step of research
   (b) The report is of lasting value
   (c) The report does not contradict the findings of the interim report
   (d) None of the above
5. A research design is:
   (a) Sacrosanct and need not be changed during course of research study
   (b) Not at all a necessary condition
   (c) Not sacrosanct and can be changed during course of research study
   (d) None of the above
6. Descriptive statistics of the data collected and analysed states:
   (a) The hidden logic in the behaviour of the variables
   (b) The inferential logic in the data set
   (c) The relationship between the variables
   (d) None of the above
7. A dummy table is usually prepared:
   (a) After the final table is prepared
   (b) From the blank questionnaire itself

(c) After cross tabulations are done
(d) None of the above

8. In preparing tables, which of the following is not true:
(a) Dummy tables must be prepared
(b) Tables must bring the hidden relations of variance under study
(c) Tables must diffuse the issue of the study
(d) None of the above

9. Doing research should unfold:
(a) The unchartered route
(b) Only affirmatives to the hypothesis that is laid down
(c) A priori recommendations suggested
(d) None of the above

10. The advent of computers in research has led to:
(a) Limitations of options in analysis
(b) Tremendous amount of flexibility with marginal increase in cost
(c) Myopic exposure of statistics to the researcher
(d) None of the above

Answers

1. (b), 2. (b), 3. (a), 4. (c), 5. (c), 6. (a), 7. (b), 8. (c), 9. (a), 10. (b)

Q2. Answer the questions

1. Briefly outline the steps in writing the final report in the case of an empirical study.
2. What are the critical issues of estimation and testing while an empirical research is carried out?
3. 'Finally, the researcher must know how to interpret the regression results', elaborate on the statement and bring out the features of regression as an inferential tool of analysis.

CHAPTER 13

Research Administration

LEARNING OBJECTIVES

After going through this chapter you will understand

- Role of a researcher in organising research
- Options in a research process
- Role of an in-house research agency
- Role of an external research agency

Key words In-house agency, external agency, custom research firms, syndicated service firms, field service firms

13.1 INTRODUCTION

It is necessary for the researcher to know what is precisely expected of him. In fact, the degree of responsibility and dimensions of work of the researcher will vary depending on the nature of the research set-up. The nature of the research set-up largely depends on the nature of the research requirement and the nature of the organisation which houses the research. A professional is trained to understand the research requirement pertaining to a research issue but more often than not, the researcher fails to deliver the best because the research set up operates at sub-optimal level. Often the best professionals do not remain aware of the fact that there are organisational issues that are to be sorted out for performing the best. This involves adjusting the working styles and knowledge of the system within which the researchers need to work. In other words, the departmental structure plays a very important role in setting up the responsibility of the researcher and the dimensions of his work which centres around the following issues: who will administer the research, who is responsible for which part of the work, how the responsibilty would be fixed, what professional commitment is expected from persons working at various levels and how the persons at various levels are linked in the structure.

13.1.1 Research Process

These issues are to be sorted out by analysing the research process.The options available for a research process are three—(i) in-house research, (ii) research through external agency and (iii) in-house research in collaboration with an external agency. We shall discuss this largely in the context of Market Research. But such analysis can be done in the context of other researches as well. Diagrammatically the options are shown in Fig. 13.1.

The administrative options that have been stated are usually decided on certain factors:

(a) The nature of research design (exploratory, descriptive or causal),
(b) The issue of research and its implications,
(c) The confidentiality of the research,
(d) The expertise available for such research,
(e) The degree of intertwined subjects in the problem settings of research,
(f) The degree of control necessary in each stage of research, and
(g) The budget for research.

Exploratory research could be needed to define the problem which could necessitate the option of in-house research. Again the issue of the research may be across industry and this may call for using an external agency for carrying out the research. In case a new product is to be launched and confidentiality is to be maintained (may be a blind test is involved), the in-house agency may do some research with some assistance or help from an external agency. Sometimes the expertise available with the in-house is too meagre for designing any research work; under such circumstances, the firm has no other course left but to assign the research to an external agency. There could be a situation where the problem is not only in sales but has its genesis in corporate policy, purchase or production. This will automatically call for collaborative work between the in-house and an external agency. In certain types of work, a degree of control may be essential. This may be more necessary in the case of experimentation when the experimental variable may need to be changed at certain specific intervals. Let us suppose a research on sales variance due to different types of promotion is being studied. This will require the in-house and external agencies to work together and study the research. At times there could be situations when the budget to solve problems is too low, under such situations the research may need to be conducted through the in-house research department.

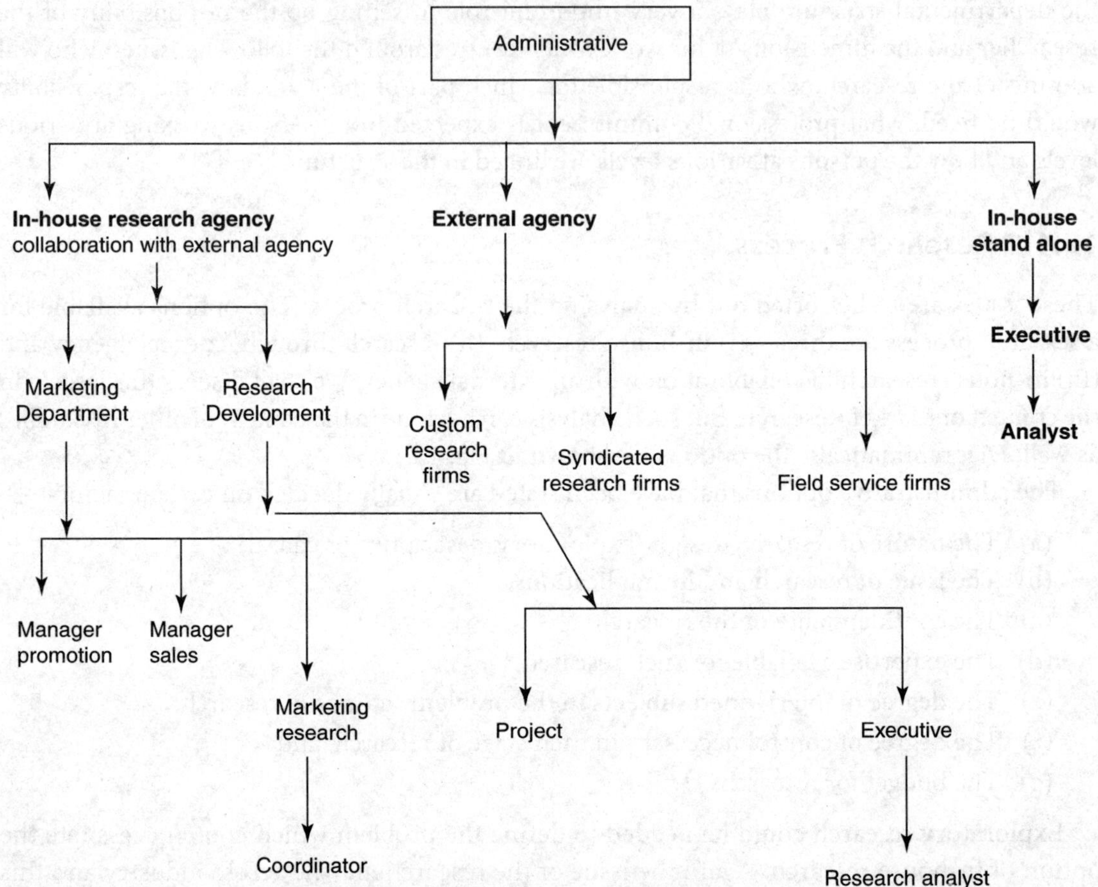

Fig. 13.1 Options of a research process

13.2 IN-HOUSE AGENCY

Let us take a more critical look into the *in-house* and external agency. The advantages of in-house research are stated below:

- Understanding the research problem and proper benchmarking is possible.
- Proper control on direction of research is possible, especially when experimental methods are involved.
- Specificity to decisional elements is possible since the goal has to be reached within a limited time.
- The cost of such research is more reasonable than the external agency charges.
- The involvement of researchers is long-term.

The above advantages are also accompanied by disadvantages. Some of these disadvantages are enumerated below:

(a) Sometimes the time allotment of the in-house researcher on specific projects may be less.
(b) Bias of the in-house department or the management's motive may be pre-assumed or may be favourably or unfavourably interfering with the results.
(c) The expertise or updated technology or knowledge in research may not be available with the in-house department.
(d) Information on industry or research on diffusion of technology from other than the specific business will not come out through in-house research.

In the above discussion we find that these are the generalised advantages and disadvantages of in-house research. However in case of specific in-house research, some other symptoms may also be visible.

13.3 EXTERNAL AGENCY

The *external agencies* have certain advantages as well; these are enumerated below:

(a) Specialised services and updated researchers are available with quality services.
(b) Objectivity in analysis of data is maintained and possibility of bias is removed.
(c) Each research project has a specific team with a committed time frame.
(d) Cross-industry research and research on diffusion of technology from other industries is possible.
(e) Pulling of resources and superior infrastructure is visible.
(f) A research agency usually has a better ability to negotiate and bargain for quality service than an in-house research department.

The pitfalls of using an external agency are also present, some are:

(a) High overhead costs which might be avoided, had the research been in-house.
(b) The control on direction of research or on the researchers is remote.
(c) The agency may not like to part with the data set if it is valuable enough for subsequent professional need of the agency.
(d) The involvement of an agency may at times pose a threat of leakage of information regarding confidential work.
(e) The long term relationships with the research projects of the researchers are absent as many get allocated to other projects.
(f) Specific decisional funding of the agency does not match the decisional need that the firm would have expected.
(g) The objective or benchmarking of research is wrongly read by the external agency.

Now that we have discussed the advantages and disadvantage of in-house research vis-à-vis the external agency, it is most appropriate that one understands the *job and role relationship* within the in-house and the external agency.

In multinational corporations, large business houses or firms of large standing, in-house research is quite common. Many have a research and development division (internal marketing information system) with one or more research analysts. These analysts work on the secondary data and they edit and validate the data. Within such an organisation, there is also a marketing division which has sub-departments such as Advertising, Sales and Market Research. The market research department has coordinators who are able to get data through summer trainees or through cross-functional contact with the research analyst. This data is then suitably interpreted for the required analysis and further decisions. At times when the liason with the research analyst fails to give the required data, the coordinator interacts with the external agency, that is, with the syndicated data research firms (by procuring syndicated data). The data so acquired is then worked on by the in-house research department or unit to transform it into a set of required data for analysis. Certain companies get monthly or bimonthly data from such syndicated research firms for market share analysis, growth trends or products; these are analysed on a regular basis through research assistants and are used to provide support to their marketing wing.

External agencies are classified into three—custom research firms, syndicated service firms and field service firms. Custom research firms are those which take up customised research projects such as launching of new brands, the effect of advertising, the effect of sales promotion, price sensitivity research, concept development, new product development and other such marketing issues. Customer research firms are apt to handle projects of this nature. Customer research firms could be specialists in certain industries as well. In India we have many such firms—Hindustan Thompson Associates, Lintas, McCann Erickson and many more.

Syndicated service firms sell the same set of data to many firms according to their need. Such data is not client specific and is given to any client who is ready to pay for the information. Let us suppose one is a specialist in pharmaceutical research and keeps on monitoring the drugs in the market. A syndicated research service could have eight to ten pharmaceutical companies as individual accounts to whom it may sell the data regularly and these individual firms will select the required data according to their convenience for further analysis.

Let us discuss the market rating indices of Class I, II and III towns of India. This syndicated data were prepared by erstwhile Clarion Advertising Services Limited by using the consumer data published by the Government of India. The towns have been classified into three categories— Class I, Class II, Class III towns. The population is not the only variable that has been considered, consumption and expenditure of the towns are also included. The syndicated report appeared in three tables. The first table showed towns in descending order of their market sizes. The market rating indices of various towns/town groups was calculated taking the total consumption expenditures of different towns and have been expressed as a percentage in relation to that of Greater Bombay (base, that is, 100). Table II of the syndicated report shows the towns arranged by states and zones. The all India ranks of the towns as well as rank within the states have been indicated.

Table III shows all the towns in the alphabetical order. The use of such a syndicated report is immense. One such very common application is, supposing a company wants to roll out its product, from the index it may decide the priority allotted to a particular town. Again on market-testing of some consumer non-durables, the index will be used to identify the test market. One can access these erstwhile market rating indices reports from business library from any of the Chambers of Commerce.

Another syndicated research report is the SEC study of IMRB. Similarly two more syndicated reports – household survey and TRP rating – have been discussed elaborately in Chapter 3 of this book.

In syndicated service firms we find that a few are specialists in products and a few on audience and these could be named as product syndicated service firms and audience syndicated service firms respectively. This kind of specialised service improves the quality of the research service.

Field service firms are many and their prime function is to collect data. These firms do not have research analysts, they are data collection specialists. Many syndicated research firms subcontract the data collection stage to these field firms. It is also true that in many instances, the in-house corporate research departments would also subcontract the data collection to such field service firms.

The description of activities conducted by such field service firms will reveal the nature of work that these firms carry out.

Client contract	:	Client could be given services of seeking a particular kind of respondent (that is, their address and contact points, time during which they could be interviewed), contacting respondents through telephone, mails could also be arranged.
Estimate cost bid	:	It has to provide a cost estimate for the contractual service that it could provide.
Interviewer recruiting	:	The field service firms usually maintain a pool of interviewers from which a few are selected for each project.
Interviewer training	:	Each project requires a specific type of training. The primary purpose for the training is to acquaint the interviewer with requirements of that particular project.
Interviewer status report	:	The client is kept informed on the number of interviews conducted on a daily basis, the nature and response to a questionnaire. This helps the client to know the work in progress with reference to the job.

Quality control : The interviews need to be coded, validated and edited and this allows the quality of the work to remain uniform.

Despatch of data : Finally the completed, validated and edited data are sent to the client.

The purpose of appointing such a field service firm are many, a few are given below.

(a) For a large agency or in-house department to control and maintain such a force of interviewers is uneconomical and administratively unwise.
(b) Training interviewers or training supervisors needs specialised skills which these firms have and they often offer this service as well.
(c) A committed time frame regarding data procurement is maintained by such firms.
(d) Supposing the data has to be collected from a large widely dispersed geographical area such as a national survey, a syndicated research firm has no other option but to collect data through field service firms.

The third major option is joint collaborative work between the in-house research department and the external agency. At times both do not see eye-to-eye with respect to the job assignment. The usual complaints from corporate clients are the following:

(a) The research is not objective, that is, actionable results have not materialised.
(b) The researcher shows a bias towards his technique rather than concentrating on the problem of the corporate.
(c) The research is time consuming and vague.

The agencies also point out a few problems in interactions with corporates:

(a) They look at research piece-meal rather than as a sequence of problem solving.
(b) Corporates believe in other functional disciplines more and value research less.
(c) Corporates do not allow much time for conducting research. They prefer to draw preliminary conclusions based on incomplete research results.
(d) Corporate houses rely more on intuition and judgement than on research. Research only remains as a process and not a tool of proper analysis.

Under the stated circumstances, the need of the situation is to bridge the gap in perception between the company and the external agency.

(a) Placing the research project in the right perspective is important. This involves sitting with the researcher or the agency and seeking help in defining the premise of the project as well as the steps involved in the assignment. The precaution to be taken at this stage is that neither the client nor the agency should be myopic. They should at least agree on a common bench mark.

    It is often observed that both the groups are overconfident and do not possess an understanding of each others' viewpoint. Understanding this would also help in understanding their limitations. The manager may say that he would like to know precisely how much the quantity of a certain ingredient in the chocolate needs to be changed to make it more acceptable. The researcher or the agency must let the client know their limitations in making predictions on the precision in the amounts of ingredient.

(b) Specifying information needed: The corporate should be able to specify what information they specifically require for their analysis and recommendation. The research agency should similarly keep a specific note of such information and see that all the required information is present while the report is handed over to the client. Supposing the client has asked for measurement of attitude on a quantitative scale, the agency must see to it that the scales are quantitatively designed and the data is quantitatively presented.

(c) Evaluating the proposed research project: Every research organisation submits a proposal of work that needs to be approved by the company. The corporate must assess the major part of the proposal that comes in written or as oral communications as otherwise it could lead to misunderstandings. This is true for the agency as well. The agency should give most, or preferably the whole, of the proposal in writing. This will reduce the communication gap.

(d) Accepting or rejecting research findings: Ultimately the manager is the deciding authority to accept the findings or reject it. If a manager is in doubt he must first clear the doubts and then accept the finding; it is no use making the agency a scapegoat.

If the above problems and remedies have been rightly observed and followed, the fact that evolves is that if the research problem has been selected properly, then one can solve most of the above stated issues. This requires that the problem be stated with consistency. It is also necessary that in order to do so one must understand that this requires a thorough idea about the dimensions of the problem. Besides these, it is necessary to undertake a preliminary survey. This survey is known as a pilot survey and usually helps in defining and narrowing down the problem. A pilot survey may consist of an exploratory design using a survey method, observation method or mail method. The purpose is very clear, for such a survey is meant for narrowing down the research issue from general to specific.

In the case of observation method, one could use a focus group. Such a group is referred to as an *exploratory focus group*. It is also known as the pilot. Certain types of questionnaires are administered to the groups and their responses and suggestions are taken into consideration. This will not only help in defining the problem but also in stating the hypothesis clearly. Sometimes, one could also use the *clinical focus group*. These are specifically required when the work pertains to discovering the subconscious attitudes of people. Let us suppose, the study pertains to the usage of bread in an industrial town. This study is to be conducted in the conventional feudal society that is in the path of transition. A questionnaire for a pilot survey will be of no help as the diagnosis of the problem is in the subconscious mind of respondents.

This requires a clinical focus group study. The attitude of women towards the family and adoption of a certain lifestyle is another such issue. At times, such clinical focus groups for pilot testing are essential. The link between the management and the external agency could be such a pilot survey, which will aid both the groups to decide on the approach to the research problem in the best possible way.

SUMMARY

- The administration of research is based on certain important factors stemming from type of research, its implication, control and limitations.
- An in-house agency is normally recommended when the research has to be closely supervised and controlled.
- Under situations involving cost and time constraints, an in-house agency is a better option for conducting research.
- In case of cross-industry research or research pertaining to sensitive public issues, the better option is to use an external agency.
- Where regular data requirement is required and the firm has core competency in inferential analysis, the use of data from a syndicated research firm is the best option.
- In case there are some problems between the management or users, and the external agency, one has to understand that some of it is perceptual and the rest is technical and both can be circumvented.
- An in-house agency working in collaboration with an external agency is often the most balanced option.

ASSIGNMENTS

Q1 Choose the right answers

1. The administrative options of marketing research are:
   (a) In-house and external agency
   (b) In-house, external agency and in-house with external agency
   (c) External agency
   (d) None of the above
2. In case the marketing research is in-house only, the nature of the research department is:
   (a) Functional
   (b) Cross-functional
   (c) Autocratic
   (d) None of the above

3. Which of the following is true in case of research by external agency:
   (a) It is a specialised service
   (b) It is highly confidential
   (c) Research process is controlled the most
   (d) None of the above
4. Which of the following is true in case of research by the in-house department:
   (a) The direction of research can be controlled
   (b) Research on time cannot be accomplished
   (c) It is a specialised service
   (d) None of the above
5. The types of firms indicated as external agency are:
   (a) Custom research firms and syndicated research firms
   (b) Syndicated research firms and field research firms
   (c) Custom research firms, syndicated research firms and field research firms
   (d) None of the above
6. The functions of the field service firms are:
   (a) Data collection, validating and editing
   (b) Research design and data collection
   (c) Research design, data collection, data analysis
   (d) None of the above
7. The function of a syndicated research firm are:
   (a) Pool resources of other research firms
   (b) Synthesising secondary data or data collected generally on a particular project
   (c) Data for a specific firm is collected
   (d) None of the above
8. Custom research firms are those:
   (a) Who sell the same data to many organisations
   (b) Only collect data for a firm
   (c) Work of a specific research project for a specific client
   (d) None of the above
9. The focus group that studies the subconscious mind is referred to as:
   (a) Clinical focus group
   (b) Exploratory focus group
   (c) Experiencing focus group
   (d) None of the above

10. The pilot survey:
    (a) Is helpful for crystallising the research problem
    (b) Is a miniature survey
    (c) Is a snap research
    (d) None of the above

Answers

1. (b), 2. (b), 3. (a), 4. (a), 5. (c), 6. (a), 7. (b), 8. (c), 9. (a), 10. (a)

Q2 Answer the questions

1. A beverage company intends to launch a new product. It has asked the manager to arrange an administrative set up to study a new cold coffee mix it wants to launch by the middle of next year. What sort of administrative option do you think the manager should undertake in order to maintain confidentiality and what are its advantages?
2. The researcher thinks that the sale of soaps has gone down because of the competition in pricing and other marketing mixes. The management thinks that factors other than the marketing mix have forced an established brand to lose its sales. You have been asked to intervene. What will be your suggestion in such a case? Answer in the form of a research proposal.

CHAPTER 14

An Illustration of Research Methodology

Estimation of the Demand for High Speed Diesel (A Case Study)

LEARNING OBJECTIVES

After going through this chapter you will understand

- To identify a research issue
- To write the research objectives
- Types of research undertaken
- Generation of data
- Methodology to be used
- Coverage area to be chosen/given
- Tools and techniques to be used
- Data collection and tabulation
- Interpretation of data and report writing

14.1 INTRODUCTION

The best way to understand the methodology of research is to consider a real life problem and search for the appropriate methodology to solve such a problem. In order to understand how this really helps, let us consider a real life problem which a set of researchers confronted, in this chapter. While solving the problem, the researchers had to utilise most of the tools and techniques that have been discussed in this book. We shall discuss the salient features of that work. The purpose is to educate the learners on how the tools and techniques that they have learnt thus far, can be utilised for solving a real-life problem in business through a case study.

An apex body (referred as XYZ) on petroleum conservation which is also a part of the petroleum industry of India, comprising representatives from the petroleum ministry and all the oil companies, monitors the growth in demand of various petroleum products in order to help create infrastructural facilities required to meet the demand.

High Speed Diesel (HSD) is a major petroleum product and is largely sold through a vast network of retail outlets. The expansion of both passenger transport and freight transport, has seen a rapid growth in the demand of HSD. Industrial and agricultural growth have also contributed to the increasing demand for HSD.

The XYZ wanted to segment HSD sales by sectors and establish a correlation of HSD demand with relevant factors. XYZ therefore commissioned the Business and Industrial Research Division of a reputed market research organisation to conduct the study.

The study was conducted in three parts—snap study, country-wide study and follow up study.

14.2 IDENTIFYING THE RESEARCH ISSUE

The first task of the research organisation is to identify the issues on which the study depends. In the language of research methodology, this can be considered as the task of *identifying the research issues.* The research issues were identified only after specifying the objectives.

The key objectives of the study were to:

(1) Assess the profile of users of HSD in terms of consumption through retail outlets.

(2) Identify/validate factors having significant influence on HSD demand.

(3) Determine the relationship between identified factors and consumption of HSD in each end-use sector.

(4) Develop alternative forecasting models.

14.3 TYPE OF RESEARCH

As you know, the different types of research are—exploratory study, descriptive study and causal study.

In this case, plans were made to develop some descriptions in terms of statistical tables while meeting the first objective. While meeting the needs of the second, third and fourth objectives, plans to consider the factors having significant influence on HSD demand following which a relation between identified factors and the consumption of HSD in each end-use sector were to be established. Technically speaking, the second objective could be met by considering a *descriptive* type of analysis, but the remaining set of issues has to be settled by considering a *causal study*. From the objective of the study, the researcher thus identifies the types of research that he is going to take up.

14.4 GENERATION OF DATA

For an empirical research, we need data as discussed in Chapter 3. The data set is generated by the interaction between stimuli and the response. However, in a research, the researcher sometimes utilises secondary data that has been generated by other researchers. Often the researcher has to generate a set of data by his own endeavours. The first type of data is known as secondary data and the second type of data is known as primary data. In the particular case which we are studying, there was a judicious blending of both the primary and secondary data. This can be understood if we consider the methodology of research that was followed in this case.

14.5 METHODOLOGY USED

A multipronged research study was conducted comprising the following steps.

1. An observation study on end-usage of HSD retail sales—one whole day observation of HSD retail sales quantity by end-use type was carried out at selected outlets in each region.
2. Direct interviews were conducted in the following sectors:

   (a) mining and industrial sector,
   (b) transport sector (cargo/passenger),
   (c) agriculture sector,
   (d) commercial sector,
   (e) power sector, and
   (f) manufacturers of automobiles and farm equipments.

3. Information from secondary sources such as the retail and direct sales of HSD for the last 10 years and published data on the Indian economy, transport sector, agriculture sector, railways, and others were considered.
4. Trend analysis model, based on monthly sales data of HSD (retail and direct sales) for the last 10 years, to forecast future sales of HSD was computed.
5. Sector-wise multiple regression models to establish relationships of factors that have significant influence on the HSD demand and build up statistical relations (read equations) that can forecast HSD demand were focussed on.

Evidently in this research, data from both the primary and secondary sources had to be utilised if the proposed methodology was to be used. More specifically for the observation study on the end-usage of the HSD retail sales, the agency had to collect the primary data by observing the retail sales quantity by end-use type at selected retail outlets in each region of the country. Direct interviews for getting the primary data had to be taken up from six sectors of the economy. For the trends, the published data (that is, secondary data) available from various agencies were utilised.

The field survey: In order to collect primary data in this case, the researchers had to plan a field survey. The first task was to decide the sample size and the distribution of the sample units over the country. There was a feedback from an earlier study, which was done in 1992–93. Based on the result of this study the XYZ, after a few rounds of discussion with the experts, decided the coverage of the primary survey.

14.6 COVERAGE AREA

The primary survey was done in and around the following areas.

North: Delhi, rural districts of Haryana, Ghaziabad, Agra, Rae Bareli, Faizabad, Lucknow.

West: Konkan districts, Pune, Mumbai, Surat, Ahmedabad, Rajkot.

South: South Arcot district, Trichirapalli, Chennai, Ernakulam, Palakkad.

East: Muzaffarpur, Begusarai, Darbahnga, Patna, Dhanbad, Purbi Singhbhum district.

It was a two-stage random sampling in which the centres were first identified on the basis of a listing provided by the XYZ. In the second stage, the units were surveyed on the basis of a structured questionnaire. The units belonged to various segments of the study. While selecting the units, the principle of random sampling could not be honoured.

In the primary survey, a total of 884 interviews were conducted among various segments (Table 14.1).

Table 14.1 The segment-wise breakup of the number of interviews conducted

S. No.	Segments	No. of contacts
1.	HSD retail outlets	97
2.	Industrial units and mines	49
3.	FCI/STC/large mandis	22
4.	Transporters/cargo agents/ freight forwarders	69
5.	Diesel car/jeep/taxi owners and drivers	202
6.	Bus owners/drivers including STUs	44
7.	Automobile manufacturers	8
8.	Farm machinery/ pumpset/ Generator manufacturers	19
9.	Tractor/farm machinery/ pumpset owners and operators	50
10.	Farmers	152
11.	SEB/power supply corporation	7
12.	Hotels/hospitals/theatres/shopping centres/offices	157
13.	RTOs	5
14.	Others	3
	Total	884 (% of target: 97.4%)

14.7 THE QUESTIONNAIRE

While collecting primary data, the researchers decided to follow *a formal structured setting* (Chapter 4). The responses were therefore recorded in the form of a structured questionnaire. Since there were fourteen segments in which the questionnaire was run, there were fourteen sets of questionnaires, which were prepared by the researchers. In each segment there was a pilot study following which the final questionnaire was prepared. These were canvassed in the field by a set of trained investigators. As all the fourteen sets of questionnaires cannot be reproduced here, therefore, one set of questions that was canvassed among 152 farmers who were included in the primary survey is reproduced here.

STUDY ON HSD

Questionnaire for Farmers—Agriculture

Name of respondent____________________ Centre [|]

Designation____________________ Questionnaire S. No. [| |]

Name of the organisation____________________

Address____________________ Card No. [ ]

____

____

Phone: Residence____________ Office__________ Edit code [| |]

Interviewee's name: ____________ [|] Date of interview Date [|] Month [|] Year [| | |]

Accompanied		Backchecked P	T	Scrutinised	
TL	1	TL 1	5	TL	1
EIC	2	EIC 2	6	EIC	2
OFE	3	OFE 3	7	OFE	3
FM	4	FM 4	8	FM	4

Signature: __________ Signature: __________ Signature: __________

Q1. How much land (in acres) do you own and cultivate—irrigated and un-irrigated? PLEASE CONVERT TRADITIONAL LAND MEASUREMENTS (LIKE BIGHAS) INTO ACRES

	Irrigated	Un-irrigated
Land owned (net)		
Land cultivated (gross)		

Q2a. What crops do you cultivate—in Rabi, Kharif and all season?
RECORD IN GRID BELOW Q2c. MULTIPLE CODES POSSIBLE.

Q2b. What areas are cultivated for each of the crops?
RECORD IN GRID BELOW Q2c

Q2c. What is the average output per annum of these crops you cultivate?
RECORD IN GRID BELOW

Prompt	Kharif crop (acres)		Rabi crop (acres)		All season crops (acres)		Average output	
	Code	Area cultivated	Code	Area cultivated	Code	Area cultivated	Rs/ year	Quintal/ year
Paddy	1		1		1			
Wheat	2		2		2			
Maize	3		3		3			
Jowar	4		4		4			
Bajra	5		5		5			
Ragi	6		6		6			
Barley	7		7		7			
Pulses (gram, arhar and so on)	8		8		8			
Small millet	9		9		9			
Oil seeds	A		A		A			
Cotton	B		B		B			
Jute	C		C		C			
Tea	D		D		D			
Sugarcane	E		E		E			
Coffee	F		F		F			
Tobacco	G		G		G			
Other crops	H		H		H			
Vegetables	I		I		I			

Q3a. What are the sources of irrigation (diesel pump/others) that you depend on for cultivation—for Kharif, Rabi and all season crops? RECORD IN GRID BELOW.

Q3b. What are the percentage break ups of water sources used during normal/below normal monsoons for these crops? RECORD IN GRID BELOW.

Irrigation source	Kharif crops			Rabi crops			All season crops		
	Source	Normal monsoon	Below normal monsoon	Source	Normal monsoon	Below normal monsoon	Source	Normal monsoon	Below normal monsoon
Diesel pump	1			1			1		
Others	2			2			2		
		100%	100%		100%	100%		100%	100%

RECORD RESPONSES FOR Q4a TO Q4g IN GRID BELOW Q4g.

Q4a. PROMPT FROM CARD A. Do you use any of these farm machineries?

Q4b. What are the capacities (or sizes) of these machines that you use?

Q4c. How many hours do these machineries (run) on 1 litre of diesel on an average? PROMPT FOR THE MACHINES HE IS USING.

Q4d. Do you own any of the machineries (yourself or your family)?

Q4e. Do you use any of these machineries on hire?

Q4f. Could you tell us for how many hours these machines were run per season in the last year for Kharif, Rabi and all season crops ?

Q4g. Do you mix kerosene with diesel for these machines?

MULTIPLE CODES POSSIBLE FOR Q4a, Q4d and Q4e.

	Q4a	Q4b	Q4c	Q4d	Q4e	Q4f No. of hours run per season on diesel			Q4g
Prompt	**Use**	**Capcaity/ size**	**Hours run per litre of diesel**	**Own**	**On hire**	**Rabi**	**Kharif**	**All season**	**Kerosene (yes/no)**
Pumpset	1			1	1	Go toQ4g	For pump set		
Tractor	2			2	2				
Tiller	3			3	3				
Harvestor	4			4	4				
Combine	5			5	5				
Thresher	6			6	6				
None	7	xxxxxxxx	xxxxxxxxxx	x	x	xxxxx	xxxx	xxxx	xxxxxx

IF '7' CODED IN Q4a, GO TO Q5.
IF '1' CODED IN Q4a, THEN ASK Q4h INSTEAD OF Q4f.

Q4h. How many hours did /do you run your pumpset(s) per season during last year and years of normal/ below normal monsoons, on diesel/electricity?

Use of pumpset during	**No of hours run on diesel**			**No of hours run on electricity**		
Last year	Rabi	Kharif	All season	Rabi	Kharif	All season
Year of normal monsoon						
Year of below normal monsoon						

Q4i. How many hours do you run your thresher per season on electricity?

<u>Rabi</u> <u>Kharif</u> <u>All season</u>

_____ _______ __________

Q5a. What are the factors that affect (increase/decrease) usage of these machines (PUMPSET/ TRACTOR/ TILLER/ HARVESTOR/COMBINE/THRASHER/OTHERS)?
CODE

Q5b. What are the three most important factors for usage of pumps? RANK

Q5c. What are the three most important factors for usage of machines other than pumps? RANK

Factors	Code	Rank for pumps	Rank for others
Problems of labourers during sowing/harvesting/others	1		
Available source of irrigation	2		
Rental rate of using such machines	3		
Amount of rains received	4		
Bank credit available	5		
Change in price of diesel	6		
What crop is cultivated	7		
Availability of appropriate and requisite quantity of fertiliser	8		
Others (please specify)	9		
	A		
	B		
	C		

THANK RESPONDENT AND TERMINATE INTERVIEW

14.8 TABULATION AND COMPILATION

After proper scrutiny, the information in the questionnaire was entered in a computer by data entry operators. Necessary checks were taken up to see whether there were errors in data entry. Having been assured of the quality of the data, the researchers generated some primary data. Summarising the information contained in the primary tables, the researchers prepared a set of final tables. While preparing the set of final tables, sufficient care was taken to check whether the research issues that were formulated at the beginning of the study could be adequately addressed by the set of final tables.

As you may recollect, the study that we are considering had a part that could be in the form a descriptive study. The descriptive study was based on some research hypothesis. While preparing the final tables it was checked whether the information contained in the tables would be sufficient to test the research hypothesis. The analysis however also needed a few more tables containing some quantitative descriptions of the research issues. Sufficient care was taken to note whether these issues were covered in a satisfactory manner.

For example, the first objective of the study was to assess the profiles of users of high speed diesel in terms of consumption through retail outlets. In order to meet this research objective, data had been collected from end-use segments. By the observation of actual sales at retail outlets, the final table that addressed this issue came in the following form.

End-use segment	North	West	South	East	All India (%)
Private car	X_{11}	X_{12}	X_{13}	X_{14}	X_1
Taxi /cab	X_{21}	X_{22}	X_{23}	X_{24}	X_2
Jeep	X_{31}	X_{32}	X_{33}	X_{34}	X_3
3-Wheeler	X_{41}	X_{42}	X_{43}	X_{44}	X_4
Truck	....	....	....	....	....
LCV	....	....	.....	....	....
Large bus	....	....	....	....	....
Mini bus	....	....	....	....	....
Other vehicle	....	....	....	....	....
Pumpset	....	....	....	....	....
Tractor	....	....	....	....	....
Tiller/thresher/ harvestor	....	....	....	....	....
Generator-hhld	....	....	....	....	....
Generator-coml	....	....	....	....	....
Generator-indl	....	....	....	....	....
Garage	....	....	....	....	....
Others	$X_{17\,1}$	$X_{17\,2}$	$X_{17\,3}$	$X_{17\,4}$	X_{17}

We do not quote the data because the final information has not been made available for public consumption.

There had been a few causal studies that the researcher performed. This included:

(a) Identifying the factors having significant influence of the HSD demand.
(b) Determining relationship between identified factors and consumption of HSD in each end-use sector.
(c) To develop alternative forecasting models.

The study in the causal form identified a few quantitative relations. These were tested with the help of a few regression analyses. The basic structure of the causal models was as follows:

$$Y = C + b_1X_1 + b_2X_2 + ...b_{20}X_{20}$$

where $C, b_{1,} b_2$ ....b_{20} are the coefficients to be determined with

$$bi = dYi / dX_I$$

For unit change in X_i, the amount of average change in Y (HSD sales). No transformation has been applied to the original variables X_1.....X_{20}. The expected signs of the coefficients of X_1...........X_{20} are all positive.

We reproduce the regression results (done with the help of a software package) in the appendix of this chapter. As one goes through the regression results described in terms of *four models* reported in the appendix, one gets an exposure to the possibilities that might be explored by a researcher from a data set. The power of statistical tools in facilitating empirical research becomes evident as one goes through this description.

14.9 REPORT WRITING

As one gets the final tables and the results of more sophisticated statistical analyses, one understands the nature of the findings; the set of research hypotheses that the researcher started with gets also validated or otherwise with the results of the empirical research. Consequently, the researcher prepares a draft of the report in which the major research issues and the findings thereof are highlighted. In this particular case, the researchers first discussed the implications of the empirical finding among themselves and after reaching a consensus, prepared a draft of the report. Time permitting, this should be the first step in preparing the report of a research work. The draft report should be discussed in a seminar or workshop involving other experts in the field so that the errors, omissions and limitations of the study are properly understood. With necessary revisions in the draft report in the light of these discussions, the researcher then prepares the final report. The report on the case study that we present here was prepared following this guideline. We cannot reproduce the final report here. The structure of the final report and the way in which this was produced followed the general guidelines that we discussed in Chapter 11 of this book.

APPENDIX 14.1

Regression results

Model 1: A regression was run using the TSP package. The variables with significant coefficients are as follows:

Variable	Coefficient	t-Statistic
X_3 (Jeep)	32.832530	1.0281
X_5 (L bus)	96.761849	5.1242
X_7 (Trucks)	105.57319	7.1047
X_{10} (Other vehicles)	18.069541	0.5620
X_{13} (Generator-industrial)	389.53892	7.1604
X_{18} (Vehicles)	416.21066	3.3850
X_{20} (Others)	115.29710	1.7501
Constant	208.05225	0.4672

$R^2 = 0.833757$
Adjusted $R^2 = 0.790009$
Standard error = 2344.531
Significant $F = 19.05816$

The other independent variables came out to be insignificant. The assumption of linearity seems to be quite valid since

$R^2 = 0.8333757$

The final equation of the model is as follows:

$$Y = 208.05 + 32.83 \times 3 + 96.76 \times 5 + 105.57 \times 7 + 18.07 \times 10 + 389.54 \times 13 + 416.21 \times 18 + 115.30 \times 20$$

Model 2: In order to have a better insight to the data, a regional dummy was incorporated into the model. The dummy variable is defined as follows:

$X_{21} = 1$ if the pumping station belongs to the South or West zone, 0 if the pumping station belongs to the North or East zone. A regression was run using $X_1, X_2 \ldots\ldots X_{21}$ as independent variables. But, it was found that the regional server-specific dummy was not statistically significant. The variables with significant coefficients are as follows:

Variable	Coefficient	t-Statistic
X_3	30.734087	0.9312
X_5	96.845735	5.0968
X_7	104.8850	6.9214
X_{13}	389.66894	7.1190
X_{18}	423.26706	3.3518
X_{20}	116.31267	1.752
Constant	141.64440	0.2790
X_{21}	181.359997	0.2782424-insignificant

$R^2 = 0.833929$
Adjusted $R^2 = 0.787429$
Standard error = 2358.892
Significant $F = 17.93398$

Note here that there is not much difference between the coefficients in Model 1 and Model 2.

By forcibly incorporating X_{21} in the model, the equation becomes:

$$Y = 141.64 + 30.73 \times 3 + 96.85 \times 5 + 104.89 \times 7 + 389.67 \times 13 + 423.27 \times 18 + 116.31 \times 20 + 181.36 \times 21$$

This particular regional dummy did not give much insight to the data. Hence a different variation was tried.

Model 3: A dummy according to the size of the server was incorporated into the model. The dummy variable is defined as follows:

$$X_{22} = 1 \text{ for total sales } Y > 7000 \text{ litres}$$
$$= 0 \text{ otherwise}$$

The equation and R^2 changed significantly after this incorporation and X_{22} turned out to be significant. In this case, the variables with significant coefficients are as follows:

Variable	Coefficient	t- Statistic
X_5	56.607229	3.6574
X_7	69.602302	5.6126
X_{13}	249.93968	5.4530

Variable	Coefficient	t- Statistic
X_{18}	307.91665	3.2259
X_{20}	52.36249	1.2173
X_{22}	5413.7986	7.3007
Constant	814.10829	2.3171

$R^2 = 0.903483$
Adjusted $R^2 = 0.876458$
Standard error = 1798.35
Significant $F = 33.43157$
The equation in this case is as follows:

$$Y = 814.11 + 56.61 \times 5 + 69.60 \times 7 + 249.94 \times 13 + 307.92 \times 18 + 52.36 \times 20 + 5413.80 \times 22$$

Model 4: Another model similar to Model 3 was run using a modified dummy variable as follows:

$$X_{22} = 1 \text{ for total sales } Y > 3000$$
$$= 0 \text{ otherwise}$$

Including this newly defined dummy variable in the model, the significant variables and their coefficients now become:

Variable	Coefficient	t-Statistic
X_5	79.858630	4.3818
X_6	48.462848	0.6952
X_7	84.149586	5.5717
X_{13}	353.63379	6.8429
X_{18}	402.31574	3.5105
X_{20}	46.6999231	0.72586
X_{22}	2522.6686	3.5468
Constant	2679.42	3.30

$R^2 = 0.857636$
Adjusted $R^2 = 0.817774$
Standard error = 2184.44
Significant $F = 21.515138$

$$Y = 2679.42 + 79.86 \times 5 + 48.46 \times 6 + 84.15 \times 7 + 353.63 \times 13 + 402.32 \times 18 + 46.70 \times 20 + 2522.67 \times 22$$

APPENDIX 1

Table of Random Numbers

(Two-digit random numbers)

Columns

(1)	(2)	(3)	(4)	(5)	(6)	(7)	(8)	(9)	(10)	(11)	(12)	(13)	(14)	(15)	(16)
51	51	00	83	63	22	55	39	65	36	63	70	77	45	85	50
68	97	87	64	81	07	83	74	71	98	16	04	29	18	94	51
30	79	20	69	22	40	98	72	20	56	20	11	72	65	71	08
81	69	40	23	72	51	39	75	17	26	99	76	89	37	20	70
90	60	73	96	53	97	86	37	48	60	82	29	81	30	15	39
46	15	38	26	61	70	04	68	08	02	80	72	83	75	46	30
99	05	48	67	26	43	18	14	23	98	61	67	70	52	85	01
98	35	55	03	36	67	68	48	08	96	21	44	25	27	99	41
11	53	44	10	13	85	57	78	37	06	08	43	63	61	62	42
06	71	95	06	79	88	54	37	21	34	17	68	86	96	83	23
83	45	19	90	70	99	00	14	29	09	34	04	87	83	07	55
49	90	65	97	38	20	46	68	43	28	06	36	49	52	83	51
39	84	51	67	11	52	49	10	43	67	29	70	80	62	80	03
16	17	17	95	70	45	80	44	38	88	39	54	86	97	37	44
13	74	63	52	52	01	41	90	59	59	19	51	85	39	52	85
68	93	60	61	97	22	61	41	47	47	10	25	62	97	05	03
01	07	98	99	46	50	47	91	94	14	63	19	75	89	11	47
74	97	67	38	03	29	63	80	06	54	18	96	09	18	94	06
19	33	53	05	70	53	30	67	72	77	63	48	84	08	31	55
43	70	02	87	40	41	45	59	40	24	13	27	79	26	88	86
95	80	35	14	97	35	33	05	90	35	89	95	01	61	16	96
82	15	94	51	33	41	67	44	43	80	69	98	46	68	05	14
65	31	91	51	80	32	44	61	81	31	96	82	00	57	25	60
85	23	65	09	29	75	63	42	88	07	10	05	24	98	65	63
65	79	20	71	53	20	25	77	94	30	05	39	28	10	99	00
81	06	01	82	77	45	12	78	83	19	76	16	94	11	68	84
00	52	53	43	37	15	26	87	76	59	61	81	43	63	64	61
50	28	11	39	03	34	25	91	43	05	96	47	55	78	99	95
53	32	40	36	40	96	76	84	97	77	72	73	09	62	06	65
69	84	99	63	22	32	98	87	41	60	76	83	44	88	96	07

APPENDIX 2

Table of Random Numbers

Columns

(17)	(18)	(19)	(20)	(21)	(22)	(23)	(24)	(25)	(26)	(27)	(28)	(29)	(30)	(31)	(32)
65	87	08	13	50	63	04	23	25	47	51	91	13	52	62	24
43	65	42	78	66	28	55	80	47	46	41	90	08	55	98	78
62	60	53	51	57	32	22	27	12	72	72	27	77	44	67	32
54	96	72	66	86	65	64	60	56	59	75	36	75	46	44	33
46	96	86	19	83	52	47	53	65	00	51	93	51	30	80	05
18	08	51	51	78	57	26	17	34	87	96	23	95	89	99	93
13	37	00	79	68	96	26	60	70	39	83	66	56	62	03	55
40	25	24	73	52	93	70	50	48	21	47	74	63	17	27	27
90	65	77	63	99	25	69	02	09	04	03	35	78	19	79	95
53	09	48	86	28	30	02	35	71	30	32	06	47	93	74	21
40	69	80	97	96	47	59	97	56	33	24	87	36	17	18	16
96	06	68	93	41	69	96	07	97	50	81	79	59	42	37	13
07	76	21	40	24	74	36	42	40	33	04	46	24	35	63	02
27	78	37	06	06	16	25	98	17	78	80	36	85	26	41	77
44	66	88	97	81	26	03	89	39	46	67	21	17	98	10	39
58	91	63	65	99	59	97	84	90	14	79	61	55	56	16	88
00	97	26	16	91	21	32	41	60	22	66	72	17	31	85	33
00	51	72	62	03	89	26	32	35	27	99	18	15	78	12	03
15	00	41	92	25	73	40	38	37	11	05	75	16	98	81	99
30	92	30	45	51	94	69	04	00	84	14	36	37	95	66	39
19	94	91	67	48	57	10	25	19	64	82	84	62	74	29	92
10	70	49	92	05	12	07	23	02	41	46	04	44	31	52	43
23	13	67	95	07	76	30	55	85	66	96	28	28	30	62	58
63	71	54	50	06	44	76	68	45	19	69	59	35	14	82	56
19	29	56	23	27	19	03	69	31	46	29	85	18	88	26	95
39	79	11	28	94	15	52	37	31	61	28	98	94	61	47	03
86	57	77	55	33	62	02	66	42	19	24	94	13	13	38	69
51	26	35	96	29	00	45	33	65	78	12	35	91	59	11	38
07	21	02	84	48	51	97	76	32	06	19	35	22	95	30	19
86	33	49	90	21	60	74	43	33	42	02	59	20	39	84	95

APPENDIX 3

Table of Random Numbers

(Three-digit random numbers)

Columns

(1)	(2)	(3)	(4)	(5)	(6)	(7)	(8)	(9)	(10)	(11)	(12)
642	807	270	546	029	835	828	386	010	216	322	045
790	186	608	897	265	257	276	134	111	614	930	921
435	410	099	205	689	786	313	094	883	382	695	654
218	345	226	433	905	298	385	904	803	854	968	739
263	626	225	267	531	617	134	416	101	081	503	908
296	340	928	403	526	048	138	609	602	807	331	986
835	883	273	307	700	226	101	762	243	049	471	774
058	569	858	422	469	850	647	050	958	217	564	686
452	341	221	191	226	645	614	734	201	633	887	868
757	094	479	348	407	575	377	095	239	675	527	886
149	322	243	302	047	427	832	247	827	331	045	500
639	252	212	801	325	032	719	795	702	411	141	913
648	047	384	924	748	096	704	732	188	117	519	249
573	469	233	958	782	058	134	047	833	897	686	154
879	632	569	615	352	706	787	428	114	305	629	806
676	183	092	227	221	143	760	061	915	362	366	778
235	417	572	035	884	979	255	034	163	387	717	660
749	782	410	000	437	057	074	404	742	573	618	017
364	969	700	077	762	551	646	702	616	517	361	377
406	697	651	823	196	747	742	202	473	049	634	182
749	604	596	495	370	532	952	843	214	125	162	641
355	217	237	436	308	679	812	164	651	367	825	191
392	184	954	851	986	202	732	640	447	515	829	158
627	816	252	418	490	869	332	852	772	438	864	281
709	349	671	505	855	905	549	550	489	101	527	041
876	219	495	418	943	864	864	424	200	164	054	452
687	529	928	822	641	033	948	299	058	732	974	113
836	884	465	379	779	348	217	195	359	232	948	907
262	484	430	807	965	329	181	438	896	614	551	306
406	292	730	137	235	154	714	114	506	375	139	077

APPENDIX 4

Table of Random Numbers

(Three-digit random numbers)

Columns											
(13)	(14)	(15)	(16)	(17)	(18)	(19)	(20)	(21)	(22)	(23)	(24)
288	302	957	018	109	053	044	058	849	285	898	732
965	943	462	554	146	318	313	540	090	553	340	096
870	654	605	967	968	085	085	370	252	657	094	056
813	728	351	266	619	151	079	473	763	886	097	893
506	662	573	866	835	785	689	529	992	283	964	416
304	855	222	564	247	726	626	370	569	002	759	996
232	804	271	605	536	173	607	504	020	357	975	079
547	746	272	659	500	487	039	821	904	130	633	750
579	419	722	753	519	962	836	477	033	320	248	817
113	008	777	675	351	395	656	463	578	647	736	959
526	559	446	464	308	899	620	172	197	937	171	423
224	878	732	433	005	993	355	727	995	421	816	713
199	107	231	637	192	397	865	512	072	863	904	818
491	049	367	154	956	911	777	635	102	349	675	392
674	920	950	500	232	289	553	962	844	902	272	428
857	512	776	644	719	415	362	900	851	169	852	504
002	072	305	756	036	523	026	453	977	744	132	319
519	302	585	845	931	731	642	365	632	333	831	719
648	414	669	196	462	612	192	781	061	420	943	216
284	604	628	959	985	898	494	235	935	259	394	334
627	443	283	351	188	946	131	915	229	203	877	693
429	152	062	486	826	147	338	911	530	984	319	317
922	430	588	568	966	031	699	384	192	956	384	030
461	744	365	022	401	047	667	423	957	158	754	211
039	060	686	065	021	808	697	314	744	220	369	155
122	309	242	226	403	441	624	875	320	402	098	046
486	341	451	395	054	268	134	740	902	999	108	084
494	983	308	978	800	884	383	530	025	978	343	269
631	946	604	987	264	596	101	084	367	788	322	601
507	294	628	614	385	914	324	632	069	382	626	724

APPENDIX 5

Values of normal deviate (*X*) for chosen levels of *P*

	0.01	0.02	0.03	0.04	0.05	0.06	0.07	0.08	0.09	0.10
0.00	2.5758	2.3263	2.1701	2.0537	1.9600	1.8808	1.8119	1.7507	1.6954	1.6449
0.10	1.5982	1.5548	1.5141	1.4758	1.4395	1.4051	1.3722	1.3408	1.3106	1.2816
0.20	1.2536	1.2265	1.2004	1.1750	1.1503	1.1264	1.1031	1.0803	1.0581	1.0364
0.30	1.0152	0.9945	0.9741	0.9542	0.9346	0.9154	0.8965	0.8779	0.8596	0.8416
0.40	0.8239	0.8064	0.7892	0.7722	0.7554	0.7388	0.7225	0.7063	0.6903	0.6745
0.50	0.6588	0.6433	0.6230	0.6128	0.5978	0.5828	0.5681	0.5534	0.5388	0.5244
0.60	0.5101	0.4958	0.4817	0.4677	0.4538	0.4399	0.4261	0.4125	0.3989	0.3853
0.70	0.3719	0.3585	0.3451	0.3319	0.3186	0.3055	0.2924	0.2793	0.2663	0.2533
0.80	0.2404	0.2275	0.2147	0.2019	0.1891	0.1764	0.1637	0.1510	0.1383	0.1257
0.90	0.1130	0.1004	0.0878	0.0753	0.0627	0.0502	0.0376	0.0251	0.0125	0

The value of ***P*** for each entry is found by adding the column heading to the value in the hand margin. The corresponding value of x is the deviation such that the probability of an observation falling outside the range from $-x$ to $+x$ is P. For example $\boldsymbol{P} = 0.03$ for $x = 2.1701$ so that 3 per cent of normally distributed values will have positive or negative deviations exceeding the standard deviation in the ration 2.1701 at least.

APPENDIX 6

Values of t for $P = 0.05$ and $P = 0.01$

n'	$P = 0.05$	$P = 0.01$	n'	$P = 0.05$	$P = 0.01$
1	12.706	63.657	17	2.110	2.898
2	4.303	9.925	18	2.101	2.878
3	3.182	5.841	19	2.093	2.861
4	2.776	4.604	20	2.086	2.845
5	2.571	4.032	21	2.080	2.831
6	2.447	3.707	22	2.074	2.819
7	2.365	3.499	23	2.069	2.807
8	2.306	3.355	24	2.064	2.797
9	2.262	3.250	25	2.060	2.787
10	2.228	3.169	26	2.056	2.779
11	2.201	3.106	27	2.052	2.771
12	2.179	3.055	28	2.048	2.763
13	2.160	3.012	29	2.045	2.756
14	2.145	2.977	30	2.042	2.750
15	2.131	2.947			
16	2.120	2.921	∞	1.960	2.576

APPENDIX 7

Values of *f* (Variance ratio)

5 per cent points of e^{2z}

n_2 \ n_1	1	2	3	4	5	6	8	12	24	∞
1	161.40	199.50	215.70	224.60	230.20	234.00	238.90	243.90	249.00	254.30
2	18.51	19.00	19.16	19.25	19.30	19.33	19.37	19.41	19.45	19.50
3	10.13	9.55	9.28	9.12	9.01	8.94	8.84	8.74	8.64	8.53
4	7.71	6.94	6.59	6.39	6.26	6.16	6.04	5.91	5.77	5.63
5	6.61	5.79	5.41	5.19	5.05	4.95	4.82	4.68	4.53	4.36
6	5.99	5.14	4.76	4.53	4.39	4.28	4.15	4.00	3.84	3.67
7	5.59	4.74	4.35	4.12	3.97	3.87	3.73	3.57	3.41	3.23
8	5.32	4.46	4.07	3.84	3.69	3.58	3.44	3.28	3.12	2.93
9	5.12	4.26	3.86	3.63	3.48	3.37	3.23	3.07	2.90	2.71
10	4.96	4.10	3.71	3.48	3.33	3.22	3.07	2.91	2.74	2.54
11	4.84	3.98	3.59	3.36	3.20	3.09	2.95	2.79	2.61	2.40
12	4.75	3.88	3.49	3.26	3.11	3.00	2.85	2.69	2.50	2.30
13	4.67	3.80	3.41	3.18	3.02	2.92	2.77	2.60	2.42	2.21
14	4.60	3.74	3.34	3.11	2.96	2.85	2.70	2.53	2.35	2.13
15	4.54	3.68	3.29	3.06	2.90	2.79	2.64	2.48	2.29	2.07
16	4.49	3.63	3.24	3.01	2.85	2.74	2.59	2.42	2.24	2.01
17	4.45	3.59	3.20	2.96	2.81	2.70	2.55	2.38	2.19	1.96
18	4.41	3.55	3.16	2.93	2.77	2.66	2.51	2.34	2.15	1.92
19	4.38	3.52	3.13	2.90	2.74	2.63	2.48	2.31	2.11	1.88
20	4.35	3.49	3.10	2.87	2.71	2.60	2.45	2.28	2.08	1.84
21	4.32	3.47	3.07	2.84	2.68	2.57	2.42	2.25	2.05	1.81
22	4.30	3.44	3.05	2.82	2.66	2.55	2.40	2.23	2.03	1.78
23	4.28	3.42	3.03	2.80	2.64	2.53	2.38	2.20	2.00	1.76
24	4.26	3.40	3.01	2.78	2.62	2.51	2.36	2.18	1.98	1.73
25	4.24	3.38	2.99	2.76	2.60	2.49	2.34	2.16	1.96	1.71
26	4.22	3.37	2.98	2.74	2.59	2.47	2.32	2.15	1.95	1.69
27	4.21	3.35	2.96	2.73	2.57	2.46	2.30	2.13	1.93	1.67
28	4.20	3.34	2.95	2.71	2.56	2.44	2.29	2.12	1.91	1.65
29	4.18	3.33	2.93	2.70	2.54	2.43	2.28	2.10	1.90	1.64
30	4.17	3.32	2.92	2.69	2.53	2.42	2.27	2.09	1.89	1.62
40	4.03	3.23	2.84	2.61	2.45	2.34	2.18	2.00	1.79	1.51
60	4.00	3.16	2.76	2.52	2.37	2.25	2.10	1.92	1.70	1.39
120	3.92	3.07	2.68	2.45	2.29	2.17	2.02	1.83	1.61	1.25
∞	3.84	2.99	2.60	2.37	2.21	2.09	1.94	1.75	1.52	1.00

Lower 5 per cent points are found by interchange of n_1 and n_2, *i.e.* n_1 must always correspond with the greater mean square.

APPENDIX 8

Values of *f* (Variance ratio)

1 per cent points of e^{2z}

					n_1					
n_2	1	2	3	4	5	6	8	12	24	∞
1	4052	4999	5403	5625	5764	5859	5981	6106	6234	6366
2	98.49	99.01	99.17	99.25	99.30	99.33	99.36	99.42	99.46	99.50
3	34.12	30.81	29.46	28.71	28.24	27.91	27.49	27.05	26.60	26.12
4	21.20	18.00	16.69	15.98	15.52	15.21	14.80	14.37	13.93	13.46
5	16.26	13.27	12.06	11.39	10.97	10.67	10.27	9.89	9.47	9.02
6	13.74	10.92	9.78	9.15	8.75	8.47	8.10	7.72	7.31	6.88
7	12.25	9.55	8.45	7.85	7.46	7.19	6.84	6.47	6.07	5.65
8	11.26	8.65	7.59	7.01	6.63	6.37	6.03	5.67	5.28	4.86
9	10.56	8.02	6.99	6.42	6.06	5.80	5.47	5.11	4.73	4.31
10	10.04	7.56	6.55	5.99	5.64	5.39	5.06	4.71	4.33	3.91
11	9.65	7.20	6.22	5.67	5.32	5.07	4.74	5.40	4.02	3.60
12	9.33	6.93	5.95	5.41	5.06	4.82	4.50	4.16	3.78	3.36
13	9.07	6.70	5.74	5.20	4.86	4.62	4.30	3.96	3.59	3.16
14	8.86	6.51	5.56	5.03	4.69	4.46	4.14	3.80	3.43	3.00
15	8.68	6.36	5.42	4.89	4.56	4.32	4.00	3.67	3.29	2.87
16	8.53	6.23	5.29	4.77	4.44	4.20	3.89	3.55	3.18	2.75
17	8.40	6.11	5.18	4.67	4.34	4.10	3.79	3.45	3.08	2.65
18	8.28	6.01	5.09	4.58	4.25	4.01	3.71	3.37	3.00	2.57
19	8.18	5.93	5.01	4.50	4.17	3.94	3.63	3.30	2.92	2.49
20	8.10	5.85	4.94	4.43	4.10	3.87	3.56	3.23	2.86	2.42
21	8.02	5.78	4.87	4.37	4.04	3.81	3.51	3.17	2.80	2.36
22	7.94	5.72	4.82	4.31	3.99	3.76	3.45	3.12	2.75	2.31
23	7.88	5.66	4.76	4.26	3.94	3.71	3.41	3.07	2.70	2.26
24	7.82	5.61	4.72	4.22	3.90	3.67	3.36	3.03	2.66	2.21
25	7.77	5.57	4.68	4.18	3.86	3.63	3.32	2.99	2.62	2.17
26	7.72	5.53	4.64	4.14	3.82	3.59	3.29	2.96	2.58	2.13
27	7.68	5.49	4.60	4.11	3.78	3.56	3.26	2.93	2.55	2.10
28	7.64	5.45	4.57	4.07	3.75	3.53	3.23	2.90	2.52	2.06
29	7.60	5.42	4.54	4.04	3.73	3.50	3.20	2.87	2.49	2.03
30	7.56	5.39	4.51	4.02	3.70	3.47	3.17	2.84	2.47	2.01
40	7.31	5.18	4.31	3.83	3.51	3.29	2.99	2.66	2.29	1.80
60	7.08	4.98	4.13	3.65	3.34	3.12	2.82	2.50	2.12	1.60
120	6.85	4.79	3.95	3.48	3.17	2.96	2.66	2.34	1.95	1.38
∞	6.64	4.60	3.78	3.32	3.02	2.80	2.51	2.18	1.79	1.00

Lower 1 per cent points are found by interchange of n_1 and n_2, *i.e.* n_1 must always correspond with the greater mean square.

APPENDIX 9

Values of χ^2

Probabilty

n	0.99	0.98	0.95	0.90	0.80	0.70	0.50	0.30	0.20	0.10	0.05	0.02	0.01	0.001
1	0.000157	0.000628	0.00393	0.0158	0.0642	0.148	0.455	1.074	1.642	2.706	3.841	5.412	6.635	10.827
2	0.0201	0.0404	0.103	0.211	0.446	0.713	1.386	2.408	3.219	4.605	5.991	7.824	9.210	13.815
3	0.115	0.185	0.352	0.584	1.005	1.424	2.366	3.665	4.642	6.251	7.815	9.837	11.345	16.268
4	0.297	0.429	0.711	1.064	1.649	2.195	3.357	4.878	5.989	7.779	9.488	11.668	13.277	18.465
5	0.554	0.752	1.145	1.610	2.343	3.000	4.351	6.064	7.289	9.236	11.070	13.388	15.086	20.517
6	0.872	1.134	1.635	2.204	3.070	3.828	5.348	7.231	8.558	10.645	12.592	15.033	16.812	22.457
7	1.239	1.564	2.167	2.833	3.822	4.671	6.346	8.383	9.803	12.017	14.067	16.622	18.475	24.322
8	1.646	2.032	2.733	3.490	4.594	5.527	7.344	9.524	11.030	13.362	15.507	18.168	20.090	26.125
9	2.088	2.532	3.325	4.168	5.380	6.393	8.343	10.656	12.242	14.684	16.919	19.679	21.666	27.877
10	2.558	3.059	3.940	4.865	6.179	7.267	9.342	11.781	13.442	15.987	18.307	21.161	23.209	29.588
11	3.053	3.609	4.575	5.578	6.989	8.148	10.341	12.899	14.631	17.275	19.675	22.618	24.752	31.264
12	3.571	4.178	5.226	6.304	7.806	9.034	11.340	14.011	15.812	18.549	21.026	24.054	26.217	32.909
13	4.107	4.765	5.892	7.042	8.634	9.926	12.430	15.119	16.985	19.812	22.362	25.472	27.688	34.528
14	4.660	5.368	6.571	7.790	9.467	10.821	13.339	16.222	18.151	21.064	23.685	26.873	29.141	36.123
15	5.229	5.985	7.261	8.547	10.307	11.721	14.339	17.322	19.311	22.307	24.996	28.259	30.578	37.679

APPENDIX 10

Z values

Z	.00	.01	.02	.03	.04	.05	.06	.07	.08	.09
.0	.5000	.5040	.5080	.5120	.5160	.5199	.5239	.5279	.5319	.5359
.1	.5398	.5438	.5478	.5517	.5557	.5596	.5636	.5675	.5714	.5753
.2	.5793	.5832	.5871	.5910	.5948	.5987	.6026	.6064	.6103	.6141
.3	.6179	.6217	.6255	.6293	.6331	.6368	.6406	.6443	.6480	.6517
.4	.6554	.6591	.6628	.6664	.6700	.6736	.6772	.6808	.6844	.6879
.5	.6915	.6950	.6985	.7019	.7054	.7088	.7123	.7157	.7190	.7224
.6	.7257	.7291	.7324	.7357	.7389	.7422	.7454	.7486	.7517	.7549
.7	.7580	.7611	.7642	.7673	.7704	.7734	.7764	.7794	.7823	.7852
.8	.7881	.7910	.7939	.7967	.7995	.8023	.8051	.8078	.8106	.8133
.9	.8159	.8186	.8212	.8238	.8264	.8289	.8315	.8340	.8365	.8389
1.0	.8413	.8438	.8461	.8485	.8508	.8531	.8554	.8577	.8599	.8621
1.1	.8643	.8665	.8686	.8708	.8729	.8749	.8770	.8790	.8810	.8830
1.2	.8849	.8869	.8888	.8907	.8925	.8944	.8962	.8980	.8997	.9015
1.3	.9032	.9049	.9066	.9082	.9099	.9115	.9131	.9147	.9162	.9177
1.4	.9192	.9207	.9222	.9236	.9251	.9265	.9279	.9292	.9306	.9319
1.5	.9332	.9345	.9357	.9370	.9382	.9394	.9406	.9418	.9429	.9441
1.6	.9452	.9463	.9474	.9484	.9495	.9505	.9515	.9525	.9535	.9545
1.7	.9554	.9564	.9573	.9582	.9591	.9599	.9608	.9616	.9625	.9633
1.8	.9641	.9649	.9656	.9664	.9671	.9678	.9686	.9693	.9699	.9706
1.9	.9713	.9719	.9726	.9732	.9738	.9744	.9750	.9756	.9761	.9767
2.0	.9772	.9778	.9783	.9788	.9793	.9798	.9803	.9808	.9812	.9817
2.1	.9821	.9826	.9830	.9834	.9838	.9842	.9846	.9850	.9854	.9857
2.2	.9861	.9864	.9868	.9871	.9875	.9878	.9881	.9884	.9887	.9890
2.3	.9893	.9896	.9898	.9901	.9904	.9906	.9909	.9911	.9913	.9916
2.4	.9918	.9920	.9922	.9925	.9927	.9929	.9931	.9932	.9934	.9936
2.5	.9938	.9940	.9941	.9943	.9945	.9946	.9948	.9949	.9951	.9952
2.6	.9953	.9955	.9956	.9957	.9959	.9960	.9961	.9962	.9963	.9964
2.7	.9965	.9966	.9967	.9968	.9969	.9970	.9971	.9972	.9973	.9974
2.8	.9974	.9975	.9976	.9977	.9977	.9978	.9979	.9979	.9980	.9981
2.9	.9981	.9982	.9982	.9983	.9984	.9984	.9985	.9985	.9986	.9986
3.0	.9987	.9987	.9987	.9988	.9989	.9989	.9989	.9989	.9990	.9990
3.1	.9990	.9991	.9991	.9991	.9992	.9992	.9992	.9992	.9993	.9993
3.2	.9993	.9993	.9994	.9994	.9994	.9994	.9994	.9995	.9995	.9995
3.3	.9995	.9995	.9995	.9996	.9996	.9996	.9996	.9996	.9996	.9997
3.4	.9997	.9997	.9997	.9997	.9997	.9997	.9997	.9997	.9997	.9998

APPENDIX 11

Percentiles of the χ^2 Distribution

df	$\chi^2_{0.005}$	$\chi^2_{.01}$	$\chi^2_{.025}$	$\chi^2_{.05}$	$\chi^2_{.10}$	$\chi^2_{.90}$	$\chi^2_{.95}$	$\chi^2_{.975}$	$\chi^2_{.99}$	$\chi^2_{.995}$
1	.000039	.00016	.00098	.0039	.0158	2.71	3.84	5.02	6.63	7.88
2	.0100	.0201	.0506	.1026	.2107	4.61	5.99	7.38	9.21	10.60
3	.0717	.115	.216	.352	.584	6.25	7.81	9.35	11.34	12.84
4	.207	.297	.484	.711	1.064	7.78	9.49	11.14	13.28	14.86
5	.412	.554	.831	1.15	1.61	9.24	11.07	12.83	15.09	16.75
6	.676	.872	1.24	1.64	2.20	10.64	12.59	14.45	16.81	18.55
7	.989	1.24	1.69	2.17	2.83	12.02	14.07	16.01	18.48	20.28
8	1.34	1.65	2.18	2.73	3.49	13.36	15.51	17.53	20.09	21.96
9	1.73	2.09	2.70	3.33	4.17	14.68	16.92	19.02	21.67	23.59
10	2.16	2.56	3.25	3.94	4.87	15.99	18.31	20.48	23.21	25.19
11	2.60	3.05	3.82	4.57	5.58	17.28	19.68	21.92	24.73	26.76
12	3.07	3.57	4.40	5.23	6.30	18.55	21.03	23.34	26.22	28.30
13	3.57	4.11	5.01	5.89	7.04	19.81	22.36	24.74	27.69	29.82
14	4.07	4.66	5.63	6.57	7.79	21.06	23.68	26.12	29.14	31.32
15	4.60	5.23	6.26	7.26	8.55	22.31	25.00	27.49	30.58	32.80
16	5.14	5.81	6.91	7.96	9.31	23.54	26.30	28.85	32.00	34.27
18	6.26	7.01	8.23	9.39	10.86	25.99	28.87	31.53	34.81	37.16
20	7.43	8.26	9.59	10.85	12.44	28.41	31.41	34.17	37.57	40.00
24	9.89	10.86	12.40	13.85	15.66	33.20	36.42	39.36	42.98	45.56
30	13.79	14.95	16.79	18.49	20.60	40.26	43.77	46.98	50.89	53.67
40	20.71	22.16	24.43	26.51	29.05	51.81	55.76	59.34	63.69	66.77
60	35.53	37.48	40.48	43.19	46.46	74.40	79.08	83.30	88.38	91.95
120	83.85	86.92	91.58	95.70	100.62	140.23	146.57	152.21	158.95	163.64

df = degree of freedom

For large degree of freedom $X^2 = \frac{1}{2}\left(Z + \sqrt{2v-1}\right)^2$ (approximately) where v = degree of freedom and Z is given in Table 10.

(*Source*: Dixon W and Massey J, *Introduction to Statistical Analysis*, 4th Ed., 1992, McGraw-Hill, New York; reproduced with the permission of the publisher.)

Select Bibliography

1. David A A and George D S, 1986, *Marketing Research*, John Wiley and Sons, New York.
2. Richard B P, 1994, *Advanced Methods In Marketing Research*, Basil Backwell Ltd, New York.
3. Gilbert C A, Jr, 1988, *Basic Marketing Research*, Dryden Press, New York.
4. Robert F, 1974, *Handbook of Marketing Research*, Mc Graw Hill Book Company, New York.
5. Groves L W J, 1994, *Principles of International Marketing Research*, Blackwell Publisher, New York.
6. Paul H N, 1987, *Industrial Market Research Handbook*, Kogan Page.
7. Rajan, 1998, *Encyclopedia of Marketing Research*, Vols 1, 2, 3, Anmol Publications, Delhi.
8. Harder T, 1969, *Introduction to Mathematical Models in Market and Opinion Research*, D Reidel Publishing Company, Holland.
9. Green P E, Donald T S and Gerald A, 1997, *Research for Marketing Decisions*, Prentice Hall India, New Delhi.
10. Ronald H P, 1996, *Marketing and Consumer Research in the Public Interest*, Sage Publication Inc., California.
11. William B O, Richard N G and Mary M F, 1993, *Handbook of Marketing Scales*, Sage Publication Inc., California.
12. Sunny G, 1984, *Marketing Research for Managers*, Heinemann Publication, London.
13. Beri C G, 1997, *Marketing Research*, Tata Mc Graw Hill, New Delhi.
14. Agarwal S, 1994, *Marketing Research*, Global Business Press, Delhi.
15. Paul G E, Tull T S and Gerald A, 1999, *Research for Marketing Decision*, 5th Edition, Prentice Hall India, New Delhi.
16. Harper B W Jr, Ralph W and Stanley S F, 1988, *All India Traveller*, 6th Edition, Bookseller Publication, Delhi.
17. David L J, Hugh W G and Donald T A, 1982, *Marketing Research*, Prentice Hall India, New Delhi.
18. William C G, 1963, *Sampling Techniques*, John Wiley and Sons Inc., New York.
19. Hannan M H, Hurwitz N W and Madow G W, 1953, *Sample Survey Methods and Theory*, Vols 1 and 2, John Wiley and Sons Inc., New York.
20. Stephan F F and McCarthy J P, 1963, *Sampling Opinions: An analysis of survey procedure*, John Wiley and Sons Inc., New York.

21. Fisher Sir R A, 1972, *The Designs of Experiments*, Harper and Row Publishers, New York.
22. Edward A L, 1972, *Experimental Design in Psychological Research*, Holt, Rinehart and Winston, New York.
23. Morris C R and Earnest N, 1962, *An Introduction to Logic*, Harcourt Brace and World, New York.
24. Campbell, Donald T and Julian S C, 1966, *Experimental and Quasi-experimental Design for Research*, Rand McNally and Company, Chicago.
25. Cox K K and Enis B M, 1966, *Experimentation for Marketing Decisions*, International Textbook Company, Scranton PA.
26. Abraham O N, 1966, *Questionnaire Design and Attitude Measurement*, Basic Books Inc., New York.
27. Kish L J, 1975, *Survey Sampling*, John Wiley and Sons, New York.
28. Tull, Donald and Gerald A, 1973, Survey Research, Intext Educational Publishers, New York.
29. Deming W E, 1966, *Some Theory of Sampling*, Dover Publications Inc., New York.
30. Deming W E, 1963, *Sampling Design in Business Research*, John Wiley and Sons, New York.
31. Robert F and Verdoon J P, 1962, *Research Methods in Economics and Business*, Macmillan Publishing Company Inc. New York.
32. Seymour B, 1965, *Experimentation in Marketing*, McGraw Hill Book Company, New York.
33. Fisher R A, 1951, *The Design of Experiments*, Hafner Publishing Company Inc., NewYork.
34. William G C, 1964, *Analysis of Variance*, Prentice Hall Inc., Englewood Cliffs NJ.
35. Raymond G L, 1975, *Interviewing; Strategy, Techniques and Tactics*, The Dorsey Press, Homewood Ill.
36. Annette G M, 1972, *Interviewing, Its Principles and Methods*, Family Service Association of America, New York.
37. Conover W J, 1971, Practical Nonparametric Methods, John Wiley and Sons Inc., New York.
38. John F E, 1971, *Mathematical Statistics*, Prentice Hall Inc., Englewood NJ.
39. Darell H, 1954, *How to lie with Statistics*, WW Norton and Company Inc., New York.
40. Sidney S, 1956, *Non-parametric Statistics for Behavioral Sciences*, McGraw Hill Book Company, New York.
41. Taro Y, 1964, *Statistics: An Introductory Analysis*, Harper Row, NewYork.

42. Wmer B J, 1971, *Statistical Principles in Experimental Design*, McGraw Hill Book Company, New York.

43. John P, 1971, *Statistical Design and Analysis of Experimental Design*, McGraw Hill Book Company, New York.

44. Anderson T W, 1958, *Introduction to Multivariate Statistical Analysis*, John Wiley and Sons Inc., New York.

45. Williams E J, 1959, *Regression Analysis*, John Wiley and Sons, New York.

46. Sokal R R and Sneath P H A, 1963, *Principles of Numerical Taxonomy*, W H Freeman and Company, San Frasncisco.

47. Wilkinson S T and Bhadrakar P L, 1984, *Methodology and Techniques of Social Research*, Himalaya Publishing House, Mumbai.

48. Kothari C R, 1992, *Research Methodology*, Wiley Eastern Limited, New Delhi.

49. Jhambs L C, 1996, *Cases and Problems on Quantitative Techniques*, Everest Publishing House, Pune.

50. Gupta C B and Gupta V, 1996, *An Introduction to Statistical Methods*, Vikas Publishing House, New Delhi.

51. Margaret C and Tiu W L, 1995, *The Marketing Research Process*, Prentice Hall, London. International.

52. Philip K, 2000, *Marketing Management* (Millenium Edition), Prentice Hall India, New Delhi.

53. Chisnall P, 1992, *Marketing Research*, Mc Graw Hill International, London.

54. Kent R, 1993, Marketing Research in Action, Routledge, London.

55. Hague P and Jackson P, 1999, Marketing Research in Practice, Kogan Page, London.

56. Birn R, Hague P and Vangeldar P, (Eds), *A Handbook of Marketing Research Techniques*, Kogan Page, London.

57. Baker M J, 1991, *Research for Marketing*, Macmillan, London.

58. Jackson P, 1997, *Quality in Marketing Research*, Kogan Page, London.

59. Das N G, 1996, *Statistical Method*, M Das & Co, Calcutta.

60. Gupta S P, 1995, *Statistical Methods*, Sultan Chand & Sons, Delhi.

61. Majumdar R, 1996, *Marketing Research*, New Age International (P) Ltd, New Delhi.

62. Gottschalk K A, 1945, *The Use of Personal Documents in History, Anthropology and Sociology*, SSR Council Bulletin-53.

63. Galtung , Johan, 1967, *Theory and Methods of Social Research*, Allen and Unwin, London.

Index

A

accuracy 155
advertising research 8
alternate hypothesis (H_a) 239
ambiguity 81, 103, 106
analogous situation 15
analysis of variance 207, 208
ascertainment errors 108
auto-correlation 205

B

basic information 87
before measure 60
binomial 128
biographies 42
bipolar scaling 138
bivariate distribution 191
bivariate tables 257
block or cluster sampling (area sampling) 166
boxplot rule 112

C

causal studies 12, 18
central tendency 181
Centre for Monitoring Indian Economy (CMIE) 48
chi-square distribution 242
chi-square tests 128, 242
circular systematic sampling 162
circular triad 134
classification information 87
clinical focus group 275
clinical interview 41
closed questions 82
close-ended questionnaire 34
coefficient of determination 196
coefficient of variation 190
concordance 129
concurrent inaccuracy 104
confidence interval 261
consistency check 113
constant sum scale 135
content analysis 39, 45
content of the questionnaire 78
contingency tables 243
continuous frequency distribution 231
continuous panel 68
continuous variate 231
control group 44, 60
controlled experiment 54
controls 167
control variable 167
convenience sampling 168
conversation 32
corporate research 8
correlation 128, 190
correlation coefficient 21
cross sectional design 64, 66, 67
CSO (Central Statistical Organisation) 47
cushion question 87
custom research firms 272

D

datum 27
degree of freedom 211
dependant variable 204
depth interview method 75
descriptive research 16
descriptive studies 12, 16
destructive test 156
deterministic causation 19
dichotomous questions 81, 84
dichotomous setting 81
discussion 40
dummy tables 257

E

econometric model 22
econometrics 205
effect of the treatment 62, 63, 64
empirical mapping 260
error in response 101
estimated value 234
estimator 155

experimental
design 59, 60, 68
economics 65
error 101
group 44, 60
explained variables 18
explanatory variables 18
explorative studies 12
exploratory focus group 275
ex-post facto test control group 67
external validity 55, 56
extraneous variables 57
extreme deviation from mean (ESD) 112

F

F distribution 208
field service firms 272
filter questions 79
final report 255
Fisher's *Z* distribution 242
focussed interview 41
formal design 16
formal structured 30
formal unstructured 30
frequency polygon 181

G

Gaussian distribution 231
geometric mean 182
grand mean 211
granger causality test 54

H

harmonic mean 182
heteroscadasticity 205
histogram 181
history 58

I

identification information 87
independent variables 204
index ranking 124
Indian Market Research Bureau (IMRB) 68
inductive process 154
informal setting 30
instrumentation effect 69
instruments 59
intercept interviews 169
interim report 255
internal validity 55, 56
interpolation 175
inter-temporal design 66
interval scale 119

K

Kendall's coefficient of concordance 122
kurtosis 181

L

laboratory experiments 55
laddering technique 75
law of comparative judgement 141
law of transitivity 133
likert scale 146
logical empiricism 4
logical positivism 4
logic of induction 264

M

market research 9
maturation 58
mean 182
mean deviation 188
mean square (MS) 211
measurement error 100
measurement scales 118
median 182
method of accommodation 112
method of linear approximation 175
methods of interpolation 175
metric scaling 140
mode 182
mode of communication 31
mortality 58
multi-collinearity 205
multi-dimensional scale 135
multi-dimensional scaling (MDS) 139
multiple choice questions 83
multistage sampling 165
multi time series 64, 67

N

national sample survey organisation 47
natural experiment 54, 65

negative response 44
newspapers 47
Newton's backward method of interpolation 178
Newton's formula 178
Newton's forward method of interpolation 178
nominal scale 119
non-directive interview 42
non-parametric test 242
non-random sample 159
non-response errors 102
non-sampling error 101, 156
non-verbal 31
normal distribution 231
notational system 59
notations 59
null hypothesis (H_o) 239

O

observation technique 44
open-ended questionnaire 34
open-ended questions 81
optimum sample size 157
oral–verbal 31
ordinal scale 119
outlier 111
outlier labelling 112

P

paired comparison 132
panel data 66, 68
participant observation 32, 44
pilot survey 14, 275
population 154, 175
population distribution 230
positivism 4
positivist school 4
post-survey checks 113
post-test measures 60
precision 156
pre-coded questionnaire 88
predictive inaccuracy 104
pre-test 60, 89
primary data 28
principle of optimisation 154
principle of random sampling 154
probabilistic causation 19
probability sampling 158
product moment correlation coefficient 192
product research 9
projective questions 94
projective techniques 90
property of transitivity 120
proxy variable 260
psychodramatic technique 95
psychometric studies 77
public records and statistics 47

Q

quantitative judgement method 130
queen of scales 126
quota sampling 166

R

random 158
randomised response technique 87, 105
range 188
rating scale 135
ratio scale 119, 126
raw data 175
referral survey 14
regressant 264
regression analysis 128, 191
regressor 264
research design 11
research hypothesis 10
response 102
response approach 130, 131
root mean square deviation 188

S

sample design 158
sample frame 158
sample mean 211
sampling distribution 230
sampling error 155
sampling units 158
screening interviews 169
secondary data 28, 47
selection bias 59
semantic differential method 138
semantic differential scale 135, 138
sentence completion test 93
sequence of questions 87
sequential sampling 165

simple random sampling 159
simple random sampling without replacement 160
simple random sampling with replacement 160
simulated marketing 63
size of questionnaire 78
Snedecor's *F* distribution 242
snowball sampling 169
software packages 257
Spearman's rank correlation coefficient 122
specification errors 108
SRSWOR 159
SRSWR 159
SS within 212
standard deviation 188
statistical variance 209
stimuli 28
stimulus centred approach 130
stimulus–response interaction 30
stimulus–situation 90
story and argument-completion technique 93
strata 163
stratified random sampling 163
structured 74
structured disguised questionnaire 76
structured interview 34, 40
structured questionnaire 34
structured undisguised questionnaire 75
student's *t* distribution 242
subject centred approach 130, 131
suggestion bias 79
summated scale 146
sum of square deviations 212
sum of squares 211
syndicated data 272
syndicated report 273
syndicated service firms 272
systematic 28
systematic error 43
systematic (non-random) error 17
systematic observation 33, 44
systematic sampling 162

T

tabulation errors 108
target group 79
television rating point (TRP) 69
testing effect 58
testing of independence of classifications 243
test of concordance 122
test of goodness of fit 242
the doll play test 94
thematic apperception test (TAT) 94
theory of statistical inference 230
the Rosenweig test 94
Thurstone scale 141
time series 66
time series design 65
total error 101
trend analysis 66
trend design 66
t scores 262
type I error 239
type II error 239
types of causation 19
types of questionnaires 78

U

uni-dimensional interval scale 141
unstructured 74
unstructured disguised questionnaire 77
unstructured interview 33, 40, 41
unstructured undisguised questionnaire 77
unsystematic stimuli 28
use split ballot 87

V

variability method 130
variable 174
variance ratio 207
variate 174
verbal 31

W

weighted index rank 120, 121
weighted index ranking 123
word association test 93
written–verbal 31

Y

Yates' correction 245